Breaking peace

Manchester University Press

Breaking
peace

Brexit and Northern Ireland

Feargal Cochrane

Manchester University Press

The right of Feargal Cochrane to be identified as the author of this work has been asserted by him in accordance with the Copyright, Designs and Patents Act 1988.

Published by Manchester University Press
Altrincham Street, Manchester M1 7JA
www.manchesteruniversitypress.co.uk

British Library Cataloguing-in-Publication Data
A catalogue record for this book is available from the British Library

ISBN   978 1 5261 4255 9   hardback

First published 2020

The publisher has no responsibility for the persistence or accuracy of URLs for any external or third-party internet websites referred to in this book, and does not guarantee that any content on such websites is, or will remain, accurate or appropriate.

Typeset
by New Best-set Typesetters Ltd
Printed in Great Britain
by TJ International Ltd, Padstow

For Oisín and Rosaleen:
Forever Irish, Forever European

Contents

Introduction   *page* 1
1 Brexit and Northern Ireland: hardening positions
   during the referendum   16
2 Brexit as meteor theory: external shocks to peace
   settlements   47
3 Brexit day: the result and the fallout   76
4 The election that changed the course of Brexit:
   Westminster 2017   107
5 Aspiration or guarantee? The 'frictionless' border   136
6 Brexit and the Good Friday Agreement   167
7 From partners to rivals: Anglo-Irish relations after
   Brexit   197
Epilogue: Brexit – do or die?   226

Acknowledgements   237
Notes   241
Select bibliography   262
Index   282

Introduction

Brexit tears up the Good Friday Agreement. The DUP were against the Good Friday Agreement and this is their revenge. … They want to destroy the Good Friday Agreement and have waited twenty-one years and this is their opportunity to do that. If Brexit goes ahead in the way envisaged by the DUP and the Brexiteers, then you have effectively binned the Good Friday Agreement.

Máirtín Ó Muilleoir MLA, Sinn Féin[1]

The damage to the Belfast Agreement and the devolved institutions has not been done by Brexit but by the absence of the Assembly sitting. It is ironic that those who are most keen on cross-border institutions are ensuring that the cross-border institutions do not meet because there is no Assembly and no Ministers to go to cross-border meetings. However, what the current situation has done is to highlight one of the very weak points of the Belfast Agreement, namely that one Party can have a veto as to whether or not the institutions of the Belfast Agreement are allowed to operate.

Sammy Wilson MP, Democratic Unionist Party[2]

[Brexit] has fundamentally changed the constitutional settlement of the United Kingdom. We need to have a new future of how we look at the United Kingdom.

Steve Aiken MLA, Ulster Unionist Party[3]

I think that [during] Brexit, Northern Ireland is the most polarised it has been since the Hunger Strikes in 1981. However, clearly there

1

is nothing like the risk of violence or the appetite for violence that there was in 1981.

Ben Lowry, deputy editor, *Belfast News Letter*[4]

Brexit hit Northern Ireland like a meteor from space. No one really saw it coming – or really understood its implications. It represents the biggest political and economic challenge for Northern Ireland since its foundation in 1921. In 2021 we will be commemorating the centenary of the creation of Northern Ireland, but the implications of Brexit will likely shape Ireland's future (North and South) for the next hundred years. In the context of Northern Ireland's troubled history, Brexit sits as a counterpoint to partition, separated by nearly a century but bookending generations of political strife, cultural division and economic instability. Thus for a political scientist who has spent the last twenty-five years writing and teaching about the political conflict and troubled institutions in the region, it raises a fascinating and urgent set of questions for the future of Northern Ireland, relationships within the whole island and between Ireland and Great Britain (GB).

In this sense the book is about history as well as politics – as in Ireland, these two disciplines are notoriously difficult to disentangle. We wear our history like a comfort blanket in Ireland; it shrouds us in nostalgia, belonging and an overriding sense of victimhood. Some have wallowed in this to an unhealthy degree – even though the victim status has been hard earned. But for some the past has invaded the present and shackled them to it in a way that has been limiting rather than liberating. This point was made by Maya Angelou, one of the great voices of post-war American literature, who said that 'history, despite its wrenching pain, cannot be unlived, however, if faced with courage, need not be lived again'.[5] When Queen Elizabeth II visited Ireland in June 2011, she spoke about the importance of 'being able to bow to the past, but not be bound by it'.[6] However, in Northern Ireland history is not simply history, it is also woven into politics, culture and religion and decanted into a heady brew of ethnonational identity. The problem is that these identities are contested, and are reflected in mainly binary British and Irish terms. History is remembered (or misremembered) along divided lines, where the past is deployed in pursuit of contemporary disputes about political power and cultural belonging. Brexit encapsulates this multilayered conflict, where micro and macro issues are inextricably linked to the point where they form an amalgam. Thus the Irish border is simultaneously about a territorial demarcation and also about an existential identity crisis. Border roads that might appear sleepy backwaters are actually emotionally charged frontiers – places that for some Brexit supporters have been 'weaponised' by those on the 'Remain' side of the argument seeking to use the Irish peace process as a shield to hide behind to guilt-trip the United Kingdom (UK) government into changing its policy. Once Brexit 'happened' (and in Ireland Brexit happened on 24 June 2016 once the referendum outcome was known), border roads became more than roads. They became political and cultural totems of Irish freedom, peace, stability and the Belfast/Good Friday Agreement.

Brexit as an issue therefore connects the present and future of Ireland to the past in a number of ways – many of them not appreciated by the government that is responsible for running the Northern part of it. The border – to take one of the most immediate issues in the UK's departure from the European Union (EU) – is not just a territorial demarcator, or even just a political one. It is of course both, but it is also an historical, cultural and psychological phenomenon with a resonance in the Irish context that has just not been appreciated when viewed through a British lens. So to close a border road in Ireland would have a significance beyond traffic management for either the Irish or UK governments. Such an act would be seen as an historical throwback to malign English control, to what is popularly referred to as the 'Troubles' of the 1970s and 1980s and beyond that to the Irish Famine of the mid-nineteenth century, the Land War that followed and the rise of militant republicanism in the early twentieth century that led to the partition of Ireland in 1921 and to the very border that is once again on the front burner of contemporary Irish politics. None of this historical baggage was on the radar of those driving the Brexit project in 2016, or of those who continue to do so.

This book examines the impact of Brexit on Northern Ireland, and it is primarily concerned with the story of the negotiations and how these affected Northern Ireland and the wider set of political relationships between London and Dublin and with the European Union itself. One of the key threads that runs through the book relates to the way in which the Brexit negotiations have affected political stability in Northern Ireland and further complicated the operation of the devolved institutions, and the progress of the peace process more broadly. As the title suggests, it poses the question: Is Brexit 'breaking peace' in Northern Ireland?

It is certainly putting huge strain on what is popularly referred to as 'peace' in Northern Ireland but might more accurately be defined as political stability in the region. Ironically, this was not foreseen at any point during the peace process or the three years of multiparty negotiations that resulted in the Belfast/Good Friday Agreement (GFA).[7] Everyone back then was looking inwards at each other – rather than outwards at how changes in the external political environment might destabilise the political settlement. There was an underlying assumption within the text of the GFA that external factors would remain constant. To this extent the book presents an example for other conflict contexts about the capacity for political events to evolve and the need for negotiated agreements to build flex into their language to accommodate such unforeseen changes. As Brexit demonstrates (like the end of the Cold War before it), meteors do land on occasion and it is wise to have some shock absorbers available for fragile post-conflict political institutions when they do.

Another theme that sits at the centre of the book relates to Northern Ireland's political and cultural position within the United

Kingdom and the manner in which Brexit once again thrust the region into the forefront of British politics. While Northern Ireland quickly became an issue in the Brexit negotiations, this was not the case during the UK referendum campaign in 2016. How Brexit would impact on Northern Ireland was simply not on the political radar – or that of the media that was covering the campaign. This oversight became obvious after the referendum result, but the fact that it was largely overlooked beforehand raises a fundamental set of issues pertaining to Northern Ireland's role within the UK and how that is understood in both Ireland and in Great Britain.

Northern Ireland, of course, quickly became *the* key focus of the Brexit negotiations and has proven to be the most difficult issue to reconcile. This book focuses on the efforts to square the Irish circle, characterised by the question of how the UK government's declared aim of leaving the single market and the customs union can be achieved while also meeting its declared intention to maintain the Common Travel Area (CTA) between the UK and Ireland. The book examines these apparently mutually incompatible aspirations and how political discourse surrounding them evolved over the course of the Brexit negotiations. To reiterate a point made earlier but central to the book – Brexit as a phenomenon has been experienced differently in Britain and Ireland. In Britain the debate has largely centred around the future and what would happen once it left the European Union. However, in Ireland Brexit is spoken of in the present tense, not as a future concept. Brexit is here already, it is happening now and it is having a tangible effect on people's lives.

One of the core themes of this book is how the main political parties developed their positions and arguments during the negotiations, why they did so and the implications of these arguments for the future of the devolved institutions in Northern Ireland. The positions of the two largest political parties in Northern Ireland, the Democratic Unionist Party (DUP) and Sinn Féin, were as divided over Brexit as that of the British and Irish governments. Sinn Féin was fundamentally opposed to Brexit, campaigned for the Remain side, and has since demanded 'special status' for the region once the UK leaves the EU. The DUP was an advocate of the 'Leave' side in the 2016 referendum and has insisted on Northern Ireland exiting the EU on the same terms as the rest of the UK, rather than being seen as a special case.

All of these themes crystallise around one central question: What is going to happen to the Irish border after Brexit? The border issue haunts the negotiations, those involved in them and everyone else who will be affected by any change in the nature of the border once the UK has left the EU. This has been one of the most intractable arguments during the Brexit negotiations and one of the most vivid areas of political debate and public concern. Fear that the border will re-emerge as a point of political friction in Ireland has concentrated the minds of many, within and beyond the policy actors involved in resolving the issue.

As mentioned earlier, the border issue provides a perfect illustration as to why Northern Ireland represents a unique aspect of the Brexit negotiations and the process of leaving the EU, an aspect not faced elsewhere in the UK. While a majority of people within the region voted to remain in the referendum on 23 June 2016, (56% voting to remain, 44% voting to leave), Northern Ireland will be the only part of the UK to share a land border with another EU state after the UK ceases to be a member.[8] So once the UK has left the EU, Northern Ireland will become the UK land frontier to the EU, a fact that has potentially huge implications for politics in Northern Ireland, where the border was for many years the physical and legal manifestation of partition and a driver of violent political conflict between the late 1960s and late 1990s, until the political institutions were established on the basis of cross-community power-sharing following the GFA in 1998. Thus the nature of the Irish border is crucial for the devolved institutions and the political stability of the whole island.

It has to be remembered that another sovereign country, Ireland,[9] has significant political, economic and cultural interests in the terms of Brexit and how these outcomes may affect political stability in Northern Ireland. This inevitably links the implementation of Brexit into a wider Anglo-Irish context, with unique complications. This reality will be crucially important for the political and economic future of Ireland and the future of the peace process more broadly.

Each of the book's seven chapters focuses on a key aspect of the Brexit negotiations and its impact on Northern Ireland and broader Anglo-Irish relations. The narrative and main arguments within it are built upon a wide evidence base, including previously published academic studies, official reports, speeches and primary documents from the main political parties in Ireland and Britain, as well as a mountainous volume of newspaper and broadcast media reporting of the Brexit negotiations over the 2016–19 period. A number of interviews were also conducted for the book with key individuals who have been close observers of political events during the period. These include politicians from Northern Ireland from the unionist and nationalist communities, journalists with a close understanding of the political temperature in Northern Ireland during the period and voices from civic society with expertise on economic and community relations dimensions of the Brexit crisis in Northern Ireland. The purpose of these interviews is to illuminate the main themes within the book and in that sense they are illustrative and reflective and are used to encapsulate the core issues discussed.

Chapter 1 introduces the key themes that underpin the book and maps the emergence of Northern Ireland as a contested issue within the Brexit referendum debate in the run-up to the vote on 23 June 2016. While the central focus is on the referendum campaign and the emergence of the main party political positions, the chapter also puts into context some of the main issues that feature in subsequent chapters. This locates the central arguments within the key academic debates on the GFA, power-sharing and the centrality of the 'consent principle' as an axis of consensus for political change in Northern Ireland within the context of the Brexit negotiation process. This chapter also sets out the debate over the future status of the Irish border and how that issue has impacted on the devolved institutions and relations between the main political parties in Northern Ireland.

Chapter 2 connects the empirical dimension of the book relating to the impact of Brexit on Northern Ireland, to a wider theoretical outlook on the dynamics of peacebuilding. The chapter introduces a new conceptual focus to conflict transformation understanding by focusing on the significance of unexpected exogenous shocks to largely endogenous political agreements. The argument here is that Brexit presents a novel example of the need to provide peace-building shock absorbers that can withstand fundamental unforeseen circumstances – meteors – that hit peace processes with the potential to knock them off their conventional axes and change the local context. This theoretical chapter is intended to provide conflict studies with an example of the need for greater flex and adaptability within conflict environments. Brexit was a meteor in the context of the Northern Ireland peace process – no one saw it coming or understood, when they were negotiating in 1998, how normal political gravity would be affected when it hit the political atmosphere in June 2016.

Chapter 3 examines the outcome of the referendum vote on 23 June 2016 and the divisions that it exposed in Northern Ireland, across the political parties and within their respective electorates. The chapter assesses the political fallout from the result and the responses of the main parties to the latest evidence of political division within the region. This period saw the crystallisation of political positions and a shift from campaigning mode, towards arguments relating to the democratic legitimacy of the vote and rival interpretations of what it meant in practice.

One of the key areas this chapter focuses upon concerns the debate that followed the result and in particular the fact that the majority of those who voted in Northern Ireland chose Remain

(56%) as opposed to Leave (44%). This led to an unusual turn of events where Sinn Féin began to articulate the right of Northern Ireland to self-determination over the Brexit issue, while the DUP focused instead on the UK vote as a whole. This complicated the usual political geometry in Northern Ireland, as the DUP, normally an advocate of an 'Ulster-first' form of devolved government, suddenly veered towards a more integrationist position. Sinn Féin meanwhile, having denied the political legitimacy of Northern Ireland for most of the last hundred years, suddenly became a champion of its majoritarian political will and democratically expressed self-determination.

Chapter 4 focuses on the aftermath of the Westminster General Election of 8 June 2017, the hung parliament that resulted and the 'confidence-and-supply' deal negotiated between the Conservative Party government and the Democratic Unionist Party on 26 June 2017. This presented yet another unforeseen component of the Brexit challenge for Northern Ireland – and again arrived against expectations. The General Election was called by the newly installed Prime Minister Theresa May to help mandate her leadership and provide the public credibility and parliamentary arithmetic to help steward Brexit through the political and legal system. It was also called because the overwhelming message from the opinion polls was that the Conservative Party would win a landslide victory against the embattled leader of the Labour Party, Jeremy Corbyn. The result did not go as expected and left Theresa May clinging to office with a minority government. The subsequent confidence-and-supply agreement with the DUP kept her in power but changed the dynamics of Brexit significantly, both in terms of how the negotiations proceeded within GB, but also in terms of Northern Ireland politics as well.

The deal with the DUP needs to be understood in the political context of Northern Ireland – as well as in GB terms. Its significance was compounded by the fact that it came at a time when there was no functioning devolved government and when relations between the DUP and Sinn Féin were already tense. The result of the Conservative Party deal with the DUP had a negative impact on that relationship and thus on the appetite of those parties to restore the devolved institutions to Northern Ireland. This is a key aspect of Northern Ireland's Brexit story, as the three-year suspension of functioning institutions and lack of common purpose between the main political representatives of the people who live there made it very difficult for the specific interests of Northern Ireland to be reflected in the UK's Brexit negotiations.

Chapter 5 focuses on the epicentre of Brexit for Northern Ireland – namely the border and how the issue of Irish border arrangements was read differently by the various parties during the Brexit negotiations. At a very basic level, the process of Brexit complicates the issue of political self-determination in Ireland and raises the question of how the Common Travel Area between the UK and Ireland will be implemented outside of the customs union. This chapter explores how the border issue was defined during the Brexit negotiations, how it divided the main political parties and their wider electorates, and the degree to which this presented new political incentives to the main political parties.

The rise of the border as a political issue after the Brexit referendum cut into one of the most sensitive aspects of Northern Ireland's ethnonational conflict – and forced people to confront what the GFA had managed to de-escalate. In blunt terms: Which side of the binary line do you live on – the British part of Ireland or the Irish part of Ireland? In this sense Brexit re-weaponised the partition of Ireland and the 'constitutional question' which had been skilfully parked by the terms of the GFA since 1998 and by the existence – until recently – of a set of power-sharing institutions in Northern Ireland which also went some way to demonstrating that a new era of local democratic control was valuing the rival traditions of Britishness and Irishness equally. Mediating the 'constitutional question' was a key tenet of the GFA and the subsequent institutions established after 1998.[10] Northern Ireland's devolved political institutions were based on a form of consociational democracy that has been at the centre of scholarly debates on Northern Ireland since they were established in 1999.[11]

The capacity of the GFA to facilitate dual political identities on the basis of choice has also provided a key foundation for the development of Anglo-Irish relations since 1998.[12] The British government tried to provide repeated assurances that the process of leaving the EU would not undermine the GFA and would seek to maintain the Common Travel Area in Ireland as well as the commitment to dual citizenship rights. As this chapter demonstrates, however, it became clear very quickly that these aspirations were hard to guarantee and that little was set down or clearly fleshed out about how these dynamics would unfold in practice, once the process of Brexit had formally begun.

Chapter 6 looks specifically at the extent to which the Brexit process represents a challenge to the Good Friday Agreement. This examines the arguments relating to whether the substantive principles of the GFA were affected by the UK's decision to leave the EU. This chapter also assesses the extent to which the negotiations themselves presented challenges to the future of the GFA and the devolved institutions within Northern Ireland.

10 April 2019 marked the twenty-first anniversary of the Good Friday Agreement. This multiparty negotiation, which resulted from two years of formal talks, involved ten political parties in Northern Ireland, the British and Irish governments and included the support and involvement of senior mediators, including the White House administration of President Bill Clinton. A formal agreement was endorsed by the two sovereign parliaments in Ireland and the United Kingdom and importantly was passed by dual referendums in Northern Ireland and the Irish Republic with overwhelming majorities. It has lasted for a generation but, at the same time, the devolved power-sharing institutions that resulted have been plagued by instability, political inertia and a chronic lack of collective coherence.

Unsurprisingly, there are different narratives surrounding the extent to which Brexit has impacted on the GFA – as indicated by some of the quotes at the beginning of this chapter. Sinn Féin see Brexit as a fundamentally destabilising challenge to the GFA and its institutions. Many unionists, however, see Brexit as more of a bump in the road within the peace process and criticise Irish nationalists for talking up Brexit as a crisis. This chapter examines these conflicting narratives on whether Brexit is actually breaking peace in Northern Ireland.

Chapter 7 examines the Brexit negotiations from a wider perspective and looks at the impact it has had on Anglo-Irish relations. The reason for this wide-angled lens is that the London/ Dublin relationship has been integral to the political fortunes of Northern Ireland and will continue to play a critical role in the future viability of the peace process and political institutions in the region. UK and Irish membership of the EU has been a point of commonality since the simultaneous entry of the two countries to the European Economic Community (EEC) in 1973. Membership also brought key personnel in both jurisdictions into regular proximity on other matters but normalised diplomatic relations between the two countries to a level that had not been seen previously. The Brexit referendum changed that and sets a new course for both countries. This relates to policy towards Northern Ireland but also to wider dimensions, notably to economic interests as well as broader attitudes to security, human rights and to the European neighbourhood itself.

The chapter demonstrates how the Brexit negotiations made diplomatic relations more fraught between the two countries, primarily over the ambiguity surrounding the future of the Irish border, but also over the UK's broader commitment to the future of the GFA itself. The chapter argues that Brexit brought a structural incompatibility into the Anglo-Irish relationship that very quickly led both countries to regard one another as opponents in a zero-sum negotiation, rather than allies with a joint purpose over Northern

Ireland. This was demonstrated through public statements on both sides relatively early in the negotiating process, with trust draining out of the political relationship between them. In January 2017, for instance, the Irish EU Commissioner for Agriculture, Phil Hogan, suggested a need for a recalibrated Anglo-Irish relationship as a result of the UK's imminent departure from the EU: 'Brexit will happen and we now need to take a very strategic and far-sighted review of our relationships with both the UK and the rest of our European partners. … It is also important that our political relationship with the United Kingdom matures to reflect the changed political and legal circumstances.'[13] This chapter maps the slow fracture in the Anglo-Irish relationship, explains why this took place and assesses its implications for Northern Ireland.

A brief conclusion examines how the experience of the referendum and the Brexit negotiations that followed have affected political and economic affairs in Northern Ireland. This final section frames the key arguments within the book and the main issues that will face Northern Ireland, the UK government and the Irish Republic, as the next phase of the Brexit process begins. It will make the argument that Brexit is 'breaking peace' in Northern Ireland and that the severity with which it does so is dependent upon how Brexit is experienced. A 'no-deal'[14] Brexit with no transition period is likely to result in a more extreme decline in Anglo-Irish relations and the peace process, while some form of deal between the EU and UK with the Backstop[15] element intact is likely to cause a less immediate and urgent crisis.

On a brief biographical and editorial aspect of the book – there is no neutrality in Brexit, as in politics more broadly. As Kevin O'Rourke puts it: 'It is impossible to write about Brexit completely dispassionately and so it is important to be open about one's potential biases.'[16] From an ontological standpoint, the book is written from the position that there is no ultimate neutrality and that academics play a part in shaping the data and the research they publish. I voted Remain in the 2016 referendum. I did so enthusiastically as a European – while being fully aware of the critique of its neo-liberal nature and its inherent political and economic failings. I also did so because I felt that a Leave result would have a negative impact on the island of Ireland and on the political institutions in Northern Ireland.

I have lived in England for over twenty years and one of my last political acts before I moved away from Northern Ireland was to vote 'Yes' in the referendum on the Belfast/Good Friday Agreement in May 1998. I felt at the time that it would be the most important exercise of my democratic franchise in my lifetime.

I was wrong. My vote to remain within the EU on 23 June 2016 was the bigger issue – though, as it turned out, I was on the losing side – one of the 16 million rather than one of the 17 million. Of course, if I was still living in Northern Ireland I would have been on the winning side (the 56% of Remainers not the 44% of Leavers) – though ultimately Northern Ireland's wishes have been sublimated under those of the whole UK in the Brexit negotiations. This is the incendiary aspect of Brexit in the Irish context – it confronts us with the reality that the GFA, its devolved institutions and our democratic right to self-determination are subservient to the will of the British government, parliament and even courts in London.

I would position myself politically as being on the left on the political spectrum, sensitive to the fact that the EU is focused more on the interests of international capital and big business and dominated by its richest members rather than by its poorest ones.[17] But I am also acutely aware of the positive dimension of European membership: the contribution made by the EU to the peace process in Northern Ireland and the importance to me personally of my European colleagues and friends in the UK. At a very basic level, I was aware of the implications of the UK leaving the EU when Ireland remained within it – the implications for the place I care about most, Northern Ireland and the wider island.

I found the radical left Brexit position unconvincing, in some cases a self-indulgent vanity project, where Brexit was a convenient vehicle for broader revolutionary goals. For some on the left their desire to resist neo-liberal institutions such as the EU was pursued irrespective of the damage that it did along the way. But many people are already getting hurt by Brexit: in small businesses, in construction industries, in whatever manufacturing sector the UK has remaining. Some of these intellectuals 'are so far left – they're right' and on Brexit, at least, they have become the enablers of right-wing racism, xenophobia and austerity. Where was their voice on the damage done to livelihoods of workers in Swindon, Sunderland, Scunthorpe and other places where people had already lost their jobs before the UK had even left the EU? Where was their voice on Ireland and the peace process? It was so *sotto voce* it was inaudible. They can write their own books and try to justify the number of eggs that have to be broken to cook their revolutionary omelettes. This book takes the view that Brexit is an act of colossal self-harm by the UK and an act of criminal disregard for peace in Ireland.

The implications of Brexit for Northern Ireland are profound for everyone who lives there and for the whole island – politically, economically and culturally. In this sense the book (like most books) has a position that is not a point of neutrality. At the same time it aims to give a voice to the case of those who have argued for Brexit and who have advocated and constructed the policies aimed to engineer the UK's departure from the EU. The book aims to be faithful to that view and to represent it fairly and accurately – while pointing out the errors of judgement that lie behind it. It lies with the reader, of course, to determine whether I have done so successfully.

The majority of the book was written by October 2019 with some very limited updates added in December 2019. Brexit has been something of a moving target and it is inevitable that this narrative account will be overtaken by the pace of fast-moving events. But while the Brexit story will continue to evolve, the fundamental themes, principles and arguments within the book will prevail.

1

Brexit and Northern Ireland: hardening positions during the referendum

On Monday, I will commence the process set out in our Referendum Act and I will go to parliament and propose that the British people decide our future in Europe through an in/out referendum on Thursday 23rd of June.

Prime Minister David Cameron, 20 February 2016

The EU Withdrawal Bill receiving Royal Assent is a historic moment for our country and a significant step towards delivering on the will of the British people.

Prime Minister Theresa May, 26 June 2018

The real-time polarisation that you can see over the last two years is incredible.

Claire Hanna MLA, Social Democratic and Labour Party, 23 April 2019[1]

In retrospect it seems ironic that Northern Ireland had a relatively low profile during the Brexit referendum campaign of 2015 and 2016.[2] This was certainly true in Britain, where it was subsumed under the white-hot debate over immigration and media-friendly slogans of the Leave campaign's assertions about 'taking back control' of the UK borders. Even in the Northern Ireland context Brexit was a relatively low-key issue, at least initially – which, given subsequent events, seems a little surprising.

There are three broad explanations for this. The first was that most people thought that the Remain side was going to win the referendum. Nearly all of the polling evidence pointed towards that outcome until very close to polling day on 23 June 2016, and the experience of the Scottish referendum on independence in 2014 was that opinion took a more conservative turn – to preserve the status quo – in the final stages of the campaign. 'Project Fear', as the negative campaigning was referred to, had made a difference in Scotland and there was a complacent belief that this would also benefit the Remain side in the Brexit referendum.

For instance, Sinn Féin's manifesto for the Irish General Election which took place in February 2016, only a week after the UK Prime Minister announced the date of the 'in/out' referendum, showed just how quickly the political context can shift. While the Brexit issue was in the air, it was more of a whiff than a stink in early 2016 – and this was reflected in the party manifestos. Sinn Féin's election manifesto was built around a critique of the government's economic policies under the slogan 'For a Fair Recovery Níos Fearr le Sinn Féin', and the foreword, from president Gerry Adams, did not include one reference to Brexit as being an issue. The same was true of the governing Fine Gael party led by the Taoiseach Enda Kenny. Fine Gael's manifesto for the 2016 General Election focused on the administration's record in government and suggested that the fragile economic recovery would be jeopardised if the party lost office. However, buried towards the back of the manifesto was a sentence that alluded to Brexit – before it was known as Brexit: 'Fine Gael believes that UK membership of the EU is beneficial for Ireland, the UK and the EU. We will advocate for continued UK membership of the EU and play a positive role in Negotiations and debates.'[3]

In other words, Fine Gael saw its role as that of being an ally to a UK government that wanted to remain within the EU and had not realised by this point (or at least publicly recognised) the extent to which large sections of the political class and public opinion did not share its vision.

Fine Gael's 2016 General Election manifesto did, however, contain a statement that in retrospect seems to have been written in a bygone age – which, in the context of Brexit, it was:

> Building on the successful state visits of 2011 and 2014, we will continue to enhance Ireland's relationship with the United Kingdom, including under the Good Friday Agreement, through the British–Irish Council and the annual summits between the Taoiseach and British Prime Minister. We will strengthen cooperation with all devolved administrations.[4]

During the final leaders' debate of the Irish General Election, broadcast by RTE on 23 February – three days after David Cameron's announcement that an in/out referendum would take place on 23 June – there was not one reference to it from Enda Kenny (Fine Gael), Michael Martin (Fianna Fáil), Joan Burton (Irish Labour Party) or Gerry Adams (Sinn Féin). Even by April 2016 (two months before the referendum), the issue had not become a major talking point within the political debate in Ireland. Sinn Féin's annual conference (Ard Fheis), held that month, took a clear position on the referendum but was overwhelmingly focused on commemorating the centenary of 1916 and the Easter Rising of that year. The Ard Fheis did pass a motion opposing Brexit on the basis of its likely impact on the peace process in Northern Ireland, but there was little energy in the issue at this stage – not least because of the assumption that the Remain side would prevail.

> Sinn Féin will oppose and campaign against any attempts by the British government to withdraw from the EU. Increased or full withdrawal by the British state from the EU, has negative implications for Ireland, North and South. It would represent a major set-back for political progress in the North and directly challenge the integrity of the Good Friday Agreement as an internationally binding treaty.[5]

Also while it might not seem so now with Sinn Féin articulating a very pro-European agenda, prior to 2016 Sinn Féin was quite a

Eurosceptic party – critiquing it in similar terms to the left of the Labour Party in the UK and taking a position not dissimilar to that of then Labour leader Jeremy Corbyn: that the EU was set up to promote the neo-liberal interests of its richest members. This was the view of former Social Democratic and Labour Party (SDLP) Brexit spokesperson Claire Hanna when she reflected on the attitude of Sinn Féin during the multiparty negotiations that led to the Good Friday Agreement in 1998:

> It has been said before, but it is worth repeating, Mark Durkan [former SDLP leader] and others have said that the reason the EU isn't mentioned more and more often [in the GFA], is because the Ulster Unionists and Sinn Féin were both Eurosceptics at the time [1998] and they didn't want to have 'EU-this and EU-that' [within the GFA] to spare their blushes.[6]

This reflection was also made by unionist commentators such as Ben Lowry, deputy editor of the *Belfast News Letter*, who pointed out that Sinn Féin had traditionally been Eurosceptic, before the 2016 referendum disrupted the political centre of gravity in Northern Ireland.[7]

The second reason why Brexit had a relatively low profile in Northern Ireland during the early stages of the referendum campaign was because there were other political problems consuming energy and attention. By 2015 relations between the largest unionist party, the Democratic Unionist Party, and the largest nationalist party, Sinn Féin, were at a very low ebb. As a result of these dysfunctional relationships, the devolved institutions in Northern Ireland were similarly fragile and much of the attention was consumed by political disagreements at the local level.

The 2016 Assembly Election in Northern Ireland was held on 5 May, just over one month before the UK referendum on EU membership and again the focus of the party election literature was on internal matters relating to the record of the devolved institutions. The title of Sinn Féin's 2016 Assembly Election manifesto was *Better with Sinn Féin Níos fearr le Sinn Féin*, and again the emphasis was placed on social and economic policies, the economy and Sinn Féin's record in government, rather than on the Brexit issue. The foreword from former deputy First Minister Martin McGuinness did refer to the party's commitment to campaign against Brexit '… as it would be bad for Ireland politically, economically and socially'. Beyond that, the possibility of the UK exiting the EU barely got a mention in an election that took place one month before the referendum that changed everything.[8]

The SDLP manifesto, *Build a Better Future*, also focused for the most part on its vision for a more progressive society and effective political institutions. However, it did make its opposition to Brexit clear and its intention to oppose it in the lead-up to the referendum on 23 June:

> Withdrawal from the European Union represents the single greatest threat to Northern Ireland's economic security. In purely financial terms, it is estimated withdrawal would cost the Northern Ireland economy at least £1 billion annually. This cost is not abstract. It is a real cost which would be paid by businesses, farmers and families right across the North. The SDLP will campaign vigorously to ensure that such a burden is not placed on all of us who live here.[9]

The Ulster Unionist Party (UUP) manifesto, *Make it Work*, presented the party as an alternative to the political status quo. It criticised the record of the DUP and Sinn Féin in government and used the in/out referendum theme to map out its position on being in or out of government after the election. On the issue of the June referendum, the UUP was ambivalent and opted for a cautious Remain stance.

> While individual party members are free to vote as they choose in the Referendum on the 23rd of June, the Ulster Unionist Party believes that, on balance, Northern Ireland is better off remaining in the EU, while HM Government pushes for further reform, and

a return to the founding principle of free trade and an end to the drive for further political union.[10]

The UUP's position on EU membership was more complicated than many of the other parties in Northern Ireland as it traditionally had strong links to the business and farming sectors as well as voters who were split across the Leave and Remain sides of the argument. They were squeezed in a similar manner to Labour and the Conservatives in Great Britain, in that while many of their members felt positively disposed towards the EU, they also had just as many supporters who were more Eurosceptic and were equally concerned by the DUP narrative that emphasised the primacy of the Union. This division was there in 2016 and remains – as pointed out by UUP Brexit spokesperson Steve Aiken just prior to the local council elections in April 2019:

> It's difficult, because I could take you down a street with similar houses, similar sorts of cars and the rest of it – and you will get a different response [on Brexit] from every single house. It depends very much on people's experience and where they've worked and what they've done and the rest of it. It is very very nuanced. There is an assessment that Europe might have done something worthwhile for us, but over the last two years [2017–19] because of the Irish government's comments and Simon Coveney pulling on the green jersey, and Leo's [Varadkar] Brit-bashing, all those points along the line have actually modified [unionist] people's views, to a degree that, having knocked on the best part of about 2000 doors in the last two weeks [April 2019], … the overwhelming response is – 'just get on with it', 'don't really care', 'just get on with it'.[11]

The DUP 2016 Assembly Election manifesto, *Our Plan for Northern Ireland*, focused on the leader Arlene Foster and the party's record in government, largely ignoring the issue of Brexit completely. This is interesting in light of subsequent events and the impression given that the DUP believed in Brexit as an ideological project in the way that Brexiteers in the UK Independence Party (UKIP) and Conservative Party did. But this would be a misreading of the DUP, who were pragmatic rather than dogmatic believers in Brexit. To casual observers in Great Britain, especially after the 2017 General Election which raised the media profile of the DUP significantly, the fact that they made the case for Brexit so consistently would give the impression that this was a long-held policy goal of the party. It was not. The DUP developed a strategic alliance with Brexiteers within the European Research Group (ERG) in the Conservative Party. But this alliance and commitment to Brexit was always secondary to its concern about Northern Ireland's constitutional position within the United Kingdom.

Like the General Election in the Irish Republic a few months previously, the lack of sustained focus on the Brexit issue demonstrates that for the first half of 2016, it was not a central aspect of political debate in either part of Ireland. Attitudes within Ireland towards the EU are broadly positive, though as Kathryn Simpson has shown in her work, it is a complex and nuanced relationship.[12] But in electoral terms the issue of EU membership was not a vote-winner in a way that could distinguish one party from another and it had not yet made it into the foreground of public debate.

The important thing to remember about elections in Northern Ireland (compared to Westminster) is that they operate under a single-transferable vote (STV) system. It is also the case that in effect there are two elections rather than one taking place, as the parties hunt for votes within (rather than across) the ethnonational divide. As voters can indicate a range of preferences across the ballot paper (rather than just putting an X against one candidate's name, as is the case in first-past-the-post elections), it is important for the parties to encourage voters to transfer preferences to their candidates from other parties within their respective ethnonational blocks. Despite the Good Friday Agreement being over two decades old and the peace process now a generation on, voting transfers across the unionist/nationalist divide remain very low in Northern Ireland.[13]

Partly as a consequence of this, a common feature of elections in Northern Ireland is 'ethnic outbidding' on both sides. Unionist parties claim that they are more trustworthy than their unionist competitors and nationalist parties claim they have a more coherent/realistic vision for the future than their nationalist rivals. So while there was a nod from most of the main parties towards Brexit in the 2016 Assembly Election, the central focus for most of them was to position themselves for this intra-ethnic competition. Such ethnic outbidding is a tried and tested feature of politics in conflict areas, and Northern Ireland exhibits a textbook example of the practice. Given this blunt political reality, there was little value to be had in using Brexit as a means of maximising the vote for any of the main parties. It was much more productive to engage in harsh rhetoric that would energise and mobilise the party faithful and confirm the prejudices and fears of the electorate. The UK referendum on EU membership was thus submerged under a relatively shallow public debate between Sinn Féin and the DUP akin to the 'trash-talking' that can be seen in advance of high-profile boxing bouts. The DUP fought the 2016 Assembly Election with a new leader, Arlene Foster, replacing former leader Peter Robinson. The DUP was focused around her leadership and personality. Foster's key message to prospective voters was that voting for the DUP was the only way unionists could stop Sinn Féin's Martin McGuinness becoming First Minister.[14] This sectarian realpolitik was underlined by Steve Aiken, Ulster Unionist Party Brexit spokesperson when he shared his recollections of the period. 'It's the fear factor. … The number of people that turn round to me and say, "I'd definitely vote for the UUP – because you've got all these [good] people. But I need to vote for the DUP to keep Sinn Féin out."'[15]

Sinn Féin interpreted this mentality as a demonstration of bad faith and a lack of respect for the legitimacy of nationalists as partners in government. As a result, such was the animosity and mutual loathing between the DUP and Sinn Féin during the 2016 Assembly Election, any implications of the Brexit referendum for Northern Ireland were squeezed out of the political discourse despite the referendum being just over a month away. In retrospect this might seem to be a little short-sighted, but hindsight is not a gift that political practitioners are blessed with.

The Green Party in Northern Ireland also had little to say about the UK's in/out referendum in the 2016 Assembly Election and focused most of its attention on a range of socially progressive policies for Northern Ireland. Its manifesto for the election was entitled *A Zero Waste Strategy for Northern Ireland* and the emphasis was on the need for equality, social justice and environmental sustainability as well as an extension of human rights standards in Northern Ireland.[16] This contrasts starkly with its manifesto for the 2017 General Election, where Brexit was a central element of the party's attempt to promote a second referendum on any negotiated deal between the UK and EU. Entitled *#PuttingYouFirst*, the manifesto campaigned on the fact that Northern Ireland's voice was not being heard effectively in the Brexit negotiations and it had voted by a majority to remain in the 2016 referendum.[17] 'This election is set against turbulent political times. The decision of the UK to back Brexit, against the wishes of the majority of people in Northern Ireland, has created huge uncertainty.'[18]

The third reason why the political debate in Northern Ireland during the early stages of the referendum campaign was relatively subdued was because it had not, by that stage, been welded onto the rival ethnonational unionist and nationalist positions. The main parties did take positions on UK membership of the EU, but they were not disagreeing with one another along ethnonational lines over Brexit in the typically pugilist manner outlined above. This division came later – but only when the referendum campaign had begun in earnest and after the result became clear. Until this point, Brexit was not a unionist/nationalist 'issue' and was not connected to identity politics as something that would augment or degrade visions of Britishness or Irishness.

The one exception to this came from the relatively small – but highly energetic – unionist party Traditional Unionist Voice (TUV). The TUV was the vehicle for its leader Jim Allister, a former member of the DUP who castigated his former party for its willingness to enter government with Sinn Féin. The TUV could be termed a hyper-unionist party, with the Union flag prominent in its party logo and adopting policy positions that were to the right of the DUP, unequivocally opposed to working with Sinn Féin and to the post-GFA devolved political institutions in Northern Ireland. The TUV highlighted its support for Brexit prior to the May 2016 Assembly Election and, unlike the other parties in Northern Ireland, gave Brexit a prominent position in its *Manifesto 2016: Straight Talking Principled Politics*.[19] The first sentence of the TUV manifesto suggested that the security of the unionist position was integrally connected to the Brexit option and to the UK's need to leave the EU:

> Northern Ireland is and must remain an integral part of the United Kingdom, which needs to salvage its independence by exiting the EU: that is the TUV view. ... The European Union is a disastrous drain on our nation's resources and restraint on our economic growth. Hence TUV's strong support for Brexit.[20]

The TUV's May Assembly Election manifesto connected into the UKIP narrative surrounding what was then framed as the in/out referendum on UK membership of the EU, which emphasised 'taking back control' from the Brussels bureaucrats and resisting the 'ever-closer union', where the inability to control national borders had diminished national sovereignty and led to an inability to control trade, UK laws and immigration:

> We will either succumb to the 'ever closer union', which drives everything the EU does, for the purpose of subduing national sovereignty, or, we retake control of our own country, borders and

destiny, by wisely leaving the EU. TUV will be unambiguous and vigorous is [sic] campaigning for the UK to break the chains that bind us to Brussels.[21]

To this extent, the TUV was the first political party in Northern Ireland to connect the Brexit referendum firmly with its ethnonational position. This was a natural fit for the party and fed into the political appetites of its core support base. While less clearly articulated, this also allowed the TUV to define 'the nation' in monolithic terms and within a binary UK against the EU narrative, ignoring the fact that another ethnonational community existed in Northern Ireland who would not define themselves as being part of the British nation.

However, while the TUV was a colourful party with a relatively high media profile for its leader Jim Allister, it was less successful electorally. Despite the foregrounding of support for Brexit and the excoriation of the DUP and Sinn Féin in its manifesto, it polled modestly, winning one seat (Jim Allister in North Antrim) and a mere 3.4% of the overall vote in the May 2016 Assembly Election. Despite this, its attempt to connect the Brexit referendum to its core mission of hyper-real unionism was a harbinger of what was to follow once the referendum campaign got into full swing in June 2016. In this sense, where the TUV led before the 2016 referendum, the DUP, Sinn Féin and the SDLP would eventually follow.

The in/out referendum campaign in Northern Ireland

Today the political positions on Brexit are very clearly defined – certainly across the main political parties in Northern Ireland. Brexit has become an article of faith for some and a defining aspect of their political programmes, while it is detested by others. It is difficult to imagine today that significant numbers of voters within Sinn Féin or the DUP would take a different position or disagree with party policy on Brexit. However, this rigidity was not always the case and in the early days before the referendum campaign started in earnest there was a much greater level of fluidity over the Leave/Remain positions across the political parties. In fact 'Brexit did not mean Brexit'[22] in these early days, as the issue was more popularly known as the in/out referendum on EU membership. There was less ownership of Brexit as a concept in those days or as a policy that needed to be defended regardless of the evidence available or as a central aspect of manifesto commitments. Fundamentally, there were other much more familiar things to fight about than this comparatively new issue.

Before the referendum campaign began there was a relatively light-touch approach from the main protagonists towards the issue. While the DUP formally announced in February 2016 that it would be supporting the Leave side in the referendum, it is clear from the above discussion of the May Assembly Election that this was a secondary concern for the party – not an issue that it felt could mobilise its support base or act as a means of maximising its vote in the election.

The UUP did not take a definitive position on the referendum when the 23 June date was announced by Prime Minister David Cameron in February 2016, again in part because of its lack of direct political significance at the time and due to the fact that there were a range of views within the party and among its core support base. The UUP traditionally had been the party of business and this was a point underlined by the party's Brexit spokesperson Steve Aiken.[23] This claim was rejected by *Irish News* political correspondent John Manley, who argued that the strong identification with the business community had more relevance to the party's past than to its present.[24] During the 1990s UUP voters had been caricatured as 'garden centre unionists'[25] – relatively moderate and pragmatic, without the moral agenda on social issues favoured by DUP voters, and less carnivorous in terms of their opposition to Irish identity symbols and Catholicism. In the end the UUP came out in support for Remain in the referendum in March 2016 but, rather like the DUP position, there was some ambivalence in its stance.

This demonstrates that in the early days before the Brexit juggernaut began moving, there was some political space within Northern Ireland politics on the Brexit issue and it had not fully grafted onto the Orange/Green axis in the manner in which other issues such as flags, emblems and the Irish language had done. In its *#MakeItWork* manifesto for the 2016 Assembly Election, the UUP elaborated on its statement in March, pointing out that while it felt the EU needed reform, the deciding factors behind its decision to support remain in the referendum related to four key areas. 1) The funding Northern Ireland received from the EU; 2) the security benefits afforded by membership of the EU in an increasingly dangerous world; 3) the need to establish pan-European plans on inward migration; and 4) the need to avoid a hard border between Ireland and the UK which would occur if Britain were to leave the EU.

> Bitter experience makes clear it is not possible to fully secure the border. There will be no Donald Trump style wall. But there will need to be a hard border. As it will not be on the actual border, it is likely to be at Great Britain's ports and airports, Cairnryan, Gatwick, Heathrow. This is not a welcome prospect.[26]

This provides further evidence that the referendum was not initially an obvious means of demarcating identity politics in Northern Ireland in electoral terms and was not an immediate proxy for the core disagreements over British and Irish identity that it would become during the Brexit negotiations.

The DUP announcement in February that it would be supporting the Leave campaign was itself relatively low key and surprisingly pluralist for a party known for its unequivocal positions on most aspects of policy. Like the Conservative Party government in Britain, the DUP offered a free vote on the issue to its political representatives, not something it did over key issues related to its political identity or policy platform. Party leader Arlene Foster did not adopt the TUV language that the referendum was a great chance to regain UK sovereignty and obtain freedom from the shackles of the EU. It was instead a pragmatic rather than an ideological assessment. It was based not so much on a rejection of the EU and all its works as a concept, but on the perceived operational deficiencies and the inability of Prime Minister David Cameron to obtain a deal from the EU in his negotiations prior to announcing the referendum. Foster admitted that there were members of her party who would take different positions on EU membership and disagreed with the party's position, as would some of the party's voters – but that these should be expressed during the referendum campaign.

> As every voter has the opportunity to express a view we fully expect that DUP members and voters will hold a range of differing personal views as to what is in the best interests of the United Kingdom. They are fully entitled to do so during what will be a momentous political debate about the direction of travel our nation chooses.[27]

The key issue for the DUP in the early days of the referendum campaign therefore was less the outcome of the vote, as much as ensuring that Northern Ireland was defined as an integral part of the United Kingdom. The definition of 'our nation' was the key phrase here and one that has been a consistent aspect of DUP policy on Brexit ever since. While this framing in the language may go unnoticed outside Northern Ireland, the political radar of those living there is very well tuned to the coded implications of language. This provides an illustration of the way in which the Brexit referendum provided an external dynamic that helped to revive contentious identity politics in the region. Prior to Brexit, such articulations of preferred nationhood held less significance. The GFA had effectively anaesthetised this and allowed dual definitions of nationhood to be accommodated. Thus unionists could define themselves as British, nationalists could define themselves as Irish and both could agree to disagree. The arrival of the referendum provided these rival understandings of national identity with a new dynamic and this (more than the specific merits or otherwise of EU membership) was what provided Brexit with its incendiary impact in Northern Ireland. As Ben Lowry, deputy editor of the *Belfast News Letter* (a paper with a strong unionist profile) put it, looking back at the referendum period: 'I don't think unionism thought through Brexit – and in fairness not a lot of people did think it through.'[28]

Civil society groups were just as surprised by the 2016 referendum result as their political counterparts in Northern Ireland. While they became more vocal as the negotiations proceeded, their initial voice was muted as CEO of Retail NI, Glyn Roberts, recollected in 2019:

> I think that we were very clear that during the referendum it [Brexit] wasn't an issue that we could sit on the fence on and we were very clear that we had to take a strong Remain view. Most of the business organisations in Northern Ireland were on the fence – that wasn't an option for us. … We have always taken the view that there is no 'good Brexit' – there is only damage limitation.[29]

This reference to the relatively unclear position of the business sector in Northern Ireland during the referendum campaign was underlined by Ulster Unionist Party Brexit spokesperson Steve Aiken when he reflected on the UUP's attempts to argue for a Remain vote in the lead-up to the referendum on 23 June:

> We spent a lot of time talking to the business community and the farming community [in Northern Ireland] and one of the most annoying things was, leading up to the remain campaign [was] trying to get the business community to actually get off the fence – you would actually have needed a proctologist to get the CBI [Confederation of British Industries] and the IOD [Institute of Directors] off the fence – and I found that really infuriating.[30]

There was, however, a civic society campaign within Northern Ireland to remain in the EU. The group, called NI Stronger in Europe[31] was a broad-based and cross-community initiative, chaired by journalist Tom Kelly. It emerged in April 2016 and had a nineteen-strong advisory board including a broad spectrum of participants from business, agriculture and other sections of economic and cultural life in Northern Ireland. It was affiliated to the GB Britain Stronger in Europe group led by Sir Stuart Rose and took part in Northern Ireland-level campaigning during the referendum campaign. The thrust of their case was an economic one along the lines of its GB sister group but tweaked for a Northern Ireland audience:

> In Northern Ireland, an incredible 50,000 jobs depend on our trade with the EU. As well as that, being in the EU means that prices in our shops are lower, your rights including holiday leave and parental leave are protected, and everything from your electricity bill to petrol for your car costs less thanks to EU action. Northern Ireland also receives £460 million in EU grants for schemes to create jobs, build roads and bridges and regenerate rural and urban areas, funding that the government could not afford to replace if we left Europe.[32]

Glyn Roberts, CEO of Retail NI, was vice-chair of this group and his pitch focused on the economic benefits of EU membership for Northern Ireland and the damage that would be done to the Northern Ireland economy if it left the EU. 'Risk is bad for business. Risk is bad for jobs and ultimately this kind of risk [Brexit] is bad for our economy.'[33] On the other side, a Northern Ireland affiliate of the Leave campaign also became active, led by Lee Reynolds as regional coordinator. Reynolds was a member of the DUP and his pitch centred around reducing the democratic deficit in Northern Ireland – rather ironic given the outcome that led to Northern Ireland's democratic wish to remain in the EU being ignored after the referendum: 'If you take Value Added Tax – a highly substantial tax in terms of public revenue, we pay it every single day and our elected politicians do not control it. We have to ask permission from 27 countries if we can change it. I do not think that is appropriate or right.'[34]

The wider British context

The abandonment of party discipline during the referendum campaign at the UK level could be viewed as an example of mature democratic practice – allowing the issues to be discussed and debated free of the adversarial and often hubristic posturing of politicians. However, the decision to allow a free vote was driven by a desire to avoid internal dissent and party splits rather than a sudden commitment to cosmopolitan democratic values. The in/out referendum itself was driven by Cameron's political weakness. He was the ultimate pragmatist who shifted policy positions gradually for political advantage, rather than out of principle or ideological belief. He conceded to an in/out referendum on EU membership not because he wanted one, but in order to head off the challenge of the UK Independence Party.

The context to this is important, as in 2014 another referendum had taken place over Scottish independence. This was another example where Cameron's complacency nearly resulted in the destruction of the United Kingdom as a constitutional entity. It was only late in the campaign, when the polls suggested a lead for the independence side, that the government and the opposition Labour Party vigorously campaigned for Scotland to remain, along with promises of additional political and economic resources.

The result was a comfortable one in the end – but Cameron came perilously close to overseeing the breakup of the United Kingdom. He seems not to have learned from this near miss in both calling the in/out referendum and in allowing a free vote on the outcome. He could, for instance, have used the Scottish experience of 2014 to make good on his rhetoric that Scotland was integral to the UK national identity by allowing the devolved regions a greater influence over the Brexit decision. A requirement to have majorities in Scotland, Wales and Northern Ireland as well as England could have been imposed to demonstrate that it was a *United* Kingdom. This could have allowed Cameron to make good on his promise to hold an in/out referendum on EU membership, but provide an overwhelming advantage to the status quo position, which was his declared preference. Instead, he tacked pragmatically in order to placate the Eurosceptics within his own party and the electoral threat from UKIP.

This context from Great Britain is important and had direct impacts on how the referendum campaign unfolded in Northern Ireland. The decision to abandon party discipline over government policy led to Theresa Villiers, then Secretary of State for Northern Ireland, to declare her support for the Leave side in the campaign. In GB terms this was unproblematic, though the UK media was by this stage in a feeding frenzy over which senior politicians were declaring for which side in the campaign. This reached its apogee with Boris Johnson's last-minute decision to opt for the Leave side of the debate and undermine his party leader and former schoolmate the Prime Minister. But in Northern Ireland Theresa Villiers was a crucial political actor, less so than during the days of direct rule perhaps, but still a powerful influence. The Secretary of State was supposed to represent the interests of everyone in Northern Ireland and be seen to be an even-handed co-guarantor of the GFA and its political institutions. However, given that nationalists and their political representatives in Sinn Féin and the SDLP were strongly in the Remain camp, this presented something of a political wrinkle within the political system. SDLP leader Colum Eastwood pointed out in February 2016 that Villiers' declaration for the leave campaign rendered her incapable of fulfilling her role: 'As I have told her repeatedly, she does not represent Northern Ireland in this position. She must not attempt to speak on our behalf.'[35] In this sense the decision of the government to allow a free vote in the referendum problematised the political relationships in Northern Ireland in a manner that was not apparent in the rest of the UK.

While unionist positions initially ranged between ambivalent support for Leave and Remain, with a large 'don't know' contingent, nationalist opinion over the in/out referendum was much more consistent. They were enthusiastic in support of remaining within the EU, though the SDLP and Sinn Féin both argued that the referendum itself was an unnecessary political risk that presented a threat to peace and stability.

In December 2015 Sinn Féin decided to campaign for the UK remaining within the EU at its policy *ard chomhairle* (governing council), on the basis that a decision to leave could cause further political division in Ireland, degrade the fragile economy and put the Good Friday Agreement and wider peace process at risk. This was interesting for a number of reasons, not least because the party had previously taken a Eurosceptic stance and had campaigned against the Lisbon Treaty on the basis of its neo-liberal and monetarist approach to economic policy, as well as because of the implications that EU membership had for an overtly nationalist movement seeking Irish independence and national self-determination. Despite its critique of the EU for advancing the interests of big business at the expense of workers' rights, Sinn Féin swallowed hard at the end of 2015 and declared its support for continued UK membership of the EU. Sinn Féin's MEP Matt Carthy pointed out that this was not an easy or straightforward policy position for the party to accept – but that the dangers of a Leave vote for Ireland and Northern Ireland in particular had changed the political equation despite its long-standing critique of EU policies:

> Our position has been very clear. We critically engage in the EU. The EU, as it stands now, is not a model we would have great affinity for. We are attempting all the time to try and bridge the democratic deficit that is there and try to underscore the unequal in terms of how European institutions work in many instances. The fact that, more and more, the European Union is moving away from a social

Europe basis to a very much right-wing agenda – that is something we are challenging. And the concept of member states working together on issues of mutual concern has been eroded by some of the larger countries, particularly France and Germany, forcing, and in some cases bullying, smaller countries.[36]

Despite these misgivings, Sinn Féin's policy position at the end of 2015 focused on the impact that Brexit would have on the Northern Ireland economy and wider trade relations between Ireland and the UK.[37] When the date of the referendum was announced in February 2016, Sinn Féin's then deputy First Minister, Martin McGuinness, argued that EU membership had been politically and economically beneficial for Ireland and for political stability in the region: 'The future of Ireland, north and south, is within the European Union and Sinn Féin will be campaigning vigorously to stay in.'[38] On 3 June 2016 McGuinness launched Sinn Féin's formal referendum campaign and called on voters to 'put Ireland first'.[39] This reiterates the point made in connection to the DUP position on the referendum, namely that it inevitably sucked the Northern Ireland parties into rival interpretations of how the outcome would redefine politics and identity. Connecting the referendum to Ireland (rather than to the UK or 'the nation' as the DUP and other unionists framed it), set up a tug of war over how the outcome of the referendum would reshape the Irishness or Britishness of Northern Ireland. McGuinness said:

> Sinn Féin will be campaigning vigorously in the coming days and weeks to encourage people to vote to put Ireland first and vote Remain in the EU. The European Union is far from perfect but the only way to address that and change it is from within. Our policy towards the European Union remains one of critical engagement. Brexit would be bad for Ireland, bad for business and trade, bad for our farmers and bad for human rights and workers' rights.[40]

So the Sinn Féin position was pitched at constructive engagement with the EU based on the overriding political and economic needs of Northern Ireland and the island as a whole. However, while publicly Sinn Féin maintained a position that Brexit was bad for the Good Friday Agreement, the devolved institutions and peace and stability in Ireland more generally, there were clearly potential up sides for the overall republican project of constitutional change and Irish reunification. Belfast-based journalist John Manley of the *Irish News* recognised: '[Sinn Féin's] immediate goal is for power, it seems – and Brexit disrupts that. But if they are looking at the ultimate goal of a united Ireland, then they should be saying "bring it on". And I imagine that privately, the strategists are thinking; "yes – bring it on. But we won't say it publicly."'[41]

In March 2016, the Sinn Féin position moved up a gear, when deputy First Minister Martin McGuinness called for a vote on Irish reunification via a border poll within Northern Ireland if the UK voted to leave the EU on 23 June. This was based on the principles enshrined within the Good Friday Agreement of 1998 and the notion that the people of Northern Ireland should have the democratic right to self-determination over EU membership *separately* from any overall UK decision: 'If Britain votes to leave the European Union then that could have huge implications for the entire island of Ireland and, given all the predictions, would run counter to the democratic wishes of the Irish people.'[42] McGuinness argued that a Brexit vote would be a game-changer that justified a fundamental recalibration of relationships between North and South and between Ireland and the UK:

> If there is a vote in Britain to leave the EU, there is a democratic imperative to provide Irish citizens with the right to vote in a border poll to end partition and to retain a role within the EU. I have proposed to Northern Ireland Secretary Theresa Villiers that, given the enormous significance of these issues, the British Government now gives a firm commitment to an immediate border poll in the event that Britain votes to leave the European Union.[43]

This demonstrates the extent to which the UK referendum on EU membership was sucking the political air out of the atmosphere in Northern Ireland and forcing both Sinn Féin and the DUP to begin taking clear positions on the implications of a referendum for the constitutional future of the region. The SDLP stopped short of calling for Irish reunification but was equally clear in its support for Remain and set out its position in February 2016 after Prime Minister David Cameron had announced the date of the referendum. The SDLP approach did not emphasise an economic critique of the EU but, like Sinn Féin, its main focus was on the economic impacts on business and farming that would be felt in Northern Ireland if the UK left the EU. Party leader Colum Eastwood called for a united front between his party, Sinn Féin, Alliance, the Greens and the Ulster Unionist Party, to ensure a Remain majority in Northern Ireland on 23 June:

> This campaign will be one of the most important votes faced by people in Northern Ireland in decades. It is therefore vital that a strong and positive campaign is conducted to remain in Europe. Arlene Foster and Jim Allister need to be challenged to outline, in detail, to our farming and business communities how their incomes will be maintained and protected outside of the European Union. How will farm incomes be secured and what trade conditions will businesses face? In the absence of these answers, all they are really offering is a blind jump into the unknown.[44]

By the time the referendum campaign began in earnest in March 2016, only one of the five major parties in Northern Ireland (the DUP) had declared its support for the UK leaving the EU. The other four (Sinn Féin, the SDLP, the UUP and Alliance Party) were supporting the Remain campaign.

Heavyweights intervene

One of the most significant events that took place in Northern Ireland during the formal part of the referendum campaign was provided by a visit to Derry by former prime ministers John Major

and Tony Blair. The intention was to bolster the Remain side of
the argument by highlighting the concern of these two architects
of peace in Northern Ireland for the continued viability of the
Good Friday Agreement and the devolved political institutions that
had been built since 1998. John Major warned sternly about the
risk of a Leave vote in the referendum jeopardising peace and
stability in Northern Ireland and potentially risking the breakup
of the United Kingdom itself: 'If we throw the pieces of the
constitutional jigsaw up in to the air, no one can be certain where
they might land.'[45] During a talk at Ulster University's Magee
College in the city, the former UK Prime Minister suggested that
if the Leave side won the referendum it was likely to precipitate
another divisive referendum over Scottish independence. 'The plain,
uncomfortable truth is that the unity of the UK itself is on the
ballot paper in two weeks' time. … There is a serious risk of a
new referendum, not immediately perhaps, but eventually.'[46] He
also pointed out a less dramatic but arguably equally important
political consequence of a vote to leave the EU, namely that it
would position Ireland 'at the opposite side of the table' when the
UK sought to negotiate its way out of the EU after the vote. It
would reframe the two countries as political opponents rather than
partners. This break in the bipartisan relationship would in turn
affect other aspects of the Anglo-Irish relationship and in this, at
least, Major turned out to be correct.

Tony Blair pointed out that Brexit would result in a hard border
returning between Northern Ireland and the Irish Republic remi-
niscent of the one that existed during the years of political conflict
in the region and with the obvious negative connotations for the
peace process that would follow.[47] He rejected the argument put
forward by some advocates of the Leave side that it would be
possible to maintain the Common Travel Area between Northern
Ireland and the Irish Republic after Britain left the EU, arguing
that this was an unrealistic expectation with no basis in reality: 'It

would make a nonsense of their entire argument for leaving which is all to do with the free movement of people in the European Union.'[48]

Their visit was counterproductive, not least because the record of English people telling Irish people what to do is not an unblemished one. In truth, it was an own goal by the Remain side, symptomatic of a residual English arrogance and lack of political empathy towards Ireland. More directly, the visit of Blair and Major led to a hardening of the DUP position, which had previously been relatively porous and pluralist towards the referendum issue. Both Major and Blair had admitted in their respective memoirs that they had stretched the truth at various times during their negotiations with politicians in Northern Ireland in the 1990s – a fact not lost on the unionist leadership. Nigel Dodds, DUP leader at Westminster, accused the two former leaders of 'scaremongering' and took issue with what he argued was a destabilising intervention based on misrepresentation of the facts: 'I think it's deeply disappointing. They know that the peace process in Northern Ireland has never been more stable. They are devaluing their own legacy.'[49]

DUP leader and First Minister Arlene Foster suggested that the visit was an irresponsible intrusion into the delicate politics of Northern Ireland from two former leaders who should have known better: 'I do find it rather disgraceful for two prime ministers who know full well the importance of the peace process here in Northern Ireland to come over here and suggest that a vote in a particular direction is going to undermine that.'[50] Beyond the public denunciations, the DUP was incensed by what it saw as a crass attempt by the former prime ministers to undermine the platform that the party was delicately balanced upon over the referendum issue. There was the practical point that the appearance of these two political heavyweights required the DUP to respond by robustly defending their support for Leave in the referendum – when this was less than wholehearted to begin with.

While the visit of the two former prime ministers grabbed the media's attention, there is no evidence that it swayed the vote. If anything, it made the DUP campaign more vigorously in support of the Leave campaign when previously it had been relatively even paced. Payback did not take long; two days before the referendum, the DUP took out a full front- and back-page advertisement in the *Metro* newspaper, read mostly by London commuters and not readily available to its own voters in Northern Ireland. The front cover of the *Metro* read simply: 'We Can be even stronger If WE TAKE BACK CONTROL Vote to Leave' – an advert badged with the DUP logo at the top and with the party's 'dupvote2leave' Facebook page linked to it. It later transpired that this advertisement cost the party £282,000 and was wholly paid for by the shadowy pro-Brexit Constitutional Research Council (CRC). The source of this donation was not initially disclosed by the DUP as it was not required to do so under Northern Ireland electoral law, but it was eventually made public several months later and led to accusations that dark money from shadowy organisations such as the CRC was diminishing the democratic process.[51] DUP spokesperson Mervyn Storey defended the decision to advertise in Britain despite the paper's lack of circulation in Northern Ireland – and his response again demonstrated that one by-product of the campaign in Northern Ireland was a restatement of national identity in territorial terms:

> We are a national party, we are the fourth largest party in the House of Commons and, clearly, this is a national campaign. Northern Ireland has not been on the periphery of this campaign, we in the DUP have been a central player in the Leave campaign and, therefore, it is as conceivable to take that ad in that publication as it is to take it in Northern Ireland.[52]

In an article for the *Belfast Telegraph* on 17 June, the DUP leader and Northern Ireland First Minister Arlene Foster repeated her support for the Leave side in the referendum and elaborated on the reasons. Ironically (given the eventual result), she began the defence of her position by highlighting the importance of the local context in the act of democratic self-determination. 'I am a devolutionist and believe decisions should be as close to the people as possible. The European Union is pulling power and decision-making further away. A return of powers would not simply flow to London but to Belfast too.'[53] Later in the article, however, there was an indication that Foster's position had been influenced by the alleged 'Project Fear' approach of the Remain side epitomised by the earlier visit of Major and Blair:

> I must admit my resolve in this has grown and grown as the EU referendum campaign has developed. The remain campaign as a whole and how it has treated Northern Ireland in particular has been the source of deep frustration on my part. The remain campaign has spread so many scare stories that I could fill every page of the *Belfast Telegraph* in response. However, what has angered me the most has been the purported threats to our peace. As that is what it is, our peace. It is not the possession of one party, one government or one campaign. … It is deeply offensive to present the people of Northern Ireland as ready to return to violence in the blink of an eye, especially over a democratic vote. I know, I trust and I wholeheartedly believe we are better than that and those who have made such claims should know better as well.[54]

It seems clear that the increasingly desperate efforts of the Remain side offended and radicalised the DUP and its voters – hardening the party's support for Brexit as the campaign proceeded. Despite this there was enough unionist support for remaining within the EU to prevent the simple decanting of Brexit into the respective ethnonational camps in the region. One of the main reasons was because the UUP's position remained ambivalent during the referendum campaign. While it formally supported remain, opinion was extremely divided on the issue. While party leader Mike Nesbitt did his best to argue for remaining within the EU, it was clear that he did not speak for other senior figures within his party. On 20 June Nesbitt tried to chart a course that allowed him to endorse Remain without alienating those who took the opposite view:

> With three days to go to the EU referendum we are very conscious that there are a lot of unionists who are still undecided on how they will vote on Thursday. We have a very simple message for them; it's ok to vote to remain. In fact, if you cherish the United Kingdom of Great Britain and Northern Ireland it is a good thing to vote remain. … Northern Ireland will acutely feel the implications of a Brexit; constitutionally, financially and politically.[55]

The degree of division within the UUP on the referendum had been demonstrated only a matter of days previously, when several grandees in the party, including former party leader David Trimble, as well as stalwarts Lord Kilclooney and Ken Maginnis wrote an open letter in support of the Leave position. There was none of the ambivalence characteristic of the party leadership; the letter condemned the EU as undemocratic and unaccountable, and recommended the restoration of British sovereign control of its laws, borders and economic future: 'The European Union has got out of control. It has expanded far beyond its original remit and is heading towards a federal European State. The people of the United Kingdom have a unique opportunity to reverse this and restore sovereignty to our own democratically-elected Parliament.'[56] This was much more compatible with the statements of the DUP leadership than it was with those of the UUP or its leader. The letter once again demonstrated the counterproductive nature of the Remain campaign's attempt to link the Brexit vote with peace in Northern Ireland, epitomised by the visit of Blair and Major: 'As architects of the Belfast Agreement we utterly reject the dishonest scaremongering that a vote to leave Europe will undermine peace in Northern Ireland.'[57]

This lack of unity within the UUP did help prevent the referendum from becoming a simple proxy for unionist/nationalist identity disputes in Northern Ireland – though this did not last long after the result became known.

The diplomatic mission

While the leading nationalist and unionist parties took opposite positions over their support for the in/out referendum, the Irish government in Dublin had consistently made the point that a leave vote would have significantly negative implications for the peace process, as well as for political and economic stability across the entire island. The Irish government had been focused on the UK referendum from the moment it had been mooted as a realistic possibility and well before the date was announced in February 2016. From this point Brexit had become an overriding foreign policy priority for the Irish government and its diplomatic representatives.[58]

There were two central reasons for this. Firstly, there was a concern that a decision by the UK to leave the EU in the referendum would raise significant barriers to trade between the UK and Ireland, exposing the Irish economy to additional tariffs as well as delays and complications linked to the import and export of goods – especially in the agri-food sector and just-in-time delivery. Secondly, there was a deep concern in Dublin that a Brexit vote would result in a hard border in Ireland and the political destabilisation of Northern Ireland and the broader peace process. While the main parties in Northern Ireland largely focused on other matters until the referendum campaign had really got underway in 2016, the Irish diplomatic machine was out of the blocks quickly. No one was faster in this regard than Ireland's former ambassador to Great Britain, Dan Mulhall. Speaking to the House of Commons Northern Ireland Affairs Committee on 10 February 2016, Mulhall outlined the government's concerns politely but firmly. While he was careful to acknowledge that the referendum was a matter for the people of Britain to decide for themselves, he pointed out that Ireland had a unique perspective to offer – not least because it was the only fellow EU member state with which the UK shared a land border:

> It is estimated that Northern Ireland will receive over €3 billion in EU funding between 2014 and 2020. It seems very risky to put in jeopardy the advantages of EU membership and to forgo such substantial funding without any guarantee that it will be supplied instead from another source. These supports include funding for SMEs, research, the green economy and education, not to mention agriculture, sectors that all have a cross-border dimension or potential. EU membership also brings with it the valuable cross-border PEACE programme and the Interreg programme. The 2014–2020 programmes, which were negotiated during the last Irish Presidency of the EU, were both jointly announced by Irish and Northern Ireland ministers in recent weeks – €550 million in all, on both sides of the border, building crucial infrastructure and supporting peace and reconciliation.[59]

The view expressed here was that, while Ireland did not have a say over the referendum, it did have a view, and a legitimate interest in the outcome, due to the potential impact a Leave vote could have on political stability in Northern Ireland and the risk it posed to the estimated £1 billion of trade that flowed between Ireland and the UK every week. The previous month, Irish Taoiseach Enda Kenny had claimed that a Leave vote in the referendum would 'create serious difficulties'[60] for Northern Ireland, a comment that was seen by the Leave side as part of the 'Project Fear' campaign being waged to frighten voters. Eventually the UK government was complicit in the conduct of Irish diplomatic mobilisation against a Leave vote in the referendum, with Prime Minister Cameron turning a blind eye to his Irish counterpart Enda Kenny openly campaigning for the Remain side among the Irish ex-pat community in Britain.

Civic voices were also mobilised in the Irish Republic with the Irish Farmers' Union (IFU) focusing on the potential barriers to trade in the agri-food sector that would likely result if the UK did vote to leave the EU on 23 June. President of the IFU Joe Healy warned in the lead-up to the vote that the UK was the largest export market for Ireland, amounting to over 40% of the Irish agri-food sector. 'It is the destination for over 50% of our beef, 60% of our cheese, €350m worth of pigmeat exports and almost 100% of our mushroom exports. It is a high-value market, with customers sharing the same language and with similar consumer preferences as Irish customers.'[61]

On the eve of the referendum Enda Kenny cranked up the emotional temperature, claiming that a vote for Brexit would lead to a hard border in Ireland and set back the gains that had been made in the peace process, fuelling an agenda of division and isolation rather than one of partnership and progress. In an article in the *Guardian* on 20 June, clearly designed to mobilise turnout and support for Remain, the Taoiseach inferred that a Leave vote would allow those with malign agendas to drive a wedge between people and make reconciliation and political progress more difficult:

> Our common membership of the EU provided an important backdrop to the Irish and UK governments working together to secure peace in Northern Ireland. The peace process was built by the people of this island coming together, and that will of course continue. … We share the UK's only land border with another EU member state. Those many thousands of UK visitors to Ireland in recent years know that the border between both parts of Ireland is barely visible. There is a seamless flow of people crossing that border. If the UK's decision is to leave the EU, this will no longer be a border between two countries. It will be a border between the UK and the remaining 27 member states of the EU. It will be the EU's western boundary running from Derry to Dundalk. … What is not easy to quantify and mitigate is the psychological effect of a hardening border on the island. My fear is that it would play into an old narrative – one of division, isolation and difference.[62]

Perhaps equally desperately, the Irish government threw its weight behind a social media initiative, #phoneafriend, where people in

Ireland were encouraged to phone their family and friends in the UK and lobby them to vote for Remain in the referendum. This was started in April by pro-EU NGO European Movement Ireland and supported by notable celebrities such as Bob Geldof and by the Irish government. Its key aim was to raise awareness among Irish people living in Britain that they qualified to vote in the June referendum and to encourage them to register to vote in time for the 7 June deadline. Targeting Irish people living in the UK – and British people living in Ireland – #phoneafriend sought to use the soft power of family and friendship networks to maximise the Remain vote from these target groups.

Of course it all proved to be too little too late for the Remain side and after a hectic day of voting on 23 June and a white-knuckle ride into the next morning as the votes were counted, the UK emerged blinking and dazed early on 24 June 2016 to the news that the UK had voted to leave the EU.

The Brexit meteor had slammed into the political atmosphere and the implications for Ireland, Northern Ireland and relationships between Ireland and the UK were barely beginning to sink in around the personal carnage to political and diplomatic careers that quickly engulfed and consumed the debate. Meteor is the correct metaphor to use, as everyone emerged on 24 June and looked into the Brexit-shaped crater, dazed, disoriented, with many people in mourning over what had just happened.

The Brexit shock wave had begun to reshape politics across Britain and Ireland.

2

Brexit as meteor theory: external shocks to peace settlements

No one saw Brexit coming. Certainly not David Cameron when he announced the in/out referendum for 23 June 2016, a prime minister who had seen off two previous referendums, on Scottish independence in 2014 and on electoral reform with the alternative vote referendum in 2011. Clearly Cameron was a man who knew how to hold and win referendums and while he called the in/out referendum on EU membership, he did so fully expecting that he would win it. There was a broader general complacency, perhaps derived from previous referendums, that incumbency advantage, combined with a stiff dose of realism or the deployment of what Brexiteers liked to call 'Project Fear', would shore up the status quo and help ensure that the Remain vote prevailed. This sanguine attitude in 2016 was aided and abetted by the opinion polls, the vast majority of which put the Remain side in the lead until the latter stages of the referendum campaign. Peter Sheridan, chief executive of Co-Operation Ireland, a reconciliation and cross-community border development NGO in Ireland, reflected on the fact that the organisation had maintained a neutral position on Brexit prior to the referendum, as it had unionist Leave supporters and nationalist Remainers on its board of trustees: 'To be fair it was probably an easy [decision] because most people thought that it wouldn't happen. Even people on the board who were in favour of leaving never really believed that it would happen. So I think it caught everybody by surprise.'[1]

A generation previously, when the Good Friday Agreement was reached on 10 April 1998, Brexit was nowhere on the political landscape. The idea of the UK leaving the European Union was not part of the political discourse within mainstream UK politics or anywhere else during the 1990s – save from the more exotic reaches of the Conservative Party and UKIP. Back then the UK was confidently asserting itself under the leadership of Tony Blair – one of the most pro-European British prime ministers since Edward Heath took the UK into what was then the Common Market in 1973. Blair was an ardent Europhile and his governments during the 1990s and after the 2001 General Election reflected a strong commitment to the European project and to the institutions of the EU. Membership of the European common currency was a wrinkle, but the EU was prepared to let the UK opt out of adopting the euro as it had let previous British governments pursue an independent course to cater for their local Anglo-specific needs. In a speech about UK foreign policy delivered in December 1998 – just months after the Good Friday Agreement was concluded, Blair was explicit about his government's commitment to the EU project:

> I made very clear, before the election, that a new Government would mean a new approach in Europe. The last Government, despite what I believe were the best intentions of the last Prime Minister, allowed Britain to be taken to the margins of Europe. We are in the European Union because it is the right place to be. And as we are in, it is time we started winning arguments, rather than running away from them. The logical conclusion of the Euro-sceptic approach that says everything that comes out of Europe is bad; that says Europe is something that is done to us, rather than something that we can shape; is to get out of Europe altogether. That would at least be an honest intellectual position. But it would be a disaster for British jobs, British trade, British influence in the world.[2]

While this was prophetic in terms of subsequent events, it seems like a throwback to a different political era – and it was. This speech was made before there was a whiff of Brexit in the air and also before that other great upheaval, the 9/11 attacks on New York and Washington, altered the political landscape. It was 9/11, not Europe, that would shape the majority of Blair's tenure as prime minister – and tragically frame his political legacy.[3] However, back in the 1990s Blair was fresh from a political landslide in the 1997 General Election and by the spring of the following year he was basking in the reflected glory of the Northern Ireland peace process. While he has since been defined by Iraq, his leadership over the peace process in Northern Ireland stands in stark contrast to that of Theresa May and former Secretary of State, the hapless Karen Bradley.[4] Before his calamitous adventures in Iraq and Afghanistan, Blair was a crucial peacemaker in Northern Ireland. During the final tempestuous days in the run-up to the GFA he took up residence in Northern Ireland and directly ran the negotiations with the Irish government and the main parties involved. These were difficult and emotional times for the political parties tasked by the chair of the talks, former US Senator George Mitchell, to 'eat, sleep and negotiate', as the talks entered continuous session in the last hours of Mitchell's imposed deadline of 9 April. Former Alliance Party leader John Alderdice had emerged during this phase and gave an impromptu comment to the waiting media imploring Blair to come over to Northern Ireland to help. 'On Sunday, I spoke to Mr Blair on the telephone and told him he needed to come [to Belfast]. Today it's Tuesday, and if the Prime Minister wants a deal, then he better get here – fast.'[5]

Blair duly arrived on 7 April 1998 and there was substance and capability behind the rhetoric. Blair had a crushing majority in 1998 – few doubted his resolve or his ability to deliver on anything his government signed up to. Theresa May's ill-fated government cast a pale shadow by comparison from 2016 to 2019, and her attempts to deliver Brexit have been the delinquent sibling to Blair's negotiating progeny. When Blair felt the hand of history on his shoulder in April 1998, it is as good as certain that he did not feel it steering the United Kingdom away from the European Union.

The most astute political Nostradamus would not have been able to see such an event coming during the GFA negotiations or for most of the eighteen years between that peace agreement and the referendum in 2016. So, as it did in the rest of the UK and the EU, Brexit slammed into Northern Ireland and into the GFA like a meteor hitting Earth. Everyone was dazed after the impact on 24 June 2016 – not least those who had promoted the Brexit campaign themselves. But the political implications for Northern Ireland and its fragile peace process were profoundly different from the implications for those living in Great Britain.

It reopened what the negotiators thought had been closed – or at least permanently neutralised – in 1998: namely the identity crisis at the centre of the constitutional argument between Britishness and Irishness.[6] As explained elsewhere in this book, Brexit removed the necessary fudge (constructive ambiguity in diplomatic-speak) that allowed both unionists and nationalists to believe different things about Northern Ireland's ultimate constitutional destiny. As long as they were not confronted by the choice, they could pragmatically accommodate such ambiguity in their collective psyches. Brexit forced this choice upon them and sucked the air out of the political atmosphere. The meteor and the political fallout from its impact metastasised the GFA and attitudes to it in ways that were not conceived or catered for in 1998. This exogenous force had knocked Northern Ireland off its normal political axis and altered the context within which the parties and their electorates operated. In an ironic twist of fate, a conflict that had been undermined for generations by the inability of unionists and nationalists to reach agreement about their *internal* differences was undone by an *external* force that no one had seen coming.

More fundamentally, the Brexit meteor had changed the character of what had been agreed in 1998 to the point that it might not be agreeable after 2016. To take one example, the broad nationalist acceptance of the 'consent principle' in 1998, morphed into something else immediately after the Brexit referendum in 2016.

A pragmatic acceptance that they could be Irish within the UK
within the envelope of the European Union, *is not at all* the same
as agreeing to be Irish within the UK, outside the protective influence
of EU membership of which the rest of the imagined community
in Ireland was a member. Peter Sheridan of Co-Operation Ireland
suggested that Brexit had pulled the rug out from under the feet
of Irish nationalists in Northern Ireland and disrupted their sense
of identity that had been settled by the GFA in 1998:

> A lot of Northern nationalists here, at the time of the Good Friday
> Agreement, signed up to [it] on the basis that they could be Irish
> within the context of a wider Europe. What they were signing up
> to almost was to a new identity of being Northern Irish ... within
> the context of a wider Europe. What they weren't signing up to
> was to be Northern Irish within the context of the UK.[7]

This notion that the contested political identity at the centre of
the Northern Ireland conflict had been transformed by Brexit was
also highlighted by journalist and commentator Alex Kane and
characterised as an external shock to the political system:

> Five years ago for example, if there had been a border poll, the
> choice would have been between a United Ireland ... and the choice
> you would have had would have been that slightly nebulous thing
> and a United Kingdom they understood within the European Union
> with that multiplicity of identities – you know the John Hewitt
> [vision] you could be British, Irish, Ulster, Planter, Gael whatever.
> All of those identities were safeguarded. ... I think the problem
> now for small n nationalists and more crucially for small u unionists,
> those unionists who are very liberal and have no hang-ups about
> same-sex marriage, over abortion law reform, and licensing law and
> secularisation – the choice they now face is a United Ireland within
> the European Union, with all those identities protected, versus a
> little-England mentality, where you could have a mad right wing
> [in power] for thirty, forty, fifty years dominating politics, with the
> DUP the main unionist party here, with Scotland out of the Union
> and with the question never going away.[8]

This view was echoed on the nationalist side by *Irish News* political correspondent John Manley when reflecting on the concern within that community over the implication of Brexit for their lives and livelihoods. 'Not only are they having their European identity taken away, and there's a threat to that ability to express yourself as Irish and to move across the island [of Ireland] freely – but there's also the potential for economic hardship, which is being imposed on us by this group of English nationalists.'[9]

To take another example – Irish republican acceptance of the criminal justice system and legal recourse to European human rights standards is underwritten by EU institutions within the terms of the GFA.[10] This is not at all the same as being committed to a criminal justice system within an entirely UK political context, where European law and human rights standards after Brexit are degraded or eroded. From this angle, Europe presents an external dimension to the GFA and is integral to it – but, when removed, alters the nature of many of the other parts that were negotiated in 1998.

Exogenous shocks to endogenous agreements

The impact of the Brexit meteor on Northern Ireland has shifted the political tectonic plates on which it stands. What was firm ground before the referendum, the idea of the GFA and the devolved institutions providing the main political axis in Belfast, now looks to be much less solid. At a basic level, Brexit placed the constitutional question back onto the political agenda in Northern Ireland. As has been highlighted elsewhere in this book, the GFA had successfully parked this issue within its constructive ambiguity by allowing those who lived there to self-identify their nationality as British, Irish or both.[11] At the time and in the years that followed, this seemed like an agreeable deceit, where everyone (or almost everyone) could agree to differ on whether the GFA underpinned and secured the Union between Northern Ireland and Great Britain, or as Sinn Féin maintained, provided a jumping-off point or staging post for their ambitions of Irish reunification. Before Brexit it did not really matter who was right – so long as enough people were happy to play along with the necessary ambivalence. But after Brexit the spotlight was put on the binary reality of nationality, coupled with the focus on the Irish border, and we were confronted with a stark choice. Were we British or were we Irish? The in/out binary logic of the 2016 referendum made it very difficult to maintain an either/ and/both approach to citizenship. This was sharpened by the experience of the negotiations themselves and the declining relationship between the British and Irish governments between 2016 and 2019. It became clear in 2019 that despite the GFA and the assumption that British and Irish people living in Northern Ireland could opt into the nationality of their choice – the UK government (and Home Office especially) were interpreting nationality in much less fluid and malleable terms – as evidenced by the Emma DeSouza case discussed below.

Similarly, once the Brexit meteor had slammed into the political fabric of Northern Ireland, its shock waves turned a number of political certainties on their heads, not least the idea that the centre of political gravity would lie in Belfast rather than in Westminster. The leader of the DUP at Westminster, Nigel Dodds, had previously remarked that the DUP could not be led from London, as the locus of activity on a day-to-day basis took place at Stormont. However, Brexit and the events that followed it arguably changed that political calculation. The devolved institutions collapsed a few months after the Brexit referendum and in June 2017 the DUP at Westminster found itself right at the centre of political power. With the absence of the devolved institutions in Northern Ireland and a confidence-and-supply deal between the DUP and the government in place, the focus of attention moved very swiftly from Belfast back to London – until the devolved institutions were restored in January 2020.

Also from the unionist perspective, Brexit lifted the veil on Irish republican and broader Irish nationalist political objectives. It is important to remember that unionists have always been split in terms of their support for the GFA – it helps explain the political decline of David Trimble and the steady emasculation of his party, the UUP, at the hands of the more radical DUP. For many unionists, the GFA represented the first stage in a capitulation to Irish nationalism, not so much a peace process as a 'piece by piece' process, where the Union would be undermined to the point that Northern Ireland became an adjunct member of the UK rather than a core member. Those siren voices that claimed the GFA to be a stepping stone for Irish republicans in their long war towards Irish reunification were hushed by the relative success of the GFA in 1998 and arrival of devolved institutions a year later. The acceptance by Sinn Féin of the 'consent' principle in Northern Ireland, the eventual decommissioning of illegal weapons by the Provisional Irish Republican Army (IRA) and the acceptance by Sinn Féin of the reformed policing service and broader criminal justice system all allowed liberal unionists to claim that the GFA represented an historic compromise – a score draw rather than a victory for one side or the other.

Brexit shattered that illusion for many unionists as the increasingly loud demand for a border poll on Irish unity after the UK leaves the EU led many unionists to conclude that the GFA had never represented an end point for Irish republicans. Instead Brexit seemed to provide an opportunity to push on for the ultimate goal rather than to maintain the halfway house of the GFA – which for many unionists was already a stretch. Ironically perhaps, given unionist support for it, Brexit called into question the motives of Irish nationalists in their support of the GFA and left some unionists feeling that they were taking advantage of Brexit to secure their traditional goal of Irish reunification.

An alternative reading (from Brexit acting like some sort of Trojan horse for republicans to pursue their previously sublimated Irish separatist ambitions) would be that nationalists were forced to choose between a comfortable pragmatism and two stark realities.

They would have to accept their Britishness and leave the EU with the rest of the UK on whatever date the government finally delivered it – or they could pivot towards a greener politics and reluctantly countenance a border poll and everything that came with it. In this sense Brexit had sucked the air out of the political tyres in Northern Ireland, reducing room for manoeuvre and making people think through options they would normally have avoided.

This relates back to the point made above by Peter Sheridan from Co-Operation Ireland. Even moderate nationalists like Claire Hanna, former Brexit lead for the SDLP before she resigned her position in opposition to the party's agreement to partner with Fianna Fáil in the Irish Republic, claimed to have felt pressured to make political choices as a result of Brexit that she would not have previously been faced with:

> History will look back in confusion and amusement at the DUP's performance over the last three years. I mean they really have radicalised the most moderate nationalist people and people like me. ... I was content to live in the UK. My project was reconciliation, the economy, making Northern Ireland work. I didn't see myself doing anything else for the next twenty-five years and Irish unity was not on my agenda. ... But they have taken that comfort blanket away, that fairly social democratic, outward-looking UK that I can live with and be a part of and that doesn't wreck my world or anything but they've completely poisoned that.[12]

Hanna's perspective was underlined by Steve Aiken, Brexit spokesperson for the UUP, who claimed that the DUP was driving non-unionists towards Dublin rather than helping to strengthen the Union between Northern Ireland and the UK. Commenting before he was elected party leader in November 2019, he said:

> Let's be perfectly honest about it – the DUP are the single biggest driver towards a United Ireland. ... I mean the future of Northern Ireland is not going to be driven by the nationalist population or the unionist population. ... It's going to be the 20% of people who

would be quite content living in the United Kingdom which has a Belfast Agreement understanding for the future. ... But through the DUP's ineptitude – and it is ineptitude – they have driven that 20% from what would have been seen as a pro-Union perspective to a pro-United Ireland like perspective as well.[13]

Alex Kane, an experienced political observer in Northern Ireland, reinforced this view from beyond the party political analysis:

What [Brexit] did do, is that it took that key demographic – I've always described them as the soft n nationalists and soft u unionists ... I think we're looking at 15, 16, 17% [of the electorate] but it is enough to swing [the result of a border poll]. I think the one thing that's happened is that those people are [now] willing to listen to an argument that they wouldn't have listened to before.[14]

Kane – a former communications officer for the UUP who has become a contributor to both unionist and nationalist newspapers – can detect scents on the political wind with the expertise that a sommelier at a fine-dining restaurant can advise customers on the wine list. His general point reflected the view that Brexit was pushing the crucial centre ground further towards seeing Irish reunification as a serious option – or at least something to be explored.

In this sense Brexit had turned the political geometry of Northern Ireland on its head, making what was previously impossible possible and what would have been taken for granted before June 2016 seem highly improbable. The point here is that no one saw these changes coming back in the 1990s when the GFA was being negotiated. The ground that negotiators thought was solid has turned out to be riddled with political sink-holes pock-marking the landscape and making everyone neurotic about where the next one is going to appear. From this perspective, the Brexit meteor changed the political landscape quite fundamentally and transformed the ways in which the main political parties and their supporters interpreted their political interests. What seemed fixed has become mobile and what was previously merely a theoretical principle has morphed into a very realistic possibility.

The Brexit meteor and exogenous shocks to endogenous conflicts

Northern Ireland had plenty of problems before the Brexit meteor hit in 2016. The point has been made repeatedly that the Good Friday Agreement was capable of failing without Brexit and indeed was doing so quite effectively prior to the 2016 referendum. Steve Aiken, Brexit spokesperson for the UUP, claimed that the GFA and the devolved institutions were damaged more by subsequent negotiations within Northern Ireland than by the arrival of the Brexit meteor into the political atmosphere: 'St Andrews [Agreement] effectively bastardised what was the Belfast Agreement process of consensuality and [cross-]community consent. So the St Andrews Agreement ensured that whatever we were going to do from then on in was going to be a sectarian first-past-the-post system.'[15]

It would be wrong to set this up as a purely binary comparison, with Brexit as the external agent and the GFA as an internal peace settlement. Northern Ireland was not purely an endogenous conflict and the GFA was not merely an internal agreement – in fact not at all. While the GFA did of course focus on the conflict between unionists and nationalists, it incorporated the EU within its terms, had a crucial Irish dimension in the form of Strand Two commitment to North–South bodies and also a Strand Three component to deal with the East/West relationships between Ireland and Great Britain. This external dimension was reflected in its ratification in their respective parliaments by the UK and Irish governments, by dual referendums in Northern Ireland and the Irish Republic in May 1998 and by the status of the GFA as an international treaty lodged at the United Nations. So the GFA was not a purely endogenous settlement, but one that also contained crucial exogenous elements within it.[16]

Taking this significant caveat on board, the GFA took certain exogenous dimensions for granted. One was the commitment of the two sovereign governments to act as co-guarantors and as joint custodians of the negotiated agreement. The other was the UK and Ireland's continued membership of the European Union. The second disappeared in the early hours of 24 June 2016 when the UK voted to leave the EU, while the first was suffocated and half strangled by the decline in Anglo-Irish relations between 2017 and 2019.

The transformation of these external dimensions of the GFA has both changed the meaning and affected the interplay of its other components in crucial ways – potentially breaking peace in Northern Ireland. To give one example, the tacit nationalist agreement to remain within the UK under the terms of the GFA was transformed by Brexit and the negotiations from 2017 to 2019. Before Brexit it seemed this was a pragmatic arrangement that allowed them to self-identify as Irish within the UK in a political identity and legal status nested within a European context. Thus UK commitments would be underwritten by its treaty obligations represented by the GFA and by the authority ceded by dint of the UK's membership of the EU to European legal standards over human rights and other issues.[17] Since the Brexit referendum in 2016, this context has transformed significantly, with nationalists in Northern Ireland now forced into a bilateral relationship where their right to Irishness and their right to due process in the practice of their political and cultural rights are no longer subject to EU legal standards and can be defined – and restricted – unilaterally under UK domestic law.

As Claire Hanna, former SDLP Brexit spokesperson put it, EU membership was an accepted part of the political context during the negotiations that led to the GFA in 1998 and an integral part of the architecture within which it was supposed to operate. 'It was always assumed, like the air around it [the GFA] that they would be in the EU, and Dublin and London would be cooperating as friends and there [would be] no necessity for a border.'[18] This analysis was not restricted to those from an Irish nationalist background. Stephen Farry, deputy leader of the non-aligned centrist Alliance Party, reinforced the point that Brexit was an external dynamic that had fundamentally transformed the internal dynamic of the GFA and the relationships between the communities within Northern Ireland:

> There was, you could argue, an underlying social contract underneath the [Good Friday] Agreement. ... The essence of the bargain was basically, from a nationalist point of view, that they would be accepting of the status quo (for now), subject to equality internally [within Northern Ireland] but the set of interlocking relationships within these islands was going to be respected. So someone from an Irish nationalist background could live out and express their Irishness without that much impediment, and therefore they have been pragmatic around this. That social contract has in effect been broken by Brexit.[19]

This transformation to the political context has led to heightened insecurity within Irish nationalism over the commitment of the UK to 'parity of esteem' between Irish nationalism and British unionism and over the right of people in Northern Ireland to self-define their nationality as British, Irish or both. This is more than just a theoretical distinction, as a legal case in 2019 demonstrated the limits of nationalists living in Northern Ireland to self-identify as Irish and the appetite of the UK to contest their right to do so, irrespective of what the GFA said about the rights of citizens to opt into the nationality of their choice.

The ambiguity over the UK's commitment to the principles inherent within the GFA was thrown into sharp relief at the end of 2015 when County Derry woman Emma DeSouza was informed by the UK Home Office that her American partner did not qualify for a residency card to stay in the UK, on the basis that she was British rather than Irish. DeSouza was born in Magherafelt in Northern Ireland and the UK Home Office defined her as legally

British under the 1981 British Nationality Act, even though she had never held a British passport and defined herself as Irish under the terms of the GFA. DeSouza took the Home Office to a legal tribunal in Belfast where the judge upheld her Irish citizenship rights under the terms of the GFA in February 2018. The Home Office contested this ruling and insisted in 2019 that UK domestic law superseded any international treaties that Britain was a party to. In effect the UK was saying that previous commitments made respecting the right of nationalists in Northern Ireland to define themselves as Irish were subservient to UK law, which stated that everyone born in Northern Ireland was British, whether they wanted to be or not. More alarmingly for nationalists in the context of their faith in the GFA, the UK was demonstrating here that it disavowed the undertakings made in the GFA regarding the right of citizens in Northern Ireland to opt for Irish rather than British citizenship – and that they would not tolerate those who did so.

Brexit had changed the political context within which these claims to nationality and citizenship were being played out and this was leaking out into the wider Anglo-Irish relationship. In May 2019, Irish Taoiseach Leo Varadkar said in the Dáil that the UK 'had got it wrong' in the DeSouza case and that the GFA allowed people from Northern Ireland to define themselves as Irish, British or both.[20] Such a public articulation of disagreement reflected the decline in the relationship between Dublin and London – but made little material change to the fact that Ireland could not compel the UK to change its view.

DeSouza herself made a link between the commitments made by the UK in the GFA to inclusive self-identification of nationality and the way in which Brexit was politicising this into a stark and legally defined binary option:

> The people of Northern Ireland are unique within the UK in that we have the birthright to identify and be accepted as Irish or British or both. However, contrary to the statutory duty on the Home

Office to accept the birthright provisions of the Good Friday agreement, it is arguing through the British courts that the people of
Northern Ireland are 'automatically British' as we were 'clearly
born in the United Kingdom'. The department regularly and
repeatedly forces British citizenship on Irish citizens born in Northern
Ireland – citizens who are Irish by birth and by choice – a choice
the people of this island voted for overwhelmingly in the Good
Friday agreement referendum. With Brexit on the horizon, and EU
citizens' rights in the balance, the situation has become urgent. ...
Further, the [court] documents troublingly elaborate: 'A treaty [the
government] is a party of does not alter the laws of the United
Kingdom,' and that the 'courts do not have the power to force the
government to uphold its obligations and commitments to a treaty'.[21]

However, as Stephen Farry pointed out, the legal right to citizenship is a grey area and its basis is established in the 1981 British
Nationality Act rather than in international treaties. The GFA may
have provided a *political* right to Irish citizenship, but it did not
provide a *legal* right to it – and Brexit was exposing the gap between
these points:

The [Emma DeSouza] case is another example of cracking open
that question of identity. To put it in very stark terms, what is the
legal basis for the Irish identity in Northern Ireland? There is none.
... The British Nationality Act of [19]81 says anyone born in in the
UK is British automatically, you can't be born anything else other
than British. That begs the question – if someone in Northern
Ireland identifies solely as Irish then what is the legal basis for that?
The UK says 'look – you are British, full stop. If you want to call
yourself Irish, that's fine and if you want an Irish passport that's
fine – but you are British.'[22]

Transformation in political conflict

External changes to the political context of predominantly internal
conflicts have been well documented in the conflict studies literature
– especially in the sub-field of conflict transformation. This sees

violent political conflict and its peaceful transformation as a fluid and dynamic process and more of a continuum than marked by clear timelines with peace and conflict at opposite ends of the spectrum. In this conceptualisation, political conflict is better seen as open-ended rather than static, where 'the issues, actors and interests change over time as a consequence of the social, economic and political dynamics of societies'.[23] While most scholars in this field note the importance of seeing conflict transformation as an organic and evolving process,[24] much of the emphasis is placed on efforts to engineer cessations of violence, viable political negotiations, inclusive conflict settlements and subsequent post-conflict reconciliation strategies.[25]

The conflict transformation lens is an appropriate one through which to view the case of Brexit and Northern Ireland, as it is the most focused on conflict being an open-ended and diffused process, where political meaning is contextual, fluid and relational rather than linear or fixed in time. This could certainly be said of the impact of Brexit and Northern Ireland, where issues such as the Irish border have multiple meanings and a layered significance that connects history, politics, geography and culture together. Conflict transformation as a conceptual tool tends to make the communities themselves, and their political elites, active creators rather than passive recipients of the political process. 'Conflict transformation is an open-ended, long-term, multi-track and dynamic process, which significantly widens the scope of actors involved.'[26] Interpreting Brexit through a conflict transformation lens certainly maximises the opportunities to understand its complex interactions within and beyond the Northern Ireland context.

Conflict mapping tools have for some time focused on the interplay of external context changes and internal political conflicts.[27] Similarly scholars in the conflict studies field have included the structural drivers of conflict on political agency and have pointed to the transformative potential of external context when examining the opportunity structures facing conflict actors. Hugh Miall identifies five points of transformation which provide a useful template for assessing Brexit and conflict situations more widely.[28] Firstly, and most significantly in the context of this study of Brexit as an external driver of internal conflict dynamics, *context transformation* or changes in the external environment beyond the conflict zone can have an impact on how issues and interests are understood within that conflict. This can especially affect issues relating to external political or economic support, with the end of the Cold War and the 9/11 attacks on New York and Washington being obvious examples.

Brexit also provides a textbook example of the way in which the internal political dynamics of Northern Ireland were affected by the external dynamics beyond its territorial borders. In fact, the external context provided by the Brexit meteor landing transformed the meaning of that territorial border.

Secondly, *structural transformations* can affect the basis for conflict by altering the balance of forces or reconfiguring central grievances. Obvious examples here would include the removal of political or economic discrimination within an asymmetric conflict which were a dynamic factor in the rise of militant violence, or the addressing of horizontal inequalities, especially those that mapped onto ethnonational divisions within conflict environments. In the case of Brexit, the 2017 UK General Election and subsequent confidence-and-supply agreement between the UK government and the DUP in Northern Ireland fundamentally impacted on the structure of the conflict and the understanding of the UK's role as a non-partisan actor and co-guarantor of the GFA.

While there is a general consensus that the 2017 General Election and subsequent confidence-and-supply agreement between the UK government and the DUP damaged the former's claim to be a non-partisan third party in Northern Ireland, there were some who believed that this was an exaggerated belief in the first place. When asked about the impact of the DUP on the UK government following the 2017 election, Máirtín Ó Muilleoir, a former Sinn Féin finance minister in the Northern Ireland Executive, argued that while it perhaps did not help the political process in Northern Ireland, the idea that its close relationship with the UK government was damaging to the GFA assumed a benign approach from the British government beforehand:

> Well, I think it's a damaging partnership – damaging to the overall political process. However, I don't view the British government as a neutral guarantor in this. Their foot-dragging on the past, their refusal to deliver on their own promises, have been evidence of their failure to be a neutral party. That said, there were clear times when, under force of pressure from America, from the EU, from Dublin or from ourselves [Sinn Féin] the British had to step up. But they never impressed me as a neutral guarantor of the Good Friday Agreement. … They, in my view as much as the unionists, dug the grave of the partnership agreement and the government we had with the DUP up to the end of 2016. That said, 'Are things worse [now] that they are in this formal relationship, this toxic marriage with the DUP?' Absolutely – there is no arguing about that. It makes the [Mount] Everest we have to climb to get the government back up and running higher again, if that were possible. … Certainly the fact that Mrs May gave herself up as a hostage to the DUP was not helpful.[29]

While there is a sense in Irish republicanism that the image of the UK as a co-guarantor of the GFA is overstated, there is acceptance that the 2017 General Election provided the type of structural transformation to the political situation that fits into Miall's five-point model.

The third element of this approach focuses on *actor transformation* and relates to the arrival or replacement of key personnel who play a role in facilitating or entering into dialogue with opposing factions, or convincing their constituencies to pursue peaceful methods. In the case of Brexit there was a sizeable rogues' gallery to pick from at various points in the three-year negotiation between 2016 and 2019. The catalyst for these actor transformations was varied, ranging from the terminal illness of former deputy First Minister Martin McGuinness and his replacement by Michelle

O'Neill as vice president of Sinn Féin, and the retirement of others, notably Gerry Adams resigning as president of Sinn Féin and passing on the republican torch to Mary Lou MacDonald. Elections and the 2016 referendum itself saw other changes in the dramatis personae of Brexit, with the most spectacular change being the resignation of David Cameron as prime minister and leader of the ruling Conservative Party in the UK on 24 June 2016. The demise and fall of Theresa May and her replacement by Boris Johnson was rather more predictable but also brought with it a significant gear change in the extent to which the UK pursued a 'Brexit – do or die' agenda. There were more natural changes of personnel in the Irish Republic, with former Taoiseach Enda Kenny and his Fine Gael administration making way for his colleague Leo Varadkar and a new minority-led government in June 2017.

But it was in the 'artistic differences' between members of the British government where most of the actor transformation was to be seen over Brexit. David Davis, the Brexit Secretary, resigned in opposition to Theresa May's Chequers Deal in July 2018, as did then Foreign Secretary Boris Johnson. Davis's successor Dominic Raab also resigned as Brexit Secretary, in November 2018, over his government's Withdrawal Agreement with the EU – which subsequently failed to get through parliament. Theresa May herself became the personification of Brexit breakdown when she announced her own resignation on 7 June – an actor change that had further impacts on Brexit as the Conservative Party and the media became consumed by the race between her would-be successors during the summer of 2019. This resulted in several of the candidates suggesting that they would be willing to leave the EU without a deal on 31 October 2019 if they were unable to renegotiate the Withdrawal Agreement – Boris Johnson's 'Brexit do or die' mantra being the most memorable soundbite.

Of course not all of these actor changes were universally destabilising for Northern Ireland, and in the case of Boris Johnson's departure from the UK Foreign Office, for example, were arguably quite constructive developments for the political atmosphere in Northern Ireland. There were numerous other resignations and actor changes over the course of the Brexit negotiations – mostly from the government – but the vast majority of these, to put it charitably, were not household names and did little damage to political stability in Northern Ireland.

Fourthly, *issue transformation* relates to the way in which central policies are reframed in response to other changes taking place. An obvious example of issue transformation in the context of Northern Ireland was provided by the acceptance of power-sharing 'with an Irish dimension' by unionists in 1998 when this was unacceptable to them in the 1970s.[30] Other issues transformed after Brexit, not least the matter of Northern Ireland's constitutional status and the extent to which the region (and those within it) were British, Irish or both. Issues that had stopped being issues were revived, significantly the nature and meaning of the territorial border in Ireland between the United Kingdom and the Irish Republic.

Finally, *personal / small group transformations* can take place at crucial points that enable other aspects of political change to operate more easily, or that function to overcome particular sticking points in the wider system of political change. In the context of Brexit some of this is clearly apparent in the personal relations between Irish politicians and their European counterparts in Brussels and the rest of the European Union. The bombast, lack of competence and political dysfunctionality coming from the UK served to throw into contrast the constructive relations between the political elites in Dublin and Brussels. This was epitomised in March 2019 when chief EU negotiator Michel Barnier attended the Ireland v. France Six Nations rugby match in Dublin, 'shoulder to shoulder' with Taoiseach Leo Varadkar and Foreign Minister Simon Coveney.[31] The pictures of them posing for photos and smiling together outside the Aviva Stadium demonstrated an ease in each other's company and an empathy that seemed light years away from the repeated frosty receptions experienced by UK Prime Minister Theresa May when she attended high-profile summits with declining personal and political capital.

The Brexit meteor hit the political ground in Northern Ireland and impacted on the themes identified above. It transformed the external context of the political conflict in Northern Ireland, its structure, its key issues, the actors involved and the personal and group relationships of those most closely connected with it.[32]

In terms of *context transformation*, Northern Ireland has moved full circle, from a conflict enclosed as a matter of British domestic governance, into an international issue – especially during the 1990s while negotiations were ongoing.[33] It receded back into the margins after the arrival of devolution and as 'normal' politics began to take hold in the region after the GFA in 1998 and especially during the 2007–17 unbroken period of devolution. More specific context transformations arrived in the wake of the 9/11 attacks on the United States and subsequent 'global war on terror' pursued by the Bush administration and its allies. The international context associated with these events encouraged a tactical reassessment within paramilitary groups in Northern Ireland and their support bases in America.[34] This had a cumulative impact along with other factors, leading to other issue transformations (most obviously acts of weapons decommissioning by the Provisional IRA in 2005).[35]

Brexit can be seen as the most significant context change in the Northern Ireland peace process, in the sense that it has fundamentally reconfigured some of the structural dimensions of the GFA and its devolved institutions. It converted the UK from a co-guarantor of the GFA into a partisan actor and arguably an opponent of some of its key features. It moved the constitutional question back onto the front burner of political debate in Northern Ireland. It raised the realistic spectre of Irish reunification via a border poll on Northern Ireland's medium-term future and forced everyone to contemplate what they were quietly forgetting since 1998 – Were they British or were they Irish?

Despite all of this, there was nothing in the GFA or in its subsequent iterations in the years that followed that prepared anyone for the effects of the Brexit meteor and its impact.

Brexit as political irony

It was not just in Ireland that the topsy-turvy impact of Brexit was transforming the political context. The constitutional fabric of the UK had been turned on its head since 2016 where irony seemed to dominate the political spectrum. For a start, Brexit was never really about membership of the EU. If it had been, then the details of EU membership (both positive and negative) would have played a larger part in the 2016 referendum debate. Brexit was rather about two other covert issues: immigration and the internal politics of the Conservative Party. One of the abiding slogans of the Brexiteers was coined by Dominic Cummings, director of the Vote Leave campaign in 2016, when he cast the referendum as being an opportunity for the UK to 'take back control'. Ironically, the rhetoric about returning democracy from Brussels to the UK turned out to be just that. Over the subsequent three-year period, Theresa May's failure to deliver a coherent policy led inexorably to the EU taking back control from the UK in terms of the Article 50 timetable – to the point in May 2019 when it had forced the UK to participate in the European Parliamentary Elections and self-flagellate itself over its Brexit-driven inadequacies.

At the top of government, we had a prime minister in Theresa May who allegedly voted Remain in the 2016 Brexit referendum promoting Brexit with all the zeal of the convert. We also had a leader of the opposition who was a well-known Eurosceptic, claiming that he supported Remain. Jeremy Corbyn mumbled publicly that he supported the UK remaining in the EU – but he seemed to do very little to advance that aim despite being implored to do so by many of those in his party. Brexit then delivered an ironic conundrum that from 2017 to 2019 we had a government that appeared to be incapable of governing and a leader of the opposition who seemed to be incapable of effectively opposing it.

To add irony onto irony, Brexit turned British political convention on its head, where non-mandatory referendums were considered binding rather than advisory, and representative parliamentary sovereignty was deemed to be secondary to the direct democracy of referendums. In a final ironic twist, what saved the parliamentary system in the UK over Brexit was not parliament, but the civic engagement of Gina Miller and a small group of UK judges. Miller's legal challenge to the government and the decision of the High Court (subsequently upheld by the Supreme Court) to prevent the government from using royal prerogative powers to trigger Article 50 forced it to seek approval in parliament. So Brexit was, in the end, about taking back control – but not in the way Brexiteers had envisaged. The Supreme Court bookended this period as it was also called upon to arbitrate over whether Prime Minister Boris Johnson had misled the Queen in his decision to prorogue the House of Commons for five weeks in September 2019. The unanimous 11–0 judgment of the UK Supreme Court was a blow to Johnson's political credibility that might have led him to wonder about the desirability of taking back control after all. Special mention also needs to go to Speaker of the House John Bercow, who defended parliamentary democracy to the best of his ability against an executive that tried to ride roughshod over it.

The central architects of Brexit, meanwhile: Arron Banks, Dominic Cummings, Daniel Hannan, Jacob Rees-Mogg, Michael Gove, Nigel Farage, Boris Johnson and other bankers, hedge-fund managers, stockbrokers and privately educated, wealthy politicians, spent the three years 2016–19 presenting themselves as the authentic voice of the people fighting the metropolitan elite in the interests of the common man – and occasionally woman. But these people are the very essence of white, male, wealthy privilege. An associated and tragic irony is that it is those who have felt the most left behind politically and economically by the European project, who voted Leave in 2016 and believed in the merits of a 'no-deal' Brexit, who are the people likely to suffer the most from such an outcome.

There was of course an Irish angle to the irony of Brexit. The DUP, a party that prided itself on its strong unionist credentials, perhaps did more to undermine the Union than Sinn Féin could ever have hoped to achieve. The party's slogan on the front of its manifesto for the May 2019 European Election was 'Defend the Union: Deliver Brexit',[36] yet, as Claire Hanna (SDLP) and Steve Aiken (UUP) have suggested above, they were arguably jeopardising the very thing they sought the most.

The UUP meanwhile, the party of business in Northern Ireland, ignored the pleas of business and farming groups at the end of 2018 to support Theresa May's Withdrawal Agreement, due to the alleged catastrophic economic impact of a no-deal Brexit on Northern Ireland. It was left to Sinn Féin to highlight the importance of the majority consent within Northern Ireland for remaining within the EU and the need to respect the self-determination of the Northern Ireland electorate.

Meteors, peace agreements and coping strategies

It seems reasonable to conclude that the Brexit meteor has knocked the peace process in Northern Ireland off its political axis, and in addition to the irony produced, it has left it spinning out of the orbital path established during the peace process in the 1990s. The central points of political gravity – power-sharing between unionist and nationalist parties; eradication of fatal political violence mediated by a partnership between the UK and Irish government as co-guarantors of the GFA; the principle that citizens (or subjects) could opt into British and/or Irish nationality – are now no longer anchored within our political narrative as they were prior to the 2016 referendum. For all of these reasons, Brexit is breaking peace in Northern Ireland and setting back the prospects of political stability in the region. It can still recover and the restoration of the devolved institutions in January 2020 is a start – but the hill that has to be climbed is a higher one as a result of the Brexit process.

Hindsight is, of course, the luxury of the academic researcher not enjoyed by the political practitioner, but it does raise an interesting point, namely whether shock absorbers can be built into peace agreements that might help mitigate the impact of meteor strikes upon them. Trouble-shooting mechanisms have long been defined as an optimal design in peace negotiations, third-party intervention efforts and the implementation of peace settlements, but these usually focus around the outstanding issues and points of existing division between conflict parties, rather than being designed to cope with unforeseen impacts of the sort represented by Brexit.[37] Nevertheless the understanding within conflict transformation literature that peace negotiations need to aim for maximum inclusivity and that peacebuilding activity and third-party intervention to support it needs to be seen an as ongoing activity has to be welcomed and if possible augmented. This trend has also led to a complementary understanding that responsibility for trouble-shooting capacity in peacebuilding efforts ought to be viewed holistically rather than being regarded as the task of either just the internal actors within a conflict or those external to it. Instead it needs to be a more multidimensional and integrated approach.[38] This is consistent with the conflict transformation perspective which sees peace negotiations, settlements and their implementation as ongoing processes rather than as isolated events. As conceptualised by leading scholars in the field, the point of conflict transformation is not to 'fix' a conflict, or bargain over a specific set of issues, but to transform the context within which those issues and relationships are understood by the conflict parties.[39]

Such an approach would seem to be the optimal way for us to understand the conflict in Northern Ireland, especially as it tries to absorb the impact of Brexit on the fragile political relationships that exist and on political stability in the region. Obviously it would help to have some form of early-warning system to enable key actors, especially the political elites who might be in a position to do something about it, to see the meteor coming and warn people to brace for its impact. The idea of early-warning systems has been a key feature within the academic literature on international peacebuilding, especially following the upsurge of interest in concepts such as international conflict prevention and responsibility to protect (R2P) during the 1990s.[40] However, the problem has not been the lack of prior warning of emergent problems in peace settlements, so much as the lack of political will to do something about the problems that everyone could see coming.

Finally, it would seem sensible to have sufficient elasticity within the process to address the new circumstances that might apply in the aftermath of conflict. Quite often negotiated peace settlements have review processes or are supplemented by new iterations of the original agreement. This has been the case with the Oslo Agreements in the Israel/Palestine conflict – though to little avail in terms of delivering a comprehensive settlement. A review mechanism was also a feature of the GFA in 1998, paragraphs 7 and 8 of the 'Validation, Implementation and Review' section, setting out the conditions for the parties to take stock of progress and deal with problems or delays in implementation.[41]

In practice, however, the GFA has been revised as a result of its own incapacity via the St Andrews Agreement in 2006, the Stormont House Agreement in 2014, the Fresh Start Agreement between Sinn Féin and the DUP in 2015 and most recently the New Decade, New Approach agreement in January 2020. These iterations of the GFA attempted to develop the devolved power-sharing institutions in a way that secured consensus between the main political parties and the unionist and nationalist communities. This witnessed the evolution of consociationalism in Northern

Ireland to include the option for formal opposition in the Northern Ireland Assembly – but the Brexit referendum in June 2016, together with the inherent tensions between the main political parties (and specifically between the DUP and Sinn Féin), saw these collapse at the end of the year.[42]

The problem with all of these mitigating elements is that they require some degree of good faith between the conflict parties and sufficient capacity to act upon them. In addition, the problem in the case of Northern Ireland, is that the Brexit meteor has not been cataclysmic for all the main parties involved. The carnage and chaos so far produced has actually provided benefits for some of the political actors – at least in the short term. The DUP, while politically exposed over its rejection of the Backstop aspect of the 2018 Withdrawal Agreement, can play to its strengths in terms of commitment to the Union. Sinn Féin can advance its Irish unity project via calls for a border poll after Brexit.

Secondly, and at the risk of strangling the metaphor, the effects of the Brexit meteor have been slow acting – in that its shock wave has not yet fully arrived. There still has to be a big Brexit moment beyond the referendum in 2016 that provides the political impetus for change. At the time of writing (October 2019) Northern Ireland and the rest of the UK has not left the EU and the impacts are linked to the *prospect* of Brexit rather than its likely full impact on the economy, border and issues such as policing policy and the criminal justice system. There is not yet a hard border erected or even a backstop operationalised. No one is yet vandalising CCTV cameras on the border, refusing to pay fines imposed for non-compliance with border checks on vehicles, or paying court costs or fines for public order offences linked to Brexit. No one has been arrested yet for criminal damage as a result of any border infrastructure or other public order offences connected to the demarcation of Northern Ireland and the Irish Republic as once again distinct and clearly delineated territorial units.

It seems clear, however, that coping strategies for external meteors that tilt negotiated settlements off their political axes would be helpful for violently divided societies such as Northern Ireland that are struggling to implement those agreements. As represented by Brexit, these meteors may be unforeseen, but the case of Northern Ireland shows that it may make a negotiation process more robust and help to implement political settlements, if the partners to those agreements can agree some means to revisit the key principles and issues in light of their transformation by such exogenous shocks. This should not require any prior concessions on the substance of the issues at the heart of the negotiations, but it could provide a mechanism for emergent problems to be addressed months or years after the negotiations take place. Northern Ireland demonstrates that when no shock absorbers have been built into the political system to deflect the impact of exogenous shocks such as Brexit, the difficulties inherent within the political system are magnified and the problems become more difficult to resolve.

Again this requires some level of cross-party consensus and/or good faith on the part of external guarantors to activate such mechanisms. Notwithstanding the absence of the former, in the past it would be a reasonable assumption that in terms of the latter issue a bipartisan approach would be taken by the UK and Irish governments towards Northern Ireland. However, as Chapter 7 demonstrates, the Brexit meteor smashed though that relationship and Anglo-Irish relations have deteriorated in the aftermath of the impact and as the Brexit negotiations have developed from 2017 to 2019. A strong Dublin–London relationship was the foundation on which the GFA and the peace process was built. It is fair to say that the Brexit meteor has also transformed this beyond recognition – to the point where relations are at their lowest point since the 1981 republican hunger strikes and perhaps since the Free State adopted a formal position of neutrality during the Second World War.

The declining Anglo-Irish relationship will be examined later in the book, but now it is important to review how these two countries ended up so divided over Brexit in the first place. The next chapter looks at the immediate aftermath of the Brexit meteor's arrival in 2016 and how events unfolded to lead to such calamitous consequences for political stability in Northern Ireland, the Irish Republic and within UK politics.

3

Brexit day: the result and the fallout

I don't know that [the Assembly] would have been pulled down if it hadn't been for Brexit I really don't. I think Brexit in a lot of ways was the straw that broke the camel's back and even if you could put a front on it and polish it – they [the DUP and Sinn Féin] were pulling in two fundamentally different directions. But the collapse of the Assembly has made Brexit worse – there is no doubt in my mind about that.

Claire Hanna MLA, SDLP[1]

If people say what was the turning point in all this – it wasn't the Brexit result, it wasn't so much the shock – it was the fact that the DUP decided they were bigger than Northern Ireland and bigger than Scotland and Wales.

Alex Kane, journalist and commentator[2]

By the time the referendum was due to be held on 23 June 2016, a febrile atmosphere had taken hold across the UK. The media was awash with national politicians criss-crossing the country, making last-ditch arguments but mostly repeating well-worn slogans that had been aired throughout the previous six weeks and in some cases over several years.

Despite a late surge in the polls by the Leave campaign, most people expected the Remain side to prevail. Even the leader of UKIP, Nigel Farage, was almost conceding defeat while the polls were still open and before the results had really started to unfold.

Speaking after he cast his vote, Farage announced, 'It's been an extraordinary referendum campaign, turnout looks to be exceptionally high and [it] looks like Remain will edge it. UKIP and I are going nowhere and the party will only continue to grow stronger in the future.'[3] Polling company YouGov released its latest opinion survey after the polls closed at 10 pm on 23 June that seemed to confirm this view, suggesting a 52%–48% victory for Remain.[4]

The overall result of the referendum is of course well known and produced a majority decision for the UK to leave the EU by a margin of 52% to 48%. In terms of individual ballots cast, this translated into 17,410,742 votes to leave and 16,141,241 votes to remain. The turnout in the referendum was also high, at 71.8%, strengthening the case that a clear mandate had been delivered for the UK to leave the European Union. Behind these headline numbers lay some equally stark indicators. Bluntly, the poll pointed to a Disunited Kingdom as the devolved regions of Scotland and Northern Ireland voted strongly for Remain, as did London. Outside the capital, however, there were majorities for Leave in every English region from the north to the south of the country. The votes were counted overnight and it quickly became apparent that the result was going to be close.

All political lives end in failure

The result came as a political bombshell, not least to Prime Minister David Cameron, who announced his resignation at breakfast time the following morning. In an attempt to get on the front foot and control the news agenda, Cameron made his announcement outside Downing Street early on 24 June, claiming that 'the British people had made a very clear decision to take a different path'[5] to the one he had recommended and therefore he felt the country needed 'fresh leadership' to take it in that direction. 'I will do everything I can as Prime Minister, to steady the ship over the coming weeks and months. But I do not think it would be right for me, to try to

be the captain, that steers our country to its next destination.'[6]
Effectively he was saying to the Leave side and cabinet colleagues
such as Boris Johnson, Michael Gove and others that this was their
project and they would now have to deliver it.

Cameron's kamikaze strategy over UK membership of the EU
was cruelly exposed. After announcing his decision to resign as prime
minister, he hummed his way back into Downing Street as if he
had just given an update on the half-time football score involving
his beloved Aston Villa (or was it West Ham?).[7] History is likely
to judge him harshly as a reckless political gambler who rolled the
dice on Brexit – and lost. The man of privilege who believed in
nothing, who bent to accommodate whatever breeze came along.
His legacy is likely to be the removal of the UK from the EU – a
decision he was fighting to prevent – and potentially the destruction
of the United Kingdom as a constitutional unit. As demonstrated
in these chapters, the vote to leave the EU and the negotiations
that have followed have further destabilised politics in Northern
Ireland and re-energised the campaign for Irish reunification. This
is unlikely in the short term but when future historians look back to
the point when the UK reconfigured into separate political units,
they may well trace it back to the 23 June 2016.

While his predecessors, from Ted Heath, through Thatcher and
Major, had managed to contain the latent conflict over Europe
and muddle through in a way that allowed the factions in his party
to co-exist, Cameron forced these incompatibilities to confront
each other to the point where they exploded into open warfare.
That is one reason why he allowed a free vote over the referendum
– he did not have the authority over the parliamentary party to
do anything else. Instead, he let one side fight the other to the
finish. The outcome produced a chronically dysfunctional government and party, the victorious Leave side emboldened, driven and
determined to deliver Brexit. The vanquished Remain side were
in turn bitter, insurgent and equally determined to ensure that
government policy did not damage what they saw as the fundamental

political and economic interests of the country. Cameron was the man without a plan, who drove the UK bus into the wall and walked away from the wreckage – humming.

Theresa May would fail too – and her charge sheet as Tory leader and prime minister in 2019 is as long as that of her predecessor's three years before. However, while she fumbled the hospital pass he gave her as prime minister and leader of the party, at least she did not hum her way back into the building after announcing her resignation. Her tears and emotional crumpling at the end of her announcement at least showed that she cared – even if the show of emotion at the end was about the death of her own career rather than the political havoc she had wreaked while in office.[8]

Tony Blair is on record as saying that Brexit was a disaster for the political and economic future of the UK – not to mention the political stability of Northern Ireland and integrity of the GFA that he had helped to wrangle during the multiparty negotiations that concluded in April 1998. On the up side, even with Blair's disastrous adventure in Iraq, looking for non-existent weapons of mass destruction, followed by the pursuit of an illegal war, he is likely to be regarded as doing less damage to the UK than Cameron's period in office. Enoch Powell's observation that all political lives end in failure was certainly reflected in Cameron's and May's tenures, with Brexit their inevitable epitaph as surely as Iraq will be Blair's.

'You were only supposed to blow the bloody doors off'

Even before Cameron began his solo humming on 24 June, the atmosphere had moved from febrile into a more chaotic chain of events. Politicians emerged from all sides, trying to get a grip on the public narrative and regain some composure and control – given the events of the previous evening. Nicola Sturgeon, First Minister of Scotland and leader of the Scottish National Party (SNP), stated that her government would not allow Scotland to be removed from the EU when it had clearly indicated in the referendum its wish to remain. She also hinted that a second referendum on Scottish independence was now highly likely as a result. This demonstrated how the referendum result was very quickly having wider ripple effects on the constitutional fabric of the UK. The support for the Remain side was overwhelming in Scotland at 62% to 38% – with all thirty-two council areas backing Remain. This needs to be understood in the context of the referendum on Scottish independence in 2014 and the commitments made by the UK government in terms of respecting Scottish opinion. Two years later the political landscape looked a lot different, presenting an existential crisis within the UK over who had the right to self-determination and who did not. In other words, the UK's decision to leave the EU highlighted that while Scotland may be a nation or even a country, it did not have a right to sovereignty and was still on a chain that could be pulled by Westminster. At her news conference on 24 June, Sturgeon said that it was 'a statement of the obvious that a second referendum must be on the table, and it is on the table'.[9]

Boris Johnson, widely tipped to succeed Cameron as prime minister, looked even more flustered than usual. He made a speech on the morning of 24 June that acknowledged what he claimed was a 'glorious opportunity' for the UK to take back control of its laws, borders and economy, but his underlying message was that there was 'no need for haste' in the process of doing so. This was in part an attempt to control the frantic pace of events and prepare for his imminent (though ultimately doomed) 2016 Conservative Party leadership contest – and the office of prime minister that would automatically fall to the winner. But Johnson's call for a patient approach towards change was also due to the fact that he was acutely aware that the political ball was now at his feet and he was facing a politically split country, a bruised set of international partners in Europe and a highly volatile economy as international investors took stock of the referendum decision. 'Nothing will change in the short term' was his call to arms on 24 June following the tumultuous events of the previous evening. The value of the pound fell dramatically to its lowest level against the US dollar in thirty-one years early on 24 June as the financial markets responded with nervousness to the referendum decision. Panicked external investors contemplated the implications of the Leave vote leading to a drop for the UK pound, which fell to $1.33USD in the early hours of 24 June, compared to $1.50 when the polls closed on 23 June – its lowest level since 1985.[10] This was in part caused by a general expectation in the financial markets that the referendum would deliver a small majority decision to remain within the EU. As a result, money and decisions were lining up behind a predicted Remain outcome. At 6 pm on 23 June, online bookmaker Betfair predicted an 84% chance of a Remain majority and 16% likelihood of a Leave vote.

Despite the fall of the pound, this was more a nervous tic from the financial markets rather than a full spasm. Statements from UK Chancellor of the Exchequer George Osborne, and Governor of the Bank of England Mark Carney early on 24 June (both of whom had argued strongly for a Remain vote in the referendum) calmed the markets and led to an all-time record volume of trading on the London Stock Exchange.[11] Once the initial shock wave had passed, nerves were calmed that there was no imminent economic crash in the UK or elsewhere around Europe or North America. Politically, the UK resembled a field hospital in a war zone on 24 June 2016 and for the days that followed, operated on triage principles. Unsurprisingly, the media was on a political sugar-high as it struggled to keep up with the speed of events and to cover all the angles.

Irish politicians and policymakers were characteristically more prepared for the Leave vote than their counterparts in the UK. As the doyen of Brexit journalists Tony Connelly has documented,

Irish politicians had a game plan ready in the unlikely event that the Leave vote prevailed. A team of Irish officials drawn mainly from the Departments of the Taoiseach and Foreign Affairs had 'war gamed' the three possible scenarios: a Leave result, a Remain outcome and a dead heat. They had worked through the modalities of an Irish response for each of these, down to the wording of press releases, which documents would be circulated to which key stakeholder groups and the media management strategy for each outcome.[12] This stands in stark contrast to the reaction within UK policy circles, where there was a chaotic and uncoordinated response to the result. As Connelly wrote:

> This was not an Irish referendum but it might as well have been. Officials from virtually every government Department had been tasked with drawing up detailed explorations of how a leave vote might affect Ireland. … There had been intense preparations in Dublin in the final weeks of the referendum campaign. There was one fundamental imperative: If Britain voted to leave the EU, the Irish state would have to show its citizens and the world, that it could withstand the immediate impact and that, no matter what, Ireland would be remaining in the EU.[13]

Northern Ireland and the implications of the vote for the future of its troubled political institutions or the peace and stability of the region more generally was of secondary interest for the vast majority of politicians and journalists in Great Britain. This would soon change once the dust began to settle on the referendum outcome and the UK began to wonder how it would give substance to the slogans. Predictably, the Westminster soap opera was uppermost in the minds of both broadcast and print media – Cameron's replacement as leader of the Conservative Party and prime minister being the main focus of attention, along with the future of UKIP leader Nigel Farage. This trend would be repeated in May 2019 when Cameron's successor Theresa May was also brought down over Brexit – with the focus being on who would replace her as prime minister rather than whether the UK was going to crash out of the EU without a deal in October.

Back in 2016, Farage and his party had been a key focus of the referendum campaign, always ready with a colourful quote or available for a good photo opportunity; Farage gave good copy to lazy journalists and their editors. Part Svengali, part harrumphing cab driver, Farage had cultivated the persona of an ordinary bloke who was not afraid to expose the excesses of the fat cats in Brussels. His slogans were good ones in marketing terms and he understood the key to political communication and propaganda: that the route to success was not to change people's minds but to confirm what they already thought. Ironically, Farage – with a background in the London stock market – out-performed Cameron in the advertising and public relations department, which had been the prime minister's own turf before he went into politics. Farage was a key focus for the media the day after the referendum and he did not disappoint his supporters in his victory speech: 'Dare to dream, that the dawn is breaking on an Independent United Kingdom. … Let June 23rd go down in our history as our Independence Day.'[14] For a politician on the fringes of formal political power in Britain, he demonstrated that he wielded considerable influence over the political future of the country, despite never having been elected to political office in the UK.

In contrast to the UKIP leader, senior Conservatives on the Leave side, notably Boris Johnson and Michael Gove, dived for cover once it became clear that Cameron was not prepared to clear up the political debris. Justice Secretary Michael Gove was woken up at 5 am to be told the news that Leave had won the vote, at which point his wife (tabloid journalist Sarah Vine) quipped, 'you were only supposed to blow the bloody doors off'.[15] This reference to a line from the 1969 comedy film *The Italian Job* was an excellent metaphor for the political context immediately after the referendum. The comment came from lead character Charlie Crocker (played by Michael Caine) while planning a gold heist in

Turin with his British gang. Crocker's hapless accomplice in the crime caper had miscalculated how much explosive was needed and completely destroyed a van when what they wanted to do was force its back doors open. The end of the film is equally a metaphor for the aftermath of the referendum as it finishes with the getaway coach crashing and ending up balanced precariously on the edge of a cliff as the gang drive back over the Alps from Italy to Switzerland, the thieves at one end and their stolen gold bars at the other. Every time they move towards the gold, their prize slides further to the back of the coach, threatening to take them all over the edge with it. They are stuck and cannot move towards the gold without tipping the entire coach over the cliff. The film ends appropriately on a cliff-hanger, with a famous last line from Charlie Crocker: 'Hang on, lads; I've got a great idea.'[16] Life truly is stranger than fiction as this is where Brexit departed from the script in that it immediately became clear that nobody in the Leave campaign had any ideas about how to give life to their project in a way that would secure a negotiated deal with the other parties to the Brexit divorce. Sky News political journalist Faisal Islam reported speaking to a key source close to Boris Johnson who admitted that they had not yet developed an action plan for what to do next. 'I said to him, "Where's the plan? Can we see the Brexit plan now?" [He replied,] "There is no plan. The Leave campaign don't have a post-Brexit plan. ... No. 10 should have had a plan." Now it sounds like I'm making that up but that literally happened two hours ago.'[17]

This lack of planning carried through into the negotiations themselves. There could be no coherent plan developed because agreement was never reached by the architects of Brexit and the government that replaced Cameron's, about what they wanted – beyond the vacuous slogan 'Brexit means Brexit' solemnly declared by Theresa May, who replaced Cameron as Conservative Party leader and prime minister in July 2016.

Northern Ireland reacts

The reaction to the referendum result in Northern Ireland was intense, if predictable, given the positions of the main parties before the vote. The result sucked all remaining air out of the idea that Brexit was an issue that complicated the ethnonational divide. The DUP argued that Brexit represented an opportunity to be grasped, both for Northern Ireland for the 'nation' as a whole – the British nation that is. Sinn Féin reiterated its demand for a border poll on Irish reunification and campaigned around the need for 'special status' for Northern Ireland.

On 24 June, Sinn Féin reiterated its request for a border poll on Northern Ireland's continued membership of the UK – flagged by deputy First Minister Martin McGuinness in March. Interestingly, given its historical position that the partitioned Northern Ireland had no democratic legitimacy, Sinn Féin was now championing its right to self-determination as a democratic principle. National party chair Declan Kearney framed Brexit as an English decision which was at odds with the local wishes of voters in Northern Ireland: 'English votes have overturned the democratic will of Northern Ireland. This was a cross-community vote in favour of remaining in the EU. English voters are dragging Northern Ireland out of the EU.'[18] Northern Ireland finance minister, Sinn Féin's Máirtín Ó Muilleoir, sounded an ominous note, suggesting that the political situation was 'as grave a crisis as we have faced in four decades'.[19] Deputy First Minister Martin McGuinness suggested that, given that the result in Northern Ireland demonstrated a wish to remain within the EU, the UK had lost its democratic mandate to govern the region.

The British government now has no democratic mandate to represent the views of the North in any future negotiations with the European Union and I do believe that there is a democratic imperative for a 'border poll' to be held. We are now in uncharted waters, nobody really knows what is going to happen. The implications for all of us on the island of Ireland are absolutely massive.[20]

The DUP focused on the exercise of UK national self-determination and bought into the rhetoric of the UK government that 'the people had spoken'. Recognising that there had been a vigorous debate on both sides of the argument, the line within the DUP (and soon after that within the UUP also) was that the task was now to draw a line under the decision and to get on with Brexit in a way that best represented the interests of the people of Northern Ireland. The free vote in the referendum offered by the DUP was not extended to views once the result was declared. Everyone had now to get behind the party line regardless of their personal views. Ian Paisley Jnr, who had campaigned for Leave, sent out a rather mixed message. On the one hand he welcomed the result in an uncompromising and typically pugnacious style: 'The union is safe and we are out of Europe, No conflict just victory!'[21] This demonstrated the way in which the outcome was now being immediately filtered through the prism of Northern Ireland's ethnonational conflict. Despite this, Paisley was still able to recommend that people in Northern Ireland should apply for Irish passports if they could. He went on Twitter to say, 'My advice is if you are entitled to a second passport then take one. I sign off lots of applications for constituents.'[22] However, it was clear that people did not need much encouragement in this regard, with Belfast's central post office running out of application forms for Irish passports within days, as eligible people in Northern Ireland and across the rest of the UK stampeded towards Irish and thus European citizenship after the result. While the DUP policy calcified around a pro-Brexit pro-Union and pro-United Kingdom concept of Brexit, eventually linking up with hard Brexiteers in the Conservative Party – this was not the case before the 2016 referendum. In truth, they were pragmatic rather than ideological Brexiteers and – like everyone else – had expected the Remain side to win the referendum. As Alex Kane said, 'I think it's now accepted [wisdom] that the DUP backed Brexit in the full expectation that it wasn't going to happen.'[23]

This tit-for-tat blame game between the main political parties that immediately followed the referendum result was hugely counterproductive – pushing the local political actors further apart at the very time they needed to come together to represent the interests of Northern Ireland in the manner that the Scottish government was managing. This was also doing nothing to build external confidence with economic investors who the Executive was spending considerable effort trying to entice into Northern Ireland on the basis of the political stability that had been built in the region since the establishment of the post-GFA political institutions.

Both unionists and nationalists were nervous about the implications of Brexit for the border, the economy and for the future of political relationships more generally. It quickly became a proxy for disagreement between the political parties and a site for mutual recrimination along ethnonational lines between the unionist and nationalist communities. Once the result had become fused with the future constitutional status of Northern Ireland (as being either an integral part of the UK or requiring special status for Northern Ireland in recognition that it was not an integral element of the UK in the manner of its other regions), the narrative from the main political parties became understood through that prism.

The reaction of the UUP was interesting given that its official policy had been to support Remain in the referendum. Party leader Mike Nesbitt made a statement on 24 June 2016 that indicated acceptance of the result but connected it to a critique of the Northern Ireland Executive. The UUP had walked out of Northern Ireland's regional government and into parliamentary opposition the previous year and had taken up the role of formal opposition in the Northern Ireland Assembly. Given this context it is not surprising that the UUP sought to connect the Brexit vote and its implications into questions of political leadership within the Northern Ireland government. Nesbitt is reported as saying:

> Despite the clear majority within Northern Ireland voting to Remain within the European Union, we must respect the overall result and deal with it and its implications, political, financial and social. There is no evidence that the Executive has been planning for this outcome. They need to move very quickly to reassure the public that there is a plan, because the full implications for Northern Ireland may not be clear for up to two years.[24]

Nesbitt followed this criticism up in a special debate on Brexit in the Northern Ireland Assembly a few days after the referendum result – asking why the Executive had not made contingency plans for a result that he described as 'a calamity'.[25] He had a point, given that there were only two outcomes possible in the referendum and the difference between the response from Belfast and the reaction in Edinburgh from the Scottish government was striking. But there could be no coherent policy response to the Brexit vote from the Northern Ireland Executive because First Minister Arlene Foster's and deputy First Minister Martin McGuinness's respective parties and supporters disagreed fundamentally about the implications of the UK leaving the EU in the first place. Added to this, Brexit landed in the political in-trays of the DUP and Sinn Féin at a point when the working relationship between the two parties was beginning to disintegrate. In this context it was impossible for them to develop a coherent plan in the manner of the SNP government in Edinburgh.

The immediate political responses again demonstrated how the outcome of the referendum had confused the traditional positions on self-determination in Northern Ireland. It also highlighted how the post-GFA focus on power-sharing was quickly overtaken by definitions of the mandate of the referendum based on a simple majority. The notion of 'majority rule' lay at the heart of Northern Ireland's political dysfunction from 1921 when the region was given its own devolved parliament until its powers were suspended amid street unrest and violence in 1972. Ever since that point until the emergence of the peace process in the early 1990s, many unionists had hankered after a return to the majoritarian logic as practised in other parts of the UK, including the devolved parliaments of Scotland and Wales. The realisation that a majority-rule system was not appropriate for an ethnonational dispute such as the Northern Ireland conflict had been at the heart of the peace process, the multiparty negotiations of 1996–98 and the post-GFA political institutions. Brexit, however, brought the spectre of majoritarian democracy back into the spotlight – though with ironic results in the case of Northern Ireland. Claiming majority support for a favoured position on Brexit was, of course, highly contingent upon what territorial entity was being referenced. Unionists preferred the entire UK – which had voted by an overall majority to leave the EU – while nationalists preferred to focus on Northern Ireland, which had voted by an overall majority to remain.

During First Minister's Questions in the Northern Ireland Assembly on 27 June 2016, DUP MLA Christopher Stalford argued that the referendum was 'an exercise in democracy' and also pointed out that, like it or not, democratic politics was based on making your argument and respecting the outcome of the majority – even if the result was not the one you wanted. 'Had the vote gone the other way, I would have had to take it on the chin and move on.'[26] This view was reiterated by DUP Brexit spokesperson Sammy Wilson when he reflected back on the referendum decision three years later:

> Whilst we believe that there are certain things which should be devolved and are rightly devolved to Northern Ireland, and Northern Ireland should have freedom to make decisions on those issues, the referendum, by its very nature, had to be a national decision and as part of the United Kingdom Northern Ireland has to live with that national decision and the government of the United Kingdom has to apply that decision nationally as well.[27]

Sinn Féin and the SDLP (as well as the Greens and Alliance Party) did not see things in the same way and focused instead on the right of the people in Northern Ireland to express self-determination independently of the other constituent parts of the UK. Sinn Féin Finance Minister Máirtín Ó Muilleoir demonstrated his party's alternative interpretation of self-determination in the same Assembly debate on 27 June: 'It's our job to find a way through this maze, but also the mandate must be respected – the majority here voted to remain.'[28]

Unsurprisingly, a binary political instrument (an in/out referendum) produced an equally binary response concerning whose self-determination was paramount. The outcome, however, was to muddy the political waters that had up until then focused on the need for unionists and nationalists to view their political futures – at least in institutional terms – as being inextricably linked though the mechanisms of consociational power-sharing.

Letter to London

Despite the clashing positions taken immediately after the result, and the way in which Brexit had now come to define a new front in the enduring political conflict between British and Irish identities in Northern Ireland, there were also points of convergence once the immediate shock of the outcome had dissipated. On 10 August, in a rare show of unity, First Minister Arlene Foster and deputy First Minister Martin McGuinness sent a joint letter from the Northern Ireland Executive Office to the UK's new Prime Minister, Theresa May, who replaced the deflated David Cameron in July. This outlined their concern that Brexit should be delivered in a way that took the unique circumstances of Northern Ireland into account, and requested their involvement in the negotiations, once Article 50 was triggered. The letter was 'reassured' by the Prime Minister's previous commitment that 'we will be fully involved and represented in the negotiations ... [and] we regard this as a fundamental prerequisite of a meaningful and inclusive negotiating process'.[29] This reference to reassurance was code for a tacit demand by the two political leaders that they were given access to the negotiations to ensure that the interests of Northern Ireland were represented.

This letter is significant in that it demonstrates the importance of power-sharing institutions in the region and the way in which this devolved office required political parties, and those leading them, to cooperate together for the entire community. It would have been much more difficult for Foster and McGuinness to have done this from their respective positions within the DUP and Sinn Féin, or as individuals. However, the institutions based on a joint First Minister/deputy First Minister office changed the dynamic and gave the letter a status it would not have had if it had simply been sent to the UK government by political parties in Northern Ireland. Removing the institutions – as of course happened shortly afterwards – takes away the need for joint stewardship and returns publicly elected representatives to their respective political parties and the ethnonational divide that defines them.

Equally important in terms of this joint letter was that both leaders agreed that Northern Ireland required a bespoke solution as it would be the only part of the UK with a land border to an EU member state once Brexit had taken place. It also highlighted a joint understanding that the resulting border would need to be manifested in a way that did not create additional political or economic problems in Ireland given the contested nature of the border in the past. As the letter said:

> There have been difficult issues relating to the border throughout our history and the peace process. We therefore appreciate your stated determination that the border will not become an impediment to the movement of people, goods and services. It must not become a catalyst for illegal activity or compromise in any way the arrangements relating to criminal justice and tackling organised crime. It is equally important that the border does not create an incentive

for those who would wish to undermine the peace process and/or the political settlement.[30]

While the text of this statement was relatively vague on specific solutions to the concerns raised, the fact that any wording could be agreed at all by the two leaders of unionism and nationalism was notable, given their opposing positions on the issue. However, the harmony of the moment was fleeting. Beyond this formal expression of joint stewardship, the positions of the DUP and Sinn Féin (and unionism and nationalism at a wider level) polarised and hardened after the result of the referendum became clear.

Changes at the top

The arrival of Theresa May as prime minister on 13 July 2016 was just another episode in the political tumult that characterised the summer of 2016. May had been Home Secretary and had campaigned (quietly) for Remain in the referendum. She won the leadership race to succeed Cameron by coming through the middle, while her rivals self-destructed spectacularly in front of her. May was at a disadvantage to the extent that she had campaigned for Remain in the referendum, was close to the previous administration and there was an expectation in some quarters that the party and the country would need to be led by someone from the Leave campaign who believed in Brexit and could deliver it. May was thus not the bookies' favourite and most of the money was on Cameron's fellow Eton and Bullingdon Club alumnus, Boris Johnson, to win the race. The election to replace Cameron turned into a metaphor for the subsequent Brexit negotiations in terms of their incompetence, as Johnson withdrew from the leadership race just at the point that he had got the media together to announce his candidature. He had been ambushed by his colleague Michael Gove, who had announced two hours earlier that he was standing, after previously saying that he would not. Johnson realised that he did not have the numbers to win, as the Brexit vote would have been split across multiple candidates. In an act of considerable chutzpah – even by the ruthless standards of Tory Party leadership contests – Gove had launched a political torpedo at his close Brexit-supporting colleague that morning, saying 'I have come, reluctantly, to the conclusion that Boris cannot provide the leadership or build the team for the task ahead.'[31] This was seen by many of Gove's colleagues as an act of naked political treachery and Gove suffered as a result, failing to make the final run-off that would be between Remain supporter Theresa May and Brexit campaigner and former Energy Minister Andrea Leadsom.

This leadership election set the tone for the Brexit negotiations that were to follow in subsequent years and were of fundamental importance to those people living in Northern Ireland who hoped that the majority vote to remain within the EU would be respected by the winner of the race, who would be the next prime minister. May was vulnerable to Leadsom over Brexit as she had campaigned for Remain while her rival clearly believed in the Brexit project before it was politically expedient to do so. As a consequence, May was unequivocal in her support for the UK leaving the EU when she launched her leadership campaign on 30 June:

> Brexit means Brexit. The campaign was fought, the vote was held, turnout was high, and the public gave their verdict. There must be no attempts to remain inside the EU, no attempts to rejoin it through the back door, and no second referendum. The country voted to leave the European Union, and it is the duty of the Government and of Parliament to make sure we do just that.[32]

In the end, once exposed to media scrutiny, Leadsom's deficiencies as a candidate were laid bare and May came through – ironically, in retrospect – as the experienced 'safe pair of hands' candidate, who could be entrusted to run the difficult Brexit negotiations efficiently. Ultimately the contest ended in a whimper, as Leadsom withdrew less than two weeks into the campaign. While she cited her reasons as being the need for political stability, the writing was on the wall as senior Tories were moving to support May in large numbers. Leadsom was relatively inexperienced and some questioned her political judgement after she was quoted as saying in a newspaper interview that because she was a mother – unlike Theresa May – she had a larger stake in society than her rival for the leadership.[33] She withdrew shortly after. Leadsom's statement came just an hour after May had launched her campaign and tied herself to the 'Brexit means Brexit' theme and the other commitments and red lines that she would find so difficult to move away from during the negotiations over the next two years. Northern Ireland did not feature in May's assessment of the task in hand, but in the end she was crowned rather than elected Tory leader and prime minister.

Personally a rather awkward and gauche individual, May began her tenure as prime minister with an homage to her predecessor – a sign of the questionable political touch that would become a motif of her doomed tenure: 'In David Cameron, I follow in the footsteps of a great modern Prime Minister … But David's true legacy is not about the economy, but about social justice'.[34] Others will argue that Brexit is Cameron's legacy – a failed political risk that will dominate the political and economic future of the UK for generations to come. Theresa May's political legacy will also be defined by her chronic mismanagement of the Brexit negotiations. Her clumsy and at times woeful stewardship of the negotiations dwarfs Cameron's failure in some ways. She played the weak hand he dealt her very badly, but there is no getting away from the fact that Cameron gambled with Brexit, he gambled with the constitutional fabric of the United Kingdom and he gambled with the political stability of Northern Ireland – and he lost. As for Theresa May, her articulation of 'the vision thing' outside 10 Downing Street on a sunny morning in July 2016 would soon turn to ashes in her mouth.

Like Margaret Thatcher before her quoting St Francis of Assisi when she became prime minister in 1979, it became clear very quickly that there was a yawning chasm between May's words and her deeds. Just as Thatcher said, 'Where there is discord, may we bring harmony … Where there is doubt, may we bring faith. And where there is despair, may we bring hope',[35] May too spoke of her mission to heal: 'That means fighting against the burning injustice … If you're black, you're treated more harshly by the criminal justice system than if you're white … The government I lead will be driven not be the interests of the privileged few – but by yours'.[36] Theresa May was leader of the Conservative Party, and had been Home Secretary and part of a government that had delivered a harsh and unforgiving austerity agenda onto the very people who were 'just about managing' and whom she claimed to value so highly. The reality of her premiership was epitomised not by her inclusive rhetoric but by the *Windrush* scandal and the promotion of the 'hostile environment' against people of colour, whom she purported to value. This scandal, where members of the black Caribbean community, including those descended from the *Windrush* generation, were asked to prove their right to remain in the UK, rocked the government in 2018 and led to the resignation of Home Secretary Amber Rudd.

May's premiership was also framed by Brexit and by the abysmal record of her government in negotiating the UK's exit from the European Union. While Cameron programmed Brexit into the UK's political sat nav, it was May who drove the bus off the cliff when she could have chosen not to do so – blindly following the instructions issued by the sat nav without seeming to recognise that she was running out of road. Her speech on 13 July 2016, as she went into Downing Street for the first time to form a new government, demonstrated her determination to deliver Brexit as requested by a majority of voters in the 2016 referendum: 'Following the referendum, we face a time of great national change. And I know because we're Great Britain [sic] that we will rise to the challenge. As we leave the European Union, we will forge a bold new positive role for ourselves in the World.'[37]

She was wrong on many levels, not least that she was leading the United Kingdom – not Great Britain – and the Northern Ireland blind spot would prove to be her undoing.[38] A few months after taking over as prime minister, May responded to the August letter from Arlene Foster and Martin McGuinness in a way that seemed relatively positive and unproblematic at first glance, but contained a more ominous message within its carefully drafted prose:

> I am committed to full engagement with the Northern Ireland Executive on the UK's exit from the EU and will take full account of the specific interests of the people of Northern Ireland in order to get the best possible deal for all parts of our United Kingdom as we leave the EU.[39]

At one level this seems quite inclusive – recognising the peculiar circumstances in Northern Ireland. However, people in Northern Ireland are past masters at decoding the meaning of political rhetoric, especially that emanating from London. It was clear that the real meaning lay in the last five words: 'as we leave the EU'. This clarified that there would be no deviation from the course set on 23 June 2016 and that, regardless of the majority vote in Northern Ireland for remaining within the EU, the region would be leaving the EU along with the rest of the UK. This message was welcomed by unionists and condemned by nationalists in equal measure and, in spite of the positive tone, the Prime Minister's response indicated that there was little prospect of special treatment for Northern Ireland despite its recent history of violent conflict and political instability.

Another theme emerged from Theresa May's letter to the First and deputy First Ministers that would become a regular part of the mood music in the UK's attempts to develop a clear narrative in the Brexit negotiations. This related to concerns that the UK's decision to leave the EU would result in a hard border in Ireland with negative political economic and cultural implications for the whole island. In her response to Foster and McGuinness, however, the Prime Minister was again reassuring – or at least appeared to be:

> The UK Government, the Northern Ireland Executive and the Irish Government have all been clear that we wish to see the continuance of the free movement of people and goods across the island of Ireland and the maintenance of the Common Travel Area across the whole of the UK and Ireland, which has served us well.[40]

Again the tone here was positive and demonstrated a commitment from the Prime Minister to iron out any wrinkles that might result from the return of a border in Ireland. On closer reading, however, it was clear that no promises or *guarantees* were being made to people in Northern Ireland or to the Irish government. The key phrase here was 'we wish to see', and such aspirational language was to become a feature of the UK negotiating position on Brexit and over the future of a border in Ireland in particular. Again, observers in both parts of Ireland had decoded this in a political nanosecond, to mean that while Britain would *wish* to see the continuation of the Common Travel Area in Ireland, they were not able to promise or guarantee that this wish would come true. While the CTA was an historical UK-Ireland arrangement rather than an EU one, it has never operated with one of the countries inside the EU and one of them beyond it.

It's Leave: so what next for Northern Ireland?

As the summer of 2016 wore on, the political parties, civic society and the general public gradually recovered from the shock of the result and began to think more concretely about the implications for Northern Ireland of the UK's decision to leave the EU.

The primary focus of Sinn Féin as the negotiations got underway, was to lobby around the lack of consent for Brexit within Northern Ireland and the fact that a majority of those who voted had expressed their democratic wish to remain within the EU. This was connected to a narrative about the integrity of the Good Friday Agreement and the political safeguards written into it and supposedly guaranteed by the UK government. After that, Sinn Féin campaigned against the spectre of a hard border in Ireland as well as the perceived economic disadvantages that Brexit would produce for the entire island. Sinn Féin used its formidable networks to hold a series of community-level meetings to discuss the implications of the referendum and also demonstrated its powerful machine in Brussels led by Martina Anderson, who took centre stage there in the party's attempt to resist the referendum outcome.

The SDLP was equally vocal, though given its status as one of the smaller parties its response was generally channelled through the media and via party leader Colum Eastwood, Brexit spokesperson Claire Hanna and former leader Mark Durkan while he remained MP for Foyle.

Two things now became inevitable in light of the conflicting positions on the result of the Brexit referendum (and its implications) adopted by the main unionist and nationalist parties. Firstly, regardless of joint letters from the First Minister and deputy First Minister to Theresa May, it would be impossible for Northern Ireland to develop a coherent political response or position on Brexit in the manner of the Scottish government. By December 2016, the SNP-led Scottish government had produced a sixty-two-page report, *Scotland's Place in Europe*, which proposed a 'differentiated solution' for Scotland – effectively allowing it to remain in the EU single market while the rest of the UK left.[41] The chasm that now existed between the DUP/UUP on the one hand and Sinn Féin/SDLP/Alliance on the other made this sort of joint approach impossible. Secondly, Brexit was now fused with ethnonational politics in Northern Ireland and rival interpretations of its implications for the 1998 Good Friday/Belfast Agreement and the power-sharing institutions that flowed from it. Equally powerfully, Brexit quickly became the site of arguments over the meaning of 'consent', democracy and the right to self-determination, all of which had been less contested terms within public discourse since power-sharing devolution had emerged after 1998.

The bumpy road to Brexit

In December 2016 the UK government announced its plan to activate Article 50, which would set the clock ticking on Britain's exit from the EU two years later, in March 2017. Following this announcement, former SDLP leader Mark Durkan made an explicit connection to democratic rights in Northern Ireland and the fragile architecture of the GFA and its associated institutions:

> The principle of consent is meant to be the core of the Good Friday Agreement. It is not only housed in that agreement, but it was the principle of consent that was used to endorse the agreement. … Where is the democracy and consent for the people of Northern Ireland when it comes to Brexit? … People such as Michael Gove (and others) do not recognise the damage that they are doing. Carefully compacted layers of understanding created the bedrock of the Good Friday Agreement, and fissures are being driven into those key foundations.[42]

This became a familiar refrain within Irish nationalist opinion during the reminder of the Brexit negotiation process; unionists countered that this was an exaggeration and linked to a wider agenda of trying to destabilise Northern Ireland's position within the Union. At this point the implications of Brexit for Northern Ireland were less dominant than the high politics at Westminster between the Conservative Party government and the Labour Party. Both were chronically split by Brexit but trying at the same time to use it to their advantage.

It seems hard to believe it in light of subsequent events, but Theresa May was in a relatively strong position in the latter half of 2016. While her party was split over how to execute the Brexit policy – what that policy should be, and indeed whether she was the right person to deliver it – Labour was providing little opposition to the government at the time. While constitutionally designated as the 'Official Opposition', Labour was also seriously split and was consumed by leadership divisions and efforts by senior figures in the Parliamentary Labour Party and shadow cabinet to get rid of party leader, Jeremy Corbyn. While vilified by the mass media in the UK and undermined by several of his most senior colleagues, Corbyn was immensely popular with Labour Party members and was successfully re-elected to the leadership of the party following a challenge to his position in September 2016. Internecine warfare, together with key policy divisions over Brexit and in other areas, left Labour in a diminished state – with most of the opposition on Brexit coming from within the pro-EU wing of the Conservative Party in the House of Commons and significantly also within the House of Lords, which subjected government plans to scrutiny and amendment.

But in 2016, Prime Minister Theresa May had a parliamentary majority and seemed destined to map out the direction and the timeline to Brexit from a position of strength. In her first speech as leader, at the Conservative Party Annual Conference in October 2016, the Prime Minister made it clear during an upbeat and rhetorically confident address that; 'Brexit means Brexit – And we're going to make a success of it.'[43] So far, so unclear, and the lack of clarity about how Brexit would be operationalised beyond the vacuous slogans and how that would impact on people – not least those living in Ireland – was to become a constant drumbeat of criticism from 2016 onwards. In her October conference speech, May passed this off as sound negotiating technique, claiming that her government would not be negotiating in public and that the details would have to remain confidential in order to maximise the chances of reaching a successful conclusion. The largely sympathetic UK media gave the Prime Minister significant leeway on this point for most of 2016 – but this would not last forever. May claimed in her speech that her government would not invoke Article 50 until the end of the year, in order to 'avoid setting the clock ticking until our objectives are clear and agreed. … There will be no unnecessary delays in invoking Article Fifty. We will invoke it when we are ready. And we will be ready soon. We will invoke Article Fifty no later than the end of March next year.'[44] As it turned out, Article 50 was triggered in March 2017, but the UK was far from ready for the clock to start ticking down to 29 March 2019, the date that the UK was supposed formally to exit the EU.

May's statement in her 2016 conference speech that the government did not require parliamentary approval to trigger Article 50 was subsequently challenged in the Supreme Court by investment banker Gina Miller – who won her case. In a landmark hearing, the UK Supreme Court ruled that the government did have to obtain parliamentary approval to trigger Article 50.[45] Beyond the case itself, this pressure on the government to give parliament or indeed the UK electorate a greater say in the terms of any Brexit deal became emblematic of the entire negotiating process.

By the time the government had lost its appeal against the Supreme Court decision in January 2017, deputy First Minister Martin McGuinness had resigned, causing the collapse of the Northern Ireland Executive. Michelle O'Neill, his successor as Sinn Féin leader at Stormont, used the High Court decision to make a wider point about the need for special status for Northern Ireland after Brexit:

> Clearly the ruling again ignores the will of the people of the North who voted by a majority to stay in the European Union. We believe that the North needs to have designated status. Clearly the onus is now on the Irish government to step up to the plate. They need to act in the interests of all the citizens of this island because they will be at the negotiating table and it is important that they act in our interests and make sure that we do receive special status given the nature of where we are here.[46]

Amid all the political turmoil at Westminster, between and within the main political parties, the political disintegration in Northern Ireland was barely noticed. Here too Brexit had become a toxic influence on political relations. While it did not trigger McGuinness's resignation as deputy First Minister, it had helped to polarise the political atmosphere at the beginning of 2017. The lack of a functioning local government at the very moment when Northern Ireland needed political leadership was a tragic by-product of the political times.

A plan emerges

Much of the period from the referendum in June 2016 until the end of that year was characterised by slogans rather than any clear direction on how Brexit was to be engineered. In part this was because there was no clarity within the UK government over what they wanted their policy to achieve – beyond the headline that 'Brexit means Brexit'.

It was not until the New Year that the UK government set out its key objectives in any detail with a landmark speech by Theresa May at Lancaster House on 17 January. This was at last the moment where the government would clarify what was meant behind the 'Brexit means Brexit' mantra, put flesh on the bones of policy and provide guidance for people within the UK about what the government wanted out of the negotiations and how it proposed to achieve those objectives. In reality the Prime Minister's Lancaster House speech was a little less forthcoming than might have been hoped as, despite announcing twelve priorities for the UK in the negotiations, there was little clarity about how goals would be achieved or aspirations would be met. Alarm bells should have gone off from the beginning of the speech – which was long on aspiration but short on anything approaching a clear guarantee about what was going to happen once the UK had left the EU. On the Irish border, there was a welcome commitment to maintain the Common Travel Area but little detail on how that would be achieved:

> Nobody wants to return to the borders of the past, so we will make it a priority to deliver a practical solution as soon as we can. ... I want this United Kingdom to emerge from this period of change stronger, fairer, more united and more outward-looking than ever before. I want us to be a secure, prosperous, tolerant country – a magnet for international talent and a home to the pioneers and innovators who will shape the world ahead. I want us to be a truly Global Britain.[47]

Fine words certainly, gushing in places over the vision offered, though starkly at odds with the political mess that was the more observable reality. And the repeated dictum of what the Prime Minister and her government 'wanted', or aspired to, did little to calm nerves about what could actually be delivered as the negotiations went on.

> A stronger Britain demands that we do something else – strengthen the precious union between the 4 nations of the United Kingdom. At this momentous time, it is more important than ever that we face the future together, united by what makes us strong: the bonds that unite us as a people, and our shared interest in the UK being an open, successful trading nation in the future. ... We have already received a paper from the Scottish government, and look forward to receiving a paper from the Welsh government shortly. Both papers will be considered as part of this important process.[48]

Given the fact that Northern Ireland and Scotland had both voted by large majorities to remain within the EU and that the UK government had rejected the Scottish government's request for a 'differentiated Brexit', the scepticism in these quarters following the Prime Minister's Lancaster House speech was perhaps understandable.

The Lancaster House speech did provide some vision of what the UK's objectives were and also presented some positive language about remaining a key member of the European community – if not a member of the EU itself. But while the speech provided the UK government with some political space at home, it was not followed up with sufficient substance or detail to have a lasting effect. More immediately, while it was couched in positivity, the speech contained thinly veiled threats concerning the implications of a no-deal outcome for the UK's European neighbours, which received a hostile reception in the European media. Germany's respected *Die Welt* newspaper, for instance, carried the front-page headline 'Little Britain – Prime Minister Theresa May leads Great Britain into isolation'.[49] Italy's *La Repubblica* was equally stark, running the headline 'Brexit: London puts up its wall – out of EU and single market'.[50] Reaction from European diplomats was more … diplomatic, with many EU leaders at least giving the Lancaster House speech a cautious welcome. The EU's chief negotiator, Michel Barnier, had vaguely positive words to proffer to the effect that an orderly exit of the UK from the EU was in everyone's interests and that as soon as the UK triggered Article 50 the negotiations could begin – but not until then. Barnier used social media to clarify that the EU was ready to plan for a smooth Brexit as soon as the UK was ready to negotiate: 'Ready as soon as UK is. Only notification can kick off negotiations.'[51] German Foreign Minister Frank-Walter Steinmeier also gave Lancaster House a cautious welcome on the basis that it at least clarified some of the timing and the general tone indicated an intention on the part of the UK to maintain good relations after the negotiations were completed in the longer term.[52]

Reaction in Ireland to Theresa May's Lancaster House speech ranged from enthusiastic and cautiously upbeat at one end of the spectrum to incredulous and scathing at the other. The response of the Irish government fitted into the former category as it sought to continue its role as critical friend of the UK government in mapping a route forward. Ireland welcomed Theresa May's commitment to the maintenance of the Common Travel Area and to the avoidance of a hard border on the island of Ireland. It went on to note rather more soberly that the speech pointed to a 'hard' rather than a 'soft' Brexit but that Dublin was prepared for any scenario that subsequently emerged:

> The Government notes that the British approach is now firmly that of a country which will have left the EU but which seeks to negotiate a new, close relationship with it. While this will inevitably be seen by many as a 'hard exit', the analysis across Government has covered all possible models for the future UK relationship with the EU.[53]

The reaction from Sinn Féin was less warm – as might have been expected. The party's former education minister, John O'Dowd MLA, claimed that the speech signalled a hard border in Ireland, significant economic damage to the region and the denial of self-determination to the people of Northern Ireland:

> Exiting the single European market, exiting the customs union, creates a hard border on the island of Ireland. Warm words, soft words from Theresa May mean nothing. Her intentions to leave the Single European Market and her intentions to leave the customs union are going to have a detrimental impact on the economy in the north and across this island. It's clear today from Theresa May's Brexit statement that the views and opinions of the people of [the] north have been completely ignored.[54]

This was also the view of the SDLP and the Alliance Party, with Stephen Farry MLA suggesting that the Lancaster House speech necessitated either a hard border on the island of Ireland or in the Irish Sea between Northern Ireland and Great Britain.[55]

If Theresa May was affected by such criticism she did not show it. The course was set to Brexit meaning Brexit, to the triggering of Article 50 in March 2017 and to the UK's exit from the European Union in March 2019. True to her January speech, in a letter to EU President Donald Tusk on 29 March 2017, the government formally announced the UK's intention to leave the EU. Article

50 was triggered, and the clock began ticking inexorably down to 29 March 2019. Tragically for her and everyone affected by the policies of her government, the Prime Minister suddenly decided that it would be a good time to call a General Election. This fateful decision, taken by the UK Prime Minister on a walking holiday, was to have profound consequences for her leadership, her party, the character of the Brexit negotiations, and the future of the UK's relations with the EU – and Ireland especially. The result of this election would define her period in office and the Brexit negotiations themselves.

4

The election that changed the course of Brexit: Westminster 2017

Northern Ireland is the most polarised it's been since the hunger strikes ... Clearly the single biggest source of polarisation at the moment I think is Brexit.

Ben Lowry, deputy editor, *Belfast News Letter*[1]

There's an ambivalence about Brexit within nationalism/republicanism. Obviously, if you see it through to its logical conclusion, it strengthens nationalism – yet in the short term there's going to be hardship, upheaval, instability and lots of uncertainty.

John Manley, political correspondent, *Irish News*[2]

Retrospect is of course a wonderful thing and if we all knew then what we know now, none of us would make any mistakes and books such as this would be shorter and less complicated to write. But politics takes place in the present not the past, and Theresa May's decision to hold a General Election in June 2017 shaped her political destiny, the prospects of her party in government and, more importantly, the future well-being of the United Kingdom, Ireland, and everyone who lives within 'these islands'. The outcome of the election, which was to take place on 8 June, had a major impact on political relationships within Northern Ireland and within May's own party. The result would also determine the shape of UK negotiations with the EU and in particular affected its capacity to deliver on its commitments to maintain a frictionless border in Ireland and maintain the integrity of the Good Friday Agreement.

The context of the 2017 election

It has been said that the secret to being a successful politician is to have luck on your side. There had been early signs that Theresa May might well have been successful in this respect as she had emerged from the Brexit referendum and the subsequent Tory Party leadership campaign relatively unscathed. In fact she won the race to succeed David Cameron as leader of the Conservative Party – and thus took office as prime minister of the UK – almost before she had begun. May was the last gun-slinger left standing in the barroom and she came through the middle – as so many do. Despite supporting the Remain side in the Brexit referendum, she was the safe experienced pair of hands who would deliver Brexit and oversee the smooth transition of the UK out of the European Union. These were halcyon days, but possibly signalled the last bit of luck she would experience during her tenure as prime minister.

On 18 April 2017 Theresa May stood outside Downing Street and said, 'We need a general election and we need one now. … I have only recently and reluctantly come to this conclusion but now I have concluded it is the only way to guarantee certainty for the years ahead.'[3]

Why did she come to this decision? The answer is due to a mixture of necessity and opportunity, wrapped up in a shroud of complacency and political miscalculation. While May was given a relatively easy ride by the mass media in the UK, who were busy gorging on the feeding frenzy of Labour Party in-fighting and the attempt by some Labour MPs to depose party leader Jeremy Corbyn, the Prime Minister's control of her own party was itself brittle. This was especially true of her command over the Brexit negotiations, with Boris Johnson in the Foreign Office, David Davis heading up the Department for Leaving the European Union and Liam Fox, another key voice in cabinet, as Secretary of State for International Trade.

Her vulnerability to accusations that she was not a true Brexit Believer in part explains the tone of the Lancaster House speech in which she had made clear that the UK was leaving the EU ... and that Brexit would mean that leave means leave: 'Not partial membership of the European Union, associate membership of the European Union, or anything that leaves us half-in, half-out.'[4] Sammy Wilson, Brexit spokesperson for the DUP, later reflected on Theresa May's period as prime minister and reinforced the criticism that her approach was based on talking tough but doing what she could to remain as close as possible to the European Union – consequently getting caught between two stools:

> Looking back on it now I believe that Theresa May was actually quite keen to keep the United Kingdom tied as closely to the EU as possible and was very happy to accept the problems which people said would exist along the border with the Irish Republic. In fact she made it even worse by saying that there would not be one extra stick of infrastructure along the border, which of course then made it difficult to even consider some of the technological solutions to monitoring trade across the border.[5]

Theresa May was prime minister and Conservative Party leader, but had a popular mandate for neither position, the latter being simply a coronation after the implosion of the other candidates, while the former had been an appointment by another woman who had experienced a 'proper' coronation as Queen of England in 1953. While the Queen was able to get away with it, Theresa May was more in need of democratic accountability, especially given the significant changes that Brexit would deliver to the UK economy as well as its political and cultural future.

The opportunity was provided by the apparently hapless state of the Labour Party and its leader Jeremy Corbyn, a man vilified and scorned at the time by the vast majority of mainstream UK media and roundly condemned as being unelectable. The opinion polls seemed to bear this judgement out, and polling in April 2017 showed the Tories with a 21% lead over Labour – surely an unassailable lead for any prime minister?

Have a problem? Have an election

Before Theresa May's gamble was tested and before the UK went to the polls – it went to the polls. At least it did so in Northern Ireland, where an early Assembly Election took place due to the collapse of the political institutions that had been precipitated by the resignation of Sinn Féin's deputy First Minister Martin McGuinness in January 2017. Tensions in government between Sinn Féin and the DUP had been obvious for some time and the relationship between McGuinness and First Minister Arlene Foster broke down irretrievably over the Renewable Heating Incentive (RHI) scandal and Foster's own part in it. The RHI scheme was established in November 2012 in an attempt to provide incentives for businesses to switch from using fossil fuels to renewable energy via the use of biomass boilers. This effort to encourage businesses in Northern Ireland to become more environmentally friendly was to have terrible repercussions for the political institutions, the political parties and the wider community who were left without a government at the very time they needed strong unified representation during the Brexit negotiations.

Arlene Foster had been the minister responsible at the Department of Enterprise, Trade and Investment that developed the policy and set up the scheme before she became DUP leader and First Minister. It became clear in 2016 that there was a serious flaw in the policy that had started out with a £25 million budget but would end up costing taxpayers between £500 million and £700 million more than was originally envisaged. The reason for this was that – unlike in Great Britain, where there was a similar scheme – there was no cap placed on the heating subsidy provided. Instead a flat rate over-generous subsidy was guaranteed for twenty years so that the more heating that was used, the more profitable the scheme became for those who installed multiple boilers to game the system. A public inquiry was set up into the scandal and revealed the extent of the mistakes that were made, the systemic dysfunction of the power-sharing government at Stormont and the friction between the DUP and Sinn Féin. The RHI inquiry also lifted the lid on internal friction within the DUP between ministers and special advisers (SPADs) and the extent to which these unelected officials were influencing policy decisions – at times apparently to the benefit of themselves, their families and their business interests. Steve Aiken, UUP Brexit spokesperson, suggested that the RHI scandal demonstrated that Northern Ireland should have been placed in 'special measures' due to the level of governance failure that was apparent:

> The ten years of DUP Sinn Féin stewardship [2007–17] has rein-forced failure all the way to the point. But the more striking thing, as the RHI inquiry shows, … there has been no record within the DUP and Sinn Féin of any decisions their ministers made because the civil servants have suffered from Stockholm syndrome and didn't want to upset their political masters. Who was speaking truth to power? Nobody. … It was rule by SPADs … This is half a billion pounds' worth of complete ineptitude and nobody's responsible.[6]

When McGuinness resigned, Arlene Foster claimed that she had nothing to hide and refused to stand aside as First Minister – though it would later emerge in the public hearing of the RHI inquiry that she, by her own admission, had not even read the regulations of the scheme that she was in charge of when she brought the legislation forward to the Northern Ireland Assembly for approval. When questioned whether she had read her own regulations she responded, 'No, I don't believe I would have read them at that stage. I probably would have only read the explanatory note, but not the regulations involved.'[7] Very quickly the media dubbed it the 'Cash for Ash' scheme and in 2017 it would become the final nail in the coffin for an already dysfunctional political system.

Foster's refusal to stand aside for a period as First Minister, as Peter Robinson had done on a previous occasion while an investigation was carried out, was the last straw for McGuinness and he resigned on 9 January 2017, citing governance issues relating to Foster and the DUP. In a letter of resignation to the Speaker of the Assembly, McGuinness launched a blistering attack on Foster and the DUP over the RHI scandal but also their broader attitude towards governance standards and towards the nationalist community and vulnerable minorities within Northern Ireland which he described as one of 'shameful disrespect' emanating from 'prejudice' and 'crass bigotry'. The RHI scandal and Foster's response to it was the main focus of his resignation letter, however:

> It is my firm view that the DUP's handling of this issue has been completely out of step with a public mood which is rightly outraged at the squandering of public money and the allegations of misconduct and corruption. The public are demanding robust action and accountability but the DUP, in particular its leader Arlene Foster, have refused to accept this. The DUP leader has a clear conflict of interest. She was the Minister responsible for the RHI scheme at its inception. No cost controls were put in place and warnings were ignored. This has led to an enormously damaging pressure on our public finances and a crisis of confidence in the political institutions. The Minister responsible for the RHI scheme should have no Executive role in overseeing how this will be rectified.[8]

Foster released a video message on Facebook in response to McGuinness's resignation in which she said she was 'disappointed' by his decision but accused Sinn Féin of trying to exploit the RHI issue for 'party political gain' when her party was trying to find solutions: 'It's clear that Sinn Féin's action are not principled – they are political … but because of Sinn Féin's selfish actions, we now have instability.'[9] This was a difficult moment for Foster's leadership of the DUP and an awkward unconfident delivery, where her attempt to look composed and statesmanlike seemed a bit sanguine, given the political failure and accusations of bigotry and corruption that surrounded her.

Due to the power-sharing system in Northern Ireland, the roles of First Minister and deputy First Minister are co-dependent, so when one resigns the other must follow, and the institutions are also suspended. Under the rules, an Assembly Election is then triggered to re-appoint a new government – which is why there was an unscheduled Assembly Election in March 2017 in advance of the Westminster General Election in June.

The atmosphere within which the 2017 Assembly Election was fought was bitter and fraught – even by Northern Ireland's standards. McGuinness was clearly seriously ill when he resigned, and by the time of the Assembly Election in March, Michelle O'Neill had been chosen to replace him as leader in the North. In her foreword to the 2017 Sinn Féin Assembly Election manifesto, *Equality, Respect, Integrity*, she blamed the DUP for the failure of the political institutions in Northern Ireland and promised a new progressive politics where everyone's identities would be 'embraced and celebrated'.[10] Party president Gerry Adams, in his own introduction to the manifesto, made an explicit link to Brexit and the role of the DUP within that: 'Sinn Féin will also stand against Brexit and the threat it poses to the economy of the island and to the all-island architecture of the Good Friday Agreement. Sinn Féin proposes a special designated status for the north within the European Union that ensures Ireland is protected.'[11] While much of the Sinn Féin manifesto in 2017 repeated the policy platform of the 2016 election, the section on Brexit was significantly beefed up, with an explicit demand for 'designated special status' and suggesting that Brexit presented a threat to the Good Friday Agreement as well as the economic fortunes of the region:

> The people of the North voted to remain in the European Union. The Tory government are seeking to impose Brexit on Ireland. The DUP stand with them and not with the people, or our economic interests. Sinn Féin will defend that democratic mandate and the rights of citizens. Sinn Féin believe that the only credible approach is for a designated special status for the north within the EU that will uphold the democratic vote of citizens, but will also ensure that the frontier between the EU and Britain will not be on the island of Ireland. Brexit undermines the integrity and status of the Good Friday Agreement and the political institutions. It will be bad for our economy, our people and our public services. … Sinn Féin is totally opposed to an EU frontier across Ireland. Trade tariffs, physical checks or border passport controls are unacceptable. Sinn Féin will work to ensure the Irish government acts in the national interest to make achieving designated special status within the EU an objective of the Brexit negotiations.[12]

This demonstrates the way in which the issue of Brexit had become fused with the ethnonational DNA of politics in Northern Ireland – it was now an orange versus green issue that connected EU membership with political identity and allegiance. The DUP, for its part, blamed Sinn Féin for causing an unnecessary election barely eight months after the previous one and accused it of political opportunism when Northern Ireland desperately needed leadership and stability to deal with the challenges it faced.

In the end, the result of the 2017 Assembly Election in Northern Ireland produced a near dead heat between the DUP and Sinn Féin, with the former out-polling the latter by the tiniest of margins at 28.1% of the vote to 27.9%. In terms of seats, the DUP squeaked it by one, winning twenty-eight seats to Sinn Féin's twenty-seven. In terms of public relations, the election was a victory for Sinn Féin and a close shave for the DUP, which had nearly lost its claim on the First Minister position in any new institutions that were established. The DUP had been harmed in the election by the RHI scandal, and party leader Arlene Foster's close ties to that issue. Foster was also damaged by her handling of relations with Sinn Féin and her reluctance to step aside while an investigation was conducted, as her predecessor Peter Robinson had done. This, together with a surge of sympathy among nationalists at the recent death of Martin McGuinness and support for his successor Michelle O'Neill, left the two main parties on practical parity.

The result emphasised longer-term trends, namely that Northern Ireland had effectively become a three-party system – the DUP, Sinn Féin and others – rather than the five-party system that had been the norm for the previous thirty years, with the DUP, UUP, Sinn Féin, SDLP and the Alliance Party. While the DUP and Sinn Féin tried to negotiate an agreement over the terms of another devolved Assembly in Northern Ireland, this was soon overtaken by events, in particular the outcome of the Westminster election of 8 June 2017.

The Brexit election, the magic money tree and the DUP

The General Election was a polarising experience, reducing the political space in a number of respects in Britain, in Northern Ireland and in the UK's efforts to negotiate a withdrawal agreement with its EU partners. That the milk was beginning to curdle in relations between London and Brussels was highlighted by exchanges between the two when Theresa May announced the dissolution of parliament on 3 May 2017. In an effort to begin the electioneering early and curry favour with the electorate, May adopted a truculent stance, to the point of suggesting that European politicians were deliberately trying to interfere in the election: 'Britain's negotiating position in Europe has been misrepresented in the continental press, the European Commission's negotiating stance has hardened, threats against Britain have been issued by European politicians and officials. All of these acts have been deliberately timed to affect the result of the [snap] general election [on 8 June].'[13] While this went down well with the tabloid press in the UK, opposition leader Jeremy Corbyn censured the Prime Minister for her tone and for using Brexit and the election for party advantage, rather than thinking in the national interest:

> By winding up the public confrontation with Brussels, the Prime Minister wants to wrap the Conservative party in the Union Jack and distract attention from her government's economic failure and rundown of our public services. ... But Brexit is too important to be used as a political game in this election. These are vital negotiations for every person in Britain and for the future of our country.[14]

This riposte was an early sign that Corbyn was not going to be the electoral push-over that May had hoped for. The EU reacted dismissively to May's accusations – an EU spokesperson suggesting that they were aware of the political context in the UK and impending election – and that they were too busy to meddle in UK affairs in any case: 'This election in the United Kingdom is mainly about Brexit. But we here in Brussels, we are very busy, rather busy, with our policy work. We have too much to do on our plate. So, in a nutshell, we are very busy.'[15]

Given the previous political dynamics in Britain and the consistently positive showing in the opinion polls, the expectation was that Theresa May would enhance her position in the General Election and increase her parliamentary majority, thus giving her a mandate from the country to expedite Brexit based on her Lancaster House speech, as well as strengthening other facets of the government's economic and social policy. To it put it more bluntly, there was a popular expectation that she would trounce Jeremy Corbyn and the Labour Party in the election – which is why she took the risk of calling it in the first place.

The result did not turn out as she had hoped. The election in Britain was defined by two things. First was Prime Minister Theresa May's inability to campaign effectively or communicate with voters in a convincing way. Secondly, somewhat against the odds, it was Labour rather than the Conservatives who won the battle for ideas in terms of the policy narrative within which the campaign was fought. It was Labour who set the policy agenda with a detailed and carefully costed manifesto – while the Conservatives campaigned over a less densely written manifesto and with a number of policy commitments that proved difficult to sell to voters.

Theresa May seemed content at the beginning of the campaign to attempt to personalise the contest, ridicule her opponent and present herself as the experienced candidate who could deliver stability in turbulent political times. However, this soon became untenable as Labour's policy platform set the news agenda and needed to be addressed with convincing arguments and alternatives. The trend of the campaign was for a gradual erosion of the Tory lead in the opinion polls over Labour to the point that it had dwindled from around twenty points to single digits in the latter stage of the campaign.

The Prime Minister tried to place Brexit at the centre of the campaign at the end of May, defining it (rather amazingly given the available evidence to the contrary) as a great opportunity for national cohesion that she was best placed to deliver: 'as we come together behind this great national mission – to make a success of Brexit and of the opportunities it brings – we will build a more united country as our shared values, interests and aspirations bring us together.'[16] In the end it all rang rather hollow and the Prime Minister displayed a chronic inability to connect with voters at a human level or convince them on the key issues surrounding economic and social policy that dominated the campaign. Interestingly, considering that the election was taking place in the middle of the Brexit negotiations, Brexit did not actually dominate the campaign or even distinguish the main parties from one another. The reason for this was that both Labour and the Tories were split over Brexit and were reluctant to widen that fracture further – and in addition both parties were ostensibly committed to the same policy of a smooth exit from the EU on the basis of the democratic mandate for Brexit established in the referendum. While Labour criticised the manner in which the government was expediting the Brexit negotiations, they did not oppose the final destination that the government was pursuing.

The election manifestos of the Labour and Conservative parties demonstrate this similarity and that Brexit was not really going to be an issue that would be decisive for them in the election result. The Conservative Party manifesto, *Forward, Together*, placed Brexit at the centre of the party's policy platform, but it was less prominently used in the election campaign itself. The manifesto was centred on Theresa May as leader, and the incumbent Prime Minister introduced it as her policy agenda for the next five years with Brexit at its centre:

> The next five years are the most challenging that Britain has faced in my lifetime. Brexit will define us: our place in the world, our economic security and our future prosperity. So now more than ever, Britain needs a strong and stable government to get the best Brexit deal for our country and its people. Now more than ever, Britain needs strong and stable leadership to make the most of the opportunities Brexit brings for hardworking families. Now more than ever, Britain needs a clear plan. This manifesto, *Forward, Together: Our Plan for a Stronger Britain and a Prosperous Future* will meet the great challenges of our time, beyond Brexit.[17]

The Labour Party manifesto, *For the Many Not the Few*, focused on the inequalities within Britain in 2017 – but put forward a radical alternative agenda and the optimistic narrative of progressive change at the centre of its offering to the electorate. Brexit was presented in terms of negotiating an exit from the EU that went beyond the rhetoric and delivered an outcome that protected jobs and the economy:

> Britain needs to negotiate a Brexit deal that puts our economy and living standards first. That won't be achieved by empty slogans and posturing. We cannot put at risk our links with our largest trading partner. Instead we need a jobs-first Brexit that allows us to upgrade our economy for the 21st century.[18]

Later in the manifesto, there is an explicit acceptance of the referendum result and commitment to delivering its outcome: 'Labour accepts the referendum result and a Labour government will put the national interest first.'[19] Labour's position was very much defined by the effective delivery of Brexit rather than reversing the direction of travel towards UK exit from the EU scheduled for March 2019. This reading of the manifestos of the Conservative and Labour parties was also reflected in the BBC leaders' debate on 1 June. This was notable for the fact that Theresa May, who had refused to participate, was effectively blind-sided when Jeremy Corbyn announced that he would take part. As a result May sent Home Secretary Amber Rudd in to bat – to some grumbling from the media and derision from her opponents. Amber Rudd made clear in the televised debate that the choice facing voters was who they wanted in Downing Street as prime minister, in an attempt to personalise the issues and capitalise on Corbyn's lack of popularity beyond his core support base:

> The only question to consider is who should be in No. 10 to steer Britain to a brighter future? Jeremy Corbyn with his money tree wish-list manifesto, and no plan for Brexit? Or Theresa May and her record of delivery? With her clear plan for Brexit and her strong team behind her who can make sure the country gets to that brighter future?[20]

The election campaign therefore – at least in Great Britain – was not fought on the basis of Brexit or no Brexit, but rather on who could deliver a better Brexit. It also became a proxy for leadership styles and economic competence. A repeated theme from Theresa May and her party during the campaign was to accuse Labour of making promises on the economy and public spending that they could not afford and that lack of sober mature experience in government would also be a feature of their handling of the Brexit negotiations if they were elected to government. The media picked up on the Tory metaphor that there was not a 'magic money tree' available to government that would be needed if Labour promises were to be afforded. During a further BBC leaders' 'debate' on 2 June – a *Question Time* programme where they engaged with the studio audience rather than one another – Theresa May was challenged by a nurse who complained about the 1% pay rise given to staff in the National Health Service (NHS). May's response was typical of many during the 2017 General Election campaign in GB, pointing out how much her government valued the work of the NHS, but that pay restraints had to be enforced in order to reduce the budget deficit: 'I'm being honest with you saying we will put more money in, but there isn't a magic money tree that we can shake to get everything we want.'[21]

This metaphor would later come back to haunt Theresa May after the election, in the context of her attempts to stay in power by doing a deal with the DUP in Northern Ireland. The magic money tree was to become much more tangible for Theresa May as she struggled for political survival in the weeks and months that followed.

The 2017 General Election in Northern Ireland

The background to the General Election in Northern Ireland remained the unresolved issues from the Assembly Election just weeks earlier. The focus was on the dysfunctional relationship between the DUP and Sinn Féin, the RHI scandal and demands from Sinn Féin that the DUP sign up to an Irish Language Act as an indication of its commitment to partnership government and a broader respect for the nationalist community. The campaign itself was unedifying, as much of the time was spent by the two main parties in bickering over which of them was responsible for the collapse of the Northern Ireland Assembly. Aside from this, the main argument between the DUP and Sinn Féin concerned their opposing positions on Brexit, its significance for the Good Friday Agreement and the future of the devolved institutions in Northern Ireland.

Like the Assembly Election that preceded it, the General Election continued the trend whereby larger parties benefited at the expense of the smaller ones. This was in part a consequence of the electoral system, with the first-past-the-post form of majoritarian democracy practised at Westminster favouring larger parties as voters are only able to indicate support for one candidate – rather than selecting multiple preferences across the ballot paper as in the STV system that operates in Northern Ireland elections. Smaller parties tend to do better under STV as they benefit from voting transfers from larger parties and there tends to be a lower threshold for election. In the Westminster system, with voters only having one roll of the dice, the dominant parties tend to be rewarded more than the smaller ones, and this was certainly borne out by the results of the 8 June poll.

The big story of the election in the Northern Ireland context was that both the UUP and the SDLP lost political representation at Westminster for the first time in modern history. Bouncing back from its wobbly 2017 Assembly Election performance, the DUP won ten seats out of the eighteen available – a dominant display of superiority over its now junior rival within the unionist community. Sinn Féin won seven seats, (though would not be taking them up due its abstentionist policy at Westminster). As a result, the DUP provided an overwhelmingly dominant voice from Northern Ireland, with only an independent, Lady Sylvia Hermon (formerly of the UUP) providing alternative political representation at Westminster.

The result emboldened the DUP in its negotiations with Sinn Féin over the restoration of devolved government in Northern Ireland and sharpened the existential crisis within the SDLP as it contemplated its own future role in Northern Ireland politics. After almost forty years, the SDLP lost its Foyle seat at Westminster to Sinn Féin. This was highly symbolic as the high-profile seat had previously been held by two former leaders of the party – John Hume and his political protégé Mark Durkan. The seat had been the preserve of the SDLP since 1983 and Durkan was one of the party's best-known personalities. Media-savvy, quick-witted and unrivalled in his ability to capture the mood with a memorable phrase, Durkan lost the seat to Sinn Féin's Elisha McCallion by less than 200 votes – having boasted a majority of over 8,000 at the previous General Election in 2015. McCallion was standing in the seat for the first time but benefited from nationalist sentiment following the recent death of former deputy First Minister Martin McGuinness, as well as the intensity of the party's campaigning operation in the area. Durkan reflected on the symbolism of the seat for the history of the SDLP and in particular for the memory of John Hume:

> We've all come to take so much of what John stood for for granted, and I didn't want the result to be part of rolling up the record of John and Pat [Hume] and all they gave us and putting it in the bin … I regret now that there's a situation where the only Derry voice that'll be heard in the House of Commons is Gregory Campbell's … It means there isn't an alternative perspective to counter or challenge to what he or the rest of the DUP will be espousing.[22]

This would turn out to be a rather prophetic vision of the future on Durkan's part, as the success of the DUP over the UUP, and the parallel success of abstentionist Sinn Féin over the SDLP, were to have a significant impact on UK politics generally and Brexit policy in particular, once the seats had all been counted and attention moved to the formation of the next government. The SDLP did bounce back in the 2019 General Election, with party leader Colum

Eastwood regaining the Foyle seat from SF and with former Brexit lead Claire Hanna picking up Belfast South from the DUP. These were both impressive victories by two of the SDLP's highest profile and talented politicians.

The deal with the DUP

We have seven abstentionists and ten DUP MPs, no other political institutions [at Stormont] so they are clearly the most vocal and they seem to be driving this [Brexit] process.

John Manley, *Irish News* political correspondent, 25 April 2019[23]

The big story of the election, of course, was the relative success of Jeremy Corbyn's Labour Party and the underperformance of Theresa May's Conservative Party. Despite the Tories' significant lead in the polls prior to the election, it had dwindled during the campaign as a result of Theresa May's abject performance and Corbyn's ability to connect with voters in key areas. Aside from the personalities of the leaders, Labour had produced a very effective and well-costed manifesto that offered an attractive range of options to voters and a catchy slogan, 'For the many, not the few', which resonated during the campaign, while the Conservatives had arguably a less inspiring or well-targeted document to offer the electorate.

The election result saw the overall Conservative lead over Labour shrink to just over 2% (42.4% against 40%) but more importantly in terms of seats won, the Tories lost their overall parliamentary majority, winning 318 seats to Labour's 262 – a gain of thirty seats for Jeremy Corbyn's Labour Party, despite intense media hostility, not to mention efforts to remove him as leader by many of his senior colleagues.

In what amounted to a political earthquake, given the pre-election expectation that the Conservatives would trounce Labour, Britain had a hung parliament with no governing majority. The result reflected the wider political environment in that the UK was split over Brexit and had delivered a result that gave no party overall political control at a time when a clear policy was desperately needed in terms of making progress on Brexit negotiations with the UK's European partners. More immediately, the lack of an overall majority for the governing Conservative Party left it needing support from other parties at Westminster in order to form a new government. The parliamentary arithmetic made it very difficult for Labour to reach a figure where it could govern effectively. While there was talk of a 'progressive alliance' being formed – basically everyone else except the Tories: Labour, SNP, Liberal Democrats, Plaid Cymru and Greens (who had one seat) – it would still only have got to 314 seats, with 326 needed for an overall majority.

That left the Conservatives, who opened talks with the DUP about an arrangement that would allow them to remain in power. While not generally known at the time, it later transpired that Theresa May and her close colleagues – including then Chief Whip Gavin Williamson – initially agreed to a full coalition with the DUP that would have seen the Northern Ireland party occupy senior cabinet posts at Westminster. When it dawned on the Conservatives that this would be unpalatable to many people within GB, not least their own voters, Theresa May tried to revoke this offer but was resisted by Williamson, who was leading the negotiations.[24] In the end – luckily for Theresa May – this offer was not taken up by the DUP, who preferred a looser arrangement, with the power to bring down the government but the freedom to diverge from its policies. These negotiations took nearly two weeks to complete and required the Queen's Speech to be delayed while the tense talks lurched onwards between the two parties with little noticeable progress being made from day to day – not unlike the Brexit process itself.

The resulting 'confidence-and-supply' agreement between the Conservatives and the DUP provided the ten crucial additional seats from the Northern Ireland party and got Theresa May and her government to 328 seats – two more than needed to have a majority in parliament. Under the terms of the deal, the DUP's ten MPs would vote with the government on the Queen's Speech, the budget and on legislation relating to Brexit and national security issues – but otherwise the DUP was free to go its own way on policy issues. In return for this support, the government agreed to provide an additional £1 billion of public money for specific spending projects in Northern Ireland, including the health service, education and maintenance of the universal winter fuel allowance.

In a press conference held between the two parties, the respective chief whips – Jeffrey Donaldson for the DUP and Gavin Williamson for the Conservatives – signed the deal and posed for photographs. But the smiles were more of relief than jubilation, at least on the part of Theresa May and her government. The election was an unmitigated disaster for the Prime Minister, who had to apologise to colleagues who had lost their seats and to the party for losing its parliamentary majority at the very time that it needed one in order to make progress in the Brexit negotiations. Kathryn Simpson captured the electoral calamity for Theresa May and her party neatly: 'Giving Article 50 notification in March and then holding a general election in June has been shown to be misguided. It underlines how little Brexit mattered in May's decision to hold this vote. The Brexit election was not about Brexit, it was political opportunism. And the electorate has noticed.'[25]

The deal with the DUP was condemned by many within Britain who feared that the DUP's conservative social policy agenda – it was opposed to marriage equality and abortion rights – would move the UK government in a similar direction. Despite this unease, the new confidence-and-supply arrangement allowed Theresa May to form a government and cling to office. Having been at the brink of resignation immediately following the election result, Theresa May found herself back inside Downing Street, though it was increasingly looking as if she was in office but not in power, as she returned with her authority much diminished.

At a wider level, the confidence-and-supply agreement between the Conservative Party and the DUP shone a rather harsh light upon the nature of the latter partner in the arrangement. The media and others within Great Britain who had previously paid little attention to the DUP, now began to look more seriously at the policy platforms held by the party. Stories emerged within the mainstream media during this period concerning DUP policies on social policy, and in particular same-sex marriage rights and abortion. This criticism was not restricted to political parties in Britain, and the fear that the DUP's moral agenda would impact on UK policy over social policy issues such as abortion extended to civil society organisations. The British Pregnancy Advisory Service (BPAS) for instance, labelled the DUP as 'extremists', with BPAS spokesperson Katherine O'Brien commenting, 'The very idea that abortion rights could be used as a bargaining tool as part of these negotiations is deeply worrying.'[26]

It would be fair to say that even within Conservative Party circles there was a degree of concern that the DUP's approach on social policy issues was out of step with mainstream opinion within Great Britain. Ruth Davidson, for instance, then leader of the Conservative Party in Scotland, sought assurances from Theresa May that DUP influence on social policy issues such as same-sex marriage would not be felt within Great Britain. Davidson claimed that the Prime Minister had given her an assurance that the DUP's social policies would not affect Great Britain and that gay rights would not be eroded in return for DUP support in parliament. Green Party deputy leader Amelia Womack dubbed the deal the 'coalition of cruelty' due to the implications she felt it would have on women in Northern Ireland and their right to have an abortion within the law. Unlike in the rest of the United Kingdom, in 2017 abortion was not legal in Northern Ireland even in cases of fatal foetal abnormality (i.e. where the baby had no chance of survival) or in cases of rape or incest.[27] So groups concerned about this issue were quick to express their concern that the Conservative minority government's reliance on the DUP would corrode efforts to protect and extend reproductive rights for women.

Impact of the election result on Northern Ireland

Unsurprisingly, news of the confidence-and-supply deal was not welcomed in Northern Ireland beyond the DUP itself and its supporters. For one thing, it presented a complication locally, with the office of Secretary of State for Northern Ireland now connected to the DUP and seen by some to represent a clear conflict of interest in terms of that role being non-partisan. In this sense, the deal between the government and the DUP raised serious issues for the restoration of devolved government in Northern Ireland and the wider peace process. In blunt terms, the UK would find it more difficult to present itself as being an honest broker in Northern Ireland as it was now in partnership with one of the main political protagonists in the region. The Good Friday Agreement was based on the logic that the UK government would act with impartiality over competing political claims and disagreements within Northern Ireland, a position that looked to be called into question by the deal with the DUP as a conflict of interest seemed clear. Former Secretary of State and Labour peer Peter Hain argued that the deal 'would jeopardise the neutrality, the non-partisan stance, that a prime minister and a secretary of state must have in relation to Northern Ireland's politics'.[28] This perspective went beyond the usual suspects in Sinn Féin and the SDLP, with Jonathan Powell, Tony Blair's former chief of staff who had been directly involved in the political negotiation in 1998 and subsequently, claiming that it made the UK a partial voice within the difficult political context in Northern Ireland and in any effort to revive the devolved political institutions: 'How can it possibly be neutral when it's supported by one particular party that could pull the plug on it at any stage?'[29]

The confidence-and-supply arrangement did little, therefore, to establish trust between Sinn Féin and the DUP to a point where the devolved institutions could be re-established. It swung the political balance of power decisively towards the DUP – whose leader, Arlene Foster, had been under severe pressure to resign following her role in the RHI scandal, the consequent collapse of devolved government due to her refusal to stand aside while her role in RHI was investigated and the poor performance of the DUP in the Assembly Election earlier in 2017. The deal with the government allowed Foster to bounce back, as she could claim unrivalled political influence for her party and an ability to feed into the ongoing Brexit negotiations. The election also saw the political rout of the DUP's main unionist rival the UUP, and Foster was able to boast of a significant financial injection for Northern Ireland – wrestled from the Treasury as the price of DUP support for the government. When the deal was announced, Arlene Foster took care to point out that her party was acting for the 'national interest' rather than for narrower party political advantage – as had been alleged by some opponents:

> Throughout these discussions our guiding principle has been our commitment to acting in the national interest in accordance with our shared objectives for strengthening and enhancing our precious Union. ... Today we have reached an outcome that is good for the United Kingdom, good for Northern Ireland and allows our nation to move forward to tackle the challenges ahead. This afternoon I will be returning to NI to continue our discussions as we attempt to re-establish the Northern Ireland Executive as now, more than ever, our political leaders both locally and nationally need to work together to find solutions for all of the people we serve.[30]

The suggestion that the deal with the government would help the DUP find the basis for an agreement with Sinn Féin and other parties to restore the devolved institutions in Northern Ireland was not universally accepted. Sinn Féin, and the nationalist community more broadly, saw the deal as one that further undermined political relationships in Northern Ireland and the chances of the devolved institutions being restored. Sinn Féin's leader in the North, Michelle O'Neill, accused the DUP of propping up the pro-austerity pro-Brexit government and forecast that it would end badly for both parties:

> They have once again betrayed the interests of the people of the north by supporting a Tory party which has cut funding to our public services year on year to the tune of hundreds of millions of pounds. Experience shows us that unionists have minimal influence on any British government. They have achieved little propping up Tory governments in the past and put their own interests before those of the people.[31]

The SDLP and the Alliance Party were equally scathing; the SDLP's Colum Eastwood welcomed the additional money but warned that it had to be 'targeted at areas of need, not the parochial priorities of one political party'.[32] Ciaran McClean from the Green Party started a crowdfunding campaign to raise money to launch a legal challenge against the confidence-and-supply deal, arguing, 'My claim is that as a citizen I expect my government to honour its obligations under the Good Friday agreement and not to bribe others with money so that it can stay in power.'[33]

While there was some consternation over the possible social policy implications of the agreement with the DUP, the greater level of criticism outside Northern Ireland focused on the financial implications of the deal and the extent to which it looked to be a kickback from the government in return for its survival. This criticism was sharpened by the fact that one of the Conservative Party criticisms of their Labour opponents during the election had been the Tory suggestion that Labour believed there was a magic money tree that it could shake to find resources for good causes. The First

Minister of Wales, Carwyn Jones, was blunt in his accusation that the deal between the Conservative Party and DUP was:

> an outrageous straight bung to keep a weak prime minister and a faltering government in office. It is outrageous that the prime minister believes she can secure her own political future by throwing money at Northern Ireland whilst completely ignoring the rest of the UK. This is a short-term fix which will have far-reaching and destabilising consequences.[34]

Jones was not alone in alluding to what became known as the 'magic money tree' – a metaphor used by the Tories during the election to attack Labour spending promises in their manifesto. Having said there was no additional money available to support Labour's agenda it looked as if the Conservative Party had found its own magic money tree and had given it a good hard shake when it needed to find £1 billion in order to hang onto power. This apparent paradox was condemned as a bribe and a 'grubby deal' by the government's political opponents. There was also a sense of irritation from politicians and their electorates in other parts of Britain at a level of funding being provided for Northern Ireland that was not available to them. The financial arrangements agreed to by the government and DUP carved out an additional £400 million for the support of infrastructure projects in Northern Ireland, a further £350 million for the health service and education provision, £150 million to extend broadband provision and £100 million dedicated to tackling deprivation: 'the cash-equivalent to an extra £537 for every person in Northern Ireland'.[35]

The implications of the General Election for Brexit

The impact of the election result on UK Brexit policy would turn out to be quite profound. Theresa May had called the election in the hope of returning to Westminster with an enhanced majority that would allow her to push through her preferred policy and give her more leverage and credibility with her European negotiators that she had a mandate for her objectives and that she would be able to deliver them. Instead, she limped back into Downing Street after the election a much reduced figure and crucially with no parliamentary majority and in an awkward alliance with the DUP. From this point forwards government policy on Brexit had to gain at least the acquiescence of its junior partner. While not quite holding a formal veto over government policy on Brexit, the DUP made it very clear that its key concern related to being fully aligned with the rest of the United Kingdom and not having any special status when it came to how the UK exited the EU. This was an article of faith for the DUP – a red line that it would defend at all costs and a position that was hard-wired into the broader political psyche of the party and its supporters.

The unionists' fear that they would be sacrificed on the altar of political expediency by a British government with more pragmatic objectives than the preservation of the Union has been a recurrent theme since the Home Rule era. For many unionists, therefore, Brexit was merely the latest stress-testing of a weakness that they were all too familiar with – and that Rudyard Kipling had so lyrically and powerfully exposed in his poem 'Ulster', published in the *Morning Post* on 9 April 1912. Despite their loyalty and devotion to the Crown, there would come a point when the government would abandon the unionist community when it deemed it necessary to do so:

> Before an Empire's eyes,
> The traitor claims his price.
> What need of further lies?
> We are the sacrifice.
> ...
> We know the war prepared
> On every peaceful home,
> We know the hells declared
> For such as serve not Rome –

> The terror, threats, and dread
> In market, hearth, and field –
> We know, when all is said,
> We perish if we yield.[36]

While the UK had long since ceased to be an empire, this has never really dimmed the unionist existential nightmare that one day the British government would seek to cash in its loyalty and blood sacrifice when it became expedient to do so. In other words, for some unionists there has always been a Brexit, even if known by another name (the Good Friday Agreement, the Anglo-Irish Agreement, the Sunningdale Agreement, the Home Rule Act), and these have always carried the threat of degrading the fragile sinews holding the UK together. The DUP's Brexit spokesperson Sammy Wilson epitomised this concern with Perfidious Albion in his suggestion that Theresa May's government might well have been amenable to the Northern Ireland-only Backstop if the result of the 2017 General Election had not left his party in a position of leverage over the Prime Minister: 'I do believe that the General Election saved Unionists' interests. I think that the Theresa May Government would have settled for a border in the Irish Sea, but for the fact that she needed us and also a significant number of people in her own Party were supportive of our position.'[37]

Perhaps for this reason, unionists have never quite felt secure in their Britishness to the same extent as other regions of the UK – even Scotland, which has its own unique relationship with Britain. Unionists have not always felt accepted by the regime to which they give their political allegiance; unrequited love can be a highly corrosive emotion. But it is Team GB that you see flying the flag at the Olympics – not Team UK, despite the fact that Northern Ireland competes under that flag – and what goes on in the Olympics mirrors a broader public consciousness of the 'nation'. Northern Ireland's invisibility in sport is a painful metaphor for those of a unionist persuasion. Put bluntly, Northern Ireland is different. It exists on the political, economic and cultural periphery of the UK, rather than being integral to it.

The phrase that Britain has 'no selfish strategic or economic interest' was coined by former Secretary of State for Northern Ireland, Peter Brooke, in 1990. It was a deliberate signal to Sinn Féin and the Provisional IRA that the UK would consider Irish reunification if that was the collective consensus of people living in the region. This in turn was one of the golden keys that unlocked peace in Northern Ireland and was a central maxim of the Belfast/ Good Friday Agreement in 1998. The British government has never said this about Scotland, Wales or any other part of the UK. It is hurtful to unionists, who feel that Britain *should* have a selfish interest in Northern Ireland. But it doesn't, and it is unlikely that it ever will.

Despite the popular adage often attributed to Margaret Thatcher, that Northern Ireland was 'as British as Finchley' (her former constituency), in practice it never has been. When it comes to Northern Ireland, different rules apply. It is Team GB first and 'Team GB and Northern Ireland' a very distant second. The vast majority of people in England have never understood this historical inheritance and thus failed to appreciate why the DUP took such an uncompromising stand over the terms of Brexit.

While they campaigned for Brexit and while it looked as if they occupied a position of power and even dominance after the 2017 General Election, ironically Brexit turned into an existential crisis for unionists. They were confronted by the fact that they were a frontier community at the physical and psychological edge of the British imagined nation and an expendable part of it. As a result of the issue of a hard border in Ireland and the 'Backstop' as a potential solution to it, the DUP gradually became politically isolated, first within Great Britain and by the end of 2018 within Northern Ireland also. The fact that they held Theresa May's feet to the flames during her doomed attempt to get the Withdrawal Agreement through the House of Commons left the DUP politically exposed in Northern Ireland. The region had voted for Remain in the 2016 referendum and even those who supported Brexit were keen to avoid a hard border in Ireland.

The Withdrawal Agreement between the UK government and the European Union that emerged in November 2018 provided a legally binding guarantee that there would not be a hard border in Ireland through the Backstop mechanism enshrined within it. As a result, the DUP found itself in a shrinking pool of opponents to the deal, with erstwhile allies such as the Ulster Farmers' Union expressing a view that the deal should be supported and non-aligned business groups such as the Confederation of British Industries (NI) also distancing themselves from the DUP position. So, while Arlene Foster's party held the balance of power at Westminster, Brexit was a crisis for it as much as for everyone else involved. This was accentuated because, while the Brexit negotiations were in their latter stages in the autumn of 2018, the inquiry into the RHI scandal was holding public hearings that laid bare the DUP's failure to meet the ethical standards required in public office. For many viewers of these hearings – and not just nationalist ones – it looked as if the DUP (or influential members of the party within Stormont) were caught with their hands in the till at the taxpayer's expense. Therefore, the juxtaposition of the DUP standing upon principle in the context of Brexit while simultaneously appearing to flout the most basic standards of behaviour over the RHI case did little to enhance the party's political reputation in Northern Ireland.

For all of these reasons, the 2017 General Election and specifically the evaporation of the government's parliamentary majority and its reliance on the DUP for political survival were fundamental to the subsequent incapacity and incoherence of the British government's Brexit policy. After the election, the government found that the nature of the Irish border, and how to deliver on its own rhetoric about maintaining a frictionless border in Ireland and the integrity of the Good Friday Agreement, would be tested to destruction. The unforeseen outcome of the General Election that led to the DUP holding the balance of power had huge implications for the Brexit negotiations and especially for how the government could manage the biggest conundrum of the whole Brexit process. How was it to leave the EU and become a non-member state, with all that entailed in terms of customs and trade regulations, while part of the UK (Northern Ireland) would share a land border with an EU member state (Ireland) after it did so? The issue of what happened to the Irish border after Brexit was already a delicate one before the 2017 General Election. With the DUP holding the balance of power in the House of Commons and exerting significant leverage over government policy, it now became a toxic aspect of the whole Brexit process and would dominate the remainder of the negotiation period. Suddenly, an aspect that the government thought it could square with a decent parliamentary majority had become a huge pot-hole on the road to Brexit that the government would continue to fall into in the months and years ahead.

After the 2017 General Election, all roads towards Brexit led to the Irish border and the peace process more broadly.

5

Aspiration or guarantee? The 'frictionless' border

In this ten miles [in South Armagh during the conflict] we had twelve army watchtowers, six helicopter bases, six army bases, four police stations, forty roads permanently sealed off and six permanent checkpoints on other roads. Nobody ever set off with that intention when they built the customs post.

Peter Sheridan, CEO, Co-Operation Ireland[1]

People [in Brussels] realise that the Backstop was too much – and why would you create something that makes it impossible for the other side to agree to it? That's not diplomacy, that's not negotiation.

Steve Aiken MLA, UUP[2]

The issue that bedevilled the negotiations throughout was one that had hardly been mentioned during the 2016 referendum campaign. What would happen to the UK's border separating Northern Ireland from the Republic of Ireland after Brexit, when the former left the EU and the latter remained a member state? Given the prominence that it assumed in the negotiations, it is a little surprising that the Irish border and disruption to the still fragile peace process did not feature to a greater extent earlier than it did. This Irish blind spot in the political psyche of the British government lies at the centre of its problematic Brexit negotiation. The United Kingdom was leaving the EU but was essentially being driven by an English dynamic while Scotland and Northern Ireland wanted to remain. More fundamentally, it demonstrated that the UK government did not have its devolved regions at the forefront of its consciousness before the referendum took place in 2016. The imagined nation was perceived as being a homogeneous unified entity – when in fact it was clear that Scotland and Northern Ireland had much more complex political and cultural dynamics. The bottom line here was just a basic lack of empathy and understanding about how Brexit would impact on these devolved regions.

In addition, the way the referendum was constructed (a simple majority across the whole UK electorate) meant that the referendum campaign was fought primarily in England, where the majority of eligible voters lived. Only in the last days of the campaign did attention really turn to Northern Ireland – in addition to mobilising the Irish diaspora vote living in GB.[3] Indeed, the Irish government did more on this than the UK, with the Irish Taoiseach, Enda Kenny, openly campaigning for Remain among the Irish community in the UK. His message invoked the economic damage a Brexit vote would do to Ireland and the negative impact it would have on the Irish border, the GFA and the peace process in Northern Ireland.[4] The constitutional appropriateness of a foreign leader campaigning on a UK domestic issue was overlooked by David Cameron as he became increasingly desperate to mobilise as many votes as he could in support of Remain. But in truth Ireland and its border was nowhere in the thinking of British politicians during the referendum campaign. Even in terms of making a case for Remain' in the referendum it was largely ignored in the list of reasons put forward to protect the status quo during the campaign in 2016. Controversially, the government put out a leaflet supporting Remain and elaborating on its reasons for doing so – delivering it to every home in the UK at taxpayers' expense, despite the fact that the government was allowing a free vote on the issue.[5] The glossy leaflet (costing around £9 million to produce) that dropped through voters' letterboxes purported to set out the 'facts' about what was in the interests of people in the UK and why the government believed that voting to remain was the better and safer option. It listed the following benefits:

> The UK has secured a special status in a reformed EU:
> - we will not join the euro
> - we will keep our own border controls
> - the UK will not be part of further European political integration
> - there will be tough new restrictions on access to our welfare system for new EU migrants
> - we have a commitment to reduce EU red tape[6]

Nowhere here did the government mention that voting Remain would protect the GFA or even the survival of the devolved political institutions. Northern Ireland was not mentioned once in the leaflet. So the Irish border was not even in the peripheral vision of the government and it remained out of sight in the formal referendum campaign and in media coverage of it – apart from in Northern Ireland itself.

When the referendum debate formally began in 2016, the official campaign group, Britain Stronger in Europe, produced a short video on the home page of its website which listed six reasons to remain in the EU. None of these mentioned Northern Ireland or the Irish border issue and focused instead on jobs, economic prosperity, lower prices in the shops and security.[7] Every conceivable rationale was put forward within the website's 'Get the facts' section for voting Remain, including the rather desperate argument that a Leave result would jeopardise people's summer holidays, put up the cost of duty-free shopping at airports and put higher roaming charges on mobile phone calls.[8] But there was not a word from the official Remain campaign here about the importance *to the United Kingdom* of political stability in Northern Ireland, the peace process in the region – or the obvious problem that the invisible border in Ireland created since the GFA might re-emerge as a hard physical entity if the UK voted to leave the EU.

The title of the official campaign itself perhaps displayed the sort on unconscious bias at the heart of the problem, as *Britain* is not the UK, and Northern Ireland has no constitutional place within it. There were other party political Remain campaigns in GB too that worked alongside the cross-party official Britain Stronger in Europe campaign, such as Labour in for Britain (that B word again), headed by Labour's former Home Secretary Alan Johnston. Here too the rationale for remaining within the EU was based on a message about jobs, the economy and 'Britain's' [sic] global influence within an interconnected world.[9] Not a mention of Northern Ireland, or the peace process. Nor any reference to the fact that the UK would have a land frontier with the EU in the very place that still housed a tense and fragile ethnonational dispute about political and cultural identity, parked rather than resolved by the GFA that Labour had done so much to deliver.

While the debate in GB focused on *Britain*'s borders, linked to immigration controls to limit those arriving from other EU countries, the border in Ireland – and its impact on Northern Ireland especially – was ignored. However, mediating this border, which was the frontier line that demarcated those who lived on the British side of it and those who lived on the Irish side, was a key tenet of the GFA and the subsequent institutions established after 1998.[10] Those institutions formed part of a hard-won political settlement that tried to at least park, if not resolve, the tug of war over the constitutional future of the region that has fuelled a violent conflict in Ireland for several generations.

Northern Ireland's devolved institutions were based on a form of consociational democracy that has been at the centre of scholarly debates on Northern Ireland since they were established in 1999.[11] A vote to leave the EU would complicate the existence of these institutions and the stability of Northern Ireland's devolved settlement. The capacity of the GFA to facilitate dual political identities on the basis of choice and consent has also provided a key foundation for the development of Anglo-Irish relations since 1998.[12] This relationship was a key pillar in the peace process for well over a generation, the bedrock on which the negotiations that led to the GFA were built.

However, regardless of this context, the political parties and the attendant media coverage of the Brexit referendum in GB demonstrated little understanding of Northern Ireland as a relevant dimension of EU membership during the campaign in 2016. This was highlighted in the television debates in the last days before the referendum vote on 23 June. The ITV debate that took place on 10 June 2016 focused on immigration controls, the economy and security issues – but hardly a mention of Northern Ireland. Eventually, after nearly one and a half hours, Remain supporter Amber Rudd brought up the future of the Union and the fact that the Leave campaign had no plan for what the Irish border would look like if the UK was to leave the EU.[13] This point went unanswered by anyone in the debate, the television adjudicator or the studio audience. On the BBC's *EU Referendum: The Great Debate,* held at Wembley Arena and televised on 21 June 2016, Northern Ireland once again failed to feature. The BBC divided the two-hour programme into three sections: the economy, immigration and *Britain's* [sic] place in the world. The Irish border was simply not on the agenda for politicians, the media or most of the voters in the choice before them.

While clearly a blind spot for both the Remain and Leave sides during the referendum campaign in 2016, the question was front and centre of attention in Ireland (North and South) because of the implications it had for the economy on both sides of the border, the Good Friday Agreement and the peace process more broadly.

Brexit and the Irish border

How often do you think about your political status, the security of your identity, your entitlement to live where you live, work where you work and to move freely within that space? The chances are that if you live in a stable political region with long-standing political institutions, you do not think about such issues very much at all. These are more likely to be at the forefront of your mind if identities, borders and political allegiances are divided and contested, as is the case in Ireland. The UK's decision to leave the EU immediately complicated the issue of political self-determination in Ireland and raised the question of how the Common Travel Area between the UK and Ireland would be implemented outside of the single market and the customs union once the UK completed its departure from the EU. As explained below, the CTA was established in 1922, shortly after Irish partition, establishing the right of citizens within it to travel freely without the need for any passport controls. The CTA is established therefore within UK law and predates its entry to the EEC in 1973, along with the Irish Republic.

For anyone not steeped in an understanding of Irish history and wondering why the Irish were so keen to get legally binding guarantees from the UK, rather than just aspirational promises over the future of the border during Brexit negotiations, the Anglo-Irish Treaty of 1921 may provide a clue. The terms of the Treaty set up a Boundary Commission that was charged with establishing the final terms of the new border and potentially allowing areas to opt in or out depending on the political allegiance of the county. It was to determine the border that would divide Ireland 'in accordance with the wishes of the inhabitants, *so far as may be* [my emphasis] compatible with economic and geographic conditions'. The Boundary Commission took until 1925 to decide that the border would stay precisely where it was – regardless of local wishes. It was a political device, not a legal one, to assist compliance with British government policy, a diplomatic sleight of hand that promised Irish nationalists one thing and unionists another. When the incensed Irish Taoiseach William Cosgrave met UK Prime Minister Stanley Baldwin in 1925 to remonstrate about the final recommendations of the Commission, all he could argue was that Baldwin's predecessor Lloyd George had 'given the impression' that the Commission would cede additional territory to the Free State, possibly reducing Northern Ireland down to four counties.[14] Cosgrave – and nationalist Ireland – learned a hard lesson during that period: promises from British prime ministers might not always be everything they seem.

The border as it used to be

In truth, British politicians within GB failed to understand either the historical significance of the Irish border, or the impact that Brexit could have upon it. One of the key aspects of the political conflict in Northern Ireland during the 'Troubles' was the territorial border that demarcated Northern Ireland within the UK, making it politically, economically, legally and culturally distinct from the rest of Ireland. 'Ulster is British' was a slogan literally daubed on walls in loyalist urban areas, and political identity linked to the physical geography has been woven into the cultural DNA of Northern Ireland over several generations.

To anyone who lived or worked (or even visited) Northern Ireland during the late 1960s through into the late 1990s, the border that separated the two jurisdictions in Ireland was physical as well as highly symbolic. No one passing from one side of the border to the other was likely to do so quickly (at least on approved roads) or without being very aware that they were moving from one jurisdiction to another. Both sides of the border were 'manned' by the respective police, customs and army checkpoints. The UK side of the border was heavily militarised, with armed police and army personnel, sandbagged watchtowers positioned at border crossings and the monotonous sound of rotor blades from the omnipresent army helicopters keeping watch over traffic flows and other movement below. Long queues of vehicles at these border crossings were commonplace, which reinforced the notion that these were two different places separated by a hard legal border. During the 1970s and 1980s it was normal practice for people travelling from Northern Ireland to stop at the edge of the border at the bureaux de changes that would convert your pounds sterling into Irish 'punts' and vice versa on the way home. From this perspective the border, by imposing a political barrier within Ireland, also produced a slow-acting cultural apartheid, where, over time, both territories evolved separately, when once they had been organically connected. It has been suggested that Ireland was always partitioned, even before partition was imposed, with the plantation of Ulster in the seventeenth century, the large clustering of Protestants and the Industrial Revolution leaving an indelible mark on the North that was different to the largely Catholic, Gaelic and agricultural society in the South.[15] But the imposition of a political border and the militarisation of that boundary from the 1960s undoubtedly sharpened this further.

In short, for people living in Ireland, the border was front and centre; it was visible, had its own economic and political architecture and it demarcated political and cultural identities in binary terms: one side was British and the other side Irish and there was no ambiguity as to which side you were on. There were clear rules relating to policing of the border and any incursions by the police or army were points of heightened diplomatic tension between the British and Irish governments. The desire to make policing more flexible and to encourage cooperation across the border was one of the key aspects of the Anglo-Irish Agreement (AIA) signed by the two governments in November 1985. Security cooperation between the Royal Ulster Constabulary (RUC) and British army and the Garda Síochána and Irish army, together with the ability to pursue suspects across the border, was a key attraction of the AIA for UK Prime Minister Margaret Thatcher – and one that she never felt was fully achieved.[16] Extradition 'across the border' from Ireland to the UK required a physical handover from one regime to another; it was visible and highly contentious.

The Irish border was drawn up after partition in 1921, a simpler time, when territorial geography was two- rather than three-dimensional and when states controlled their borders and people largely remained within them. Global modernity and the digital economy have muddied the waters to a great extent and today we can have dual or multiple citizenships, bank accounts in more than one country and access to an á la carte cultural menu of our choosing. Borders are now fluid, mobile and contextual, where once they were fixed territorial and legal markers. Ireland reflects this change perfectly, as highlighted by the Northern Ireland Affairs Committee in its report on Brexit and the Irish border in 2018: 'In the Londonderry–Strabane area a person could be "earning in sterling", buy their home in euros, and simultaneously own a car registered in Ireland. School children from one jurisdiction can be educated in the other and some health services, such as Emergency Services, are a shared resource.'[17] Alongside the 'constructive ambiguity' of the peace process in the 1990s, where the GFA allowed people living in Northern Ireland to self-identify as British or Irish, or both, the digital economy blurred the line of where the rule of domestic borders ended and international regulations began.

Another aspect of this speaks to the different meanings of Brexit in Britain and Ireland. In GB, much of the debate centred on immigration before the referendum and taking back control of laws and borders after it. The majority of media coverage focused on the psycho-drama of Westminster politics for much of the period after the referendum, between 2016 and 2019, and the rival policy positions of the government and the Labour Party over Brexit. Why? Because whether Theresa May's government remained in power or Labour came into office actually mattered to people's everyday lives. The Irish border and subsequently what became known as the 'Irish Backstop', and even the GFA and peace process itself, were largely theoretical issues for most of those living in GB. In Ireland, by contrast, changes to the border and peace itself were immediate, tangible and frightening realities thrown up by the Brexit process. These were also understood in the present rather than the future tense by many people living near the Irish border, and the uncertainty of the three-year negotiation process had immediate impacts on decisions people had to make over where they lived, where they sent their children to school and employment choices.[18] The mood was summed up by one citizen: 'I have no idea what is going to happen. Just feeling generally scared about potential return to violence if there is to be a hard border. Have no idea what plans to make.'[19] For people like this – and there were many others in Ireland who experienced Brexit as a practical political and economic concern – Brexit was a *trauma experience* rather than a debate about trade rules and tariffs. There was little evidence that the UK government either knew or cared about this aspect of how their negotiations were impacting on people's lives. This lack of empathy can be seen through the history of Anglo-Irish relations and helps explain the disconnect between UK policy objectives and their unintended consequences.

At a more practical level, any new border infrastructure will mean that movement across the two jurisdictions is likely to become more difficult, and thus may diminish, producing a greater cultural distinctiveness between the two over time. It may also make it problematic for people to live in one jurisdiction and work in the other – something that the motorway between Belfast and Dublin encouraged – cutting the journey time between the two cities by 40%. The House of Commons Northern Ireland Affairs Committee recognised this point in its report on the impact of Brexit in 2018: 'Before the removal of security measures, we heard that "people in Donegal stayed in Donegal and people in the north stayed in the north". Today, open borders have enabled communities to reconnect after decades of separation.'[20] The Irish government have estimated that there are 1,852,000 car crossings a month across the border – a figure that is likely to fall significantly if a more visible border becomes more difficult to cross.[21]

The key question on many people's minds across Ireland, as the Brexit negotiations got formally underway between the UK and the EU after the British government triggered Article 50 in March

2017, was how would it impact on the GFA, the arrangements for the Irish border and the peace process in Northern Ireland? In terms of the border specifically, the uncertainty over whether the CTA would be maintained when the UK left the EU had a direct impact on political stability in Northern Ireland – where political relationships were already fraught. As the Northern Ireland Affairs Committee summed it up: 'The land border is 310 miles long with over 200 formal crossing points and probably the same number again of informal crossing points.'[22]

Redefining the Irish border

Northern Ireland represents a unique aspect of the Brexit puzzle not faced elsewhere in the UK and clearly not understood by politicians or the electorate in GB – either before or after the referendum. In short, Brexit will redefine the Irish border, from a traditional binary relationship between the UK and Ireland, into a triangular relationship between the UK, Ireland and the rest of the EU. The people of Northern Ireland are located somewhere inside that triangle. Brexit alters the Irish border from beyond its temporal territorial space and converts it into the frontier to the EU and the only territorial land border between the UK and an EU member state. This has potentially huge implications for politics in Northern Ireland – where the border was for many years the physical and legal manifestation of partition. Another blind spot in Theresa May's pursuit of Brexit was that the UK also had responsibilities to uphold the GFA – as its co-guarantor for starters, but equally importantly, to ensure the vitality of the cross-border relationship. An EU/UK Mapping Report drawn up in 2017 but kept confidential by the UK until 2019 identified 145 areas of north–south cooperation under the GFA that would be negatively impacted by Brexit, especially if border infrastructure increased. RTE journalist Tony Connelly quotes the joint report's judgement that north–south cooperation within the terms of the GFA was wholly dependent upon the avoidance of a hard border in Ireland after Brexit:

> It was consistently recognised that virtually all areas of north–south cooperation are predicated on the avoidance of a hard border, including related customs or regulatory checks and controls. Similarly, it was acknowledged that the free movement of people underpins many areas of north–south cooperation, as well as access to services on both sides of the border. The continuation of the Common Travel Area between Ireland and the UK is therefore vital in this regard.[23]

The referendum result instantly raised a politically sensitive question and one that is woven into the DNA of the peace process and the GFA. Who has a right to self-determination in the UK and on what basis? It has been claimed by Leave supporters, including former Prime Minister Theresa May, that 'the people' have spoken and that the democratic will of Britain [sic] to leave the EU was declared on 23 June 2016. In the first line of Theresa May's Lancaster House speech setting out the UK government's 'Plan for Britain' on 17 January 2017, she declared: 'A little over 6 months ago, the British people voted for change.'[24] In her ill-fated speech to the Conservative Party Annual Conference on 4 October 2017, the Prime Minister declared, 'our first and most important duty is to get Brexit right. The people have decided. We have taken their instruction. Britain is leaving the European Union in March 2019.'[25] The political message seemed clear, even if the Prime Minister's coughing gaff-prone delivery was less so. 'Brexit means Brexit' – a phrase so devoid of meaning it was perversely the perfect motto for the whole process.

However, those on the Remain side of the argument have pointed out that these instructions were not as clear as the Prime Minister and her Brexit lieutenants suggested. While over 17 million people in the UK had voted to leave the EU, over 16 million voted to remain. More specifically, the people in two of the three devolved regions, Northern Ireland and Scotland, had voted to remain and were thus demonstrably not having their instructions followed. More specifically still, one of those devolved regions, Northern Ireland, as a consequence of generations of violent political conflict, has more bespoke constitutional arrangements than the rest of the UK.

The 'frictionless' border

Everyone said that they did not want to see a return to a hard border in Ireland and that the CTA within Ireland would be maintained. The phrase that soon emerged was 'frictionless border', and the vast majority of interested parties declared their support for this as their overriding concern. There have not been many areas of the Brexit negotiation that have secured unanimous support, but commitment to a frictionless border in Ireland united the government, the Labour opposition and other parties at Westminster, the Irish government and opposition parties, all of the parties in Northern Ireland, including the DUP – and all of the negotiating partners in Brussels along with the twenty-six other EU member states. While acting as Ireland's ambassador to Great Britain, Dan Mulhall gave evidence to a House of Lords Select Committee where he emphasised the importance of the frictionless border and the cross-party consensus to maintain it: 'It is universally acknowledged that the open and virtually invisible border that exists at present confers benefits on both parts of Ireland and on all communities in Northern Ireland. I am not aware of anyone who thinks that a hardening of that border would be an acceptable outcome.'[26]

The problem was, of course, that simply stating a commitment to this principle was a long way from ensuring it would actually be delivered, and inevitably disagreements would later emerge about how to accommodate the CTA and the frictionless border within the context of a comprehensive agreement between the UK and the EU.

Aspiration or guarantee?

The main focus of the DUP, however, was less on a 'frictionless' border and more targeted at ensuring that Northern Ireland left the EU on the same terms as the rest of the UK. This overriding principle became the foundation for its post-election confidence-and-supply agreement with Theresa May's government. The DUP's concern to leave the EU on the same basis as the rest of the UK found physical form at the end of 2017, when an initial draft of a joint report on progress between the EU and UK had to be swiftly revised. Article 49 of this agreed position had initially suggested that until a comprehensive trade deal was finalised between the UK and EU, and in 'the absence of agreed solutions, the United Kingdom will maintain full alignment with those rules of the Internal Market and the Customs Union which, now or in the future, support North–South cooperation, the all-island economy and the protection of the 1998 Agreement'.[27]

At last, after a year of wrangling, it had seemed that a break-through had been reached and a 'frictionless' border in Ireland secured. However, when Theresa May was in the middle of having lunch in Brussels before unveiling the joint position with her EU negotiating partners, she was told that the DUP was not happy with it and would not support it. Their reason was that it set conditions for Northern Ireland outside those required of the rest of the UK. Lunch was hurriedly abandoned, the Prime Minster flew back to London with no deal in place and hastily patched together an additional clause (Article 50) that suggested a further option could be the full regulatory alignment of the UK with that of Ireland:

> In the absence of agreed solutions, as set out in the previous para-graph, the United Kingdom will ensure that no new regulatory barriers develop between Northern Ireland and the rest of the United Kingdom, unless, consistent with the 1998 Agreement, the Northern Ireland Executive and Assembly agree that distinct arrangements are appropriate for Northern Ireland.'[28]

While this would amount to arrangements very close to the existing customs union, the fact that *all* of the UK would be subject to them was more acceptable to the DUP than Article 49, which singled Northern Ireland out for special treatment.

The DUP had demonstrated that at this point in time it had an effective veto over the development of UK negotiating positions on Brexit. The situation of the UK government was complicated by internal tensions over what type of Brexit it actually wanted, which made it difficult to define a coherent position. The trend was instead for the articulation of aspirations over the future of the border – followed by attempts to redefine or renegotiate these positions. To put it more critically, the UK developed a profile of promising one thing but doing another. At times this was down to its lack of capacity to govern – especially after the 2017 General Election with the minority government propped up by the DUP. Hence the UK position on the border has fluctuated for reasons of the government's own political survival as it has tacked between options as a result of the confidence-and-supply agreement with the DUP. This was seen most clearly in the chaos over the December 2017 agreement between the UK and EU, with the second draft being prepared on 8 December due to the rejection of the first a few days earlier.[29]

The political paranoia of Brexit and the Irish border

To understand the impact of Brexit on Ireland it is important to appreciate the context of how the negotiations unfolded after the UK triggered Article 50 on 29 March 2017. This was the formal notification to the EU of the UK's intention to leave the EU and started the two-year countdown to 29 March 2019, when the UK was supposed to leave formally. What was not clear at the time – or over the next three years, was just how incoherent, tortuous and incompetent the UK government would become in its dealings with the EU over its terms of exit. The lack of coherent strategy for what would happen to the Irish border and the periods of diplomatic confusion about what the UK plan was, or how it would be achieved, heightened levels of frustration, anger and fear across all communities in Ireland as the negotiations limped forwards for three years. In other words, assessments of how Brexit impacted attitudes concerning the Irish border need to focus not so much on how it all shook out at the end of the negotiations but should be framed along the timeline of the journey to that destination. Brexit was a *process* not an *event*, certainly in the context of its impact on Ireland.

The political context was that Northern Ireland was already politically unstable before the Brexit referendum, and its brittle power-sharing system was in the process of collapsing. While little understood in GB, a conflict culture remains strong in Northern Ireland and this dominates political perceptions and behaviour. Insecurity, paranoia, ingrained pessimism and bitterness are the staple diet for politicians and their electorates. Hope for the best – but prepare for the worst. This is a result of the experiences of people in Northern Ireland, the violent conflict that they endured there, and the record of political failure and complacency that have shaped the political culture of the region. There is a chronic lack of empathy across GB, and from British politicians particularly, about the nature of the unique political ecosystem in Northern Ireland. This was epitomised by Theresa May herself when asked at the beginning of the negotiations about the sort of Brexit she wanted to negotiate: 'actually what we should be looking for is a red, white and blue Brexit' – a comment that managed to be simultaneously meaningless in the GB context but crass and destructive for many in Ireland on both sides of the border.[30] This casual remark was uttered not in malice but in ignorance of how it would be perceived in Ireland. In the context where she owed her position as prime minister to the grace and favour of the DUP, it showed a spectacular lack of political touch.

In fairness, it was a throwaway line to dodge a question about the type of Brexit policy she would pursue and came in the context of contributions from some of her cabinet colleagues, including Chancellor of the Exchequer, Philip Hammond, about the possibility of a 'grey Brexit' that remained close to the EU – between the black Brexit of total separation, and a white Brexit that later became known by the acronym BRINO (Brexit in Name Only). Her quip was an attempt to avoid being pinned down about whether she was going to pursue a 'hard' Brexit or a 'soft' Brexit – in other words seek to leave the single market and customs union or find a means of staying closer to these two pillars of EU member-ship. But throwaways are takeaways in conflict cultures such as Northern Ireland and the formal leader of the country had a responsibility to be aware of that. Incidents such as this typify the incremental erosion of trust that characterised the Brexit negotia-tions – where lack of certainty allowed worst-case scenarios to prosper.

In conflict cultures people have to work in worst-case scenarios because they do not have the luxury of anything else. The nature of the Irish border and the Backstop to prevent a hard border in Ireland (and the idea of an alternative arrangement where a border could be placed between Ireland and GB located in the Irish Sea) are not just theoretical ideas for people in Ireland. Technical, tedious and detailed though they are, these issues will shape people's everyday lives, define their political and cultural identities and impact directly on their economic fortunes. Given these stakes, the lofty insouciance and ignorance of British politicians such as former Brexit Secretary David Davis was hard to take for many Brexit-watchers in Ireland. The locus for much of this can be seen on social media throughout the Brexit negotiating period, perhaps most lyrically via the dedicated Twitter account of eponymous hero the Irish Border. This anony-mous account @BorderIrish, which had over 95,000 followers, provided incisive, witty and informed commentary on the gap between Irish and British understanding.

The implications of Brexit for the Irish border are significant at political, economic and cultural levels. Firstly and most obviously, any physical infrastructure (including cameras – whether they are at the border or elsewhere) will become a target for those wishing to oppose the reintroduction of a visible border. This will present a security problem for both the UK and Irish governments and any future devolved administration in Northern Ireland. This point was recognised by George Hamilton, while he was chief constable of the Police Service of Northern Ireland.[31] This has also been commented on by numerous academics with expertise in this area.[32] Survey evidence of public opinion in Northern Ireland would seem to reinforce this concern; a study published in May 2018 found 'strong expectations that protests against either North–South or East–West border checks would quickly deteriorate into violence'.[33]

There is a wider political implication – namely that the border will re-energise the issue of the constitutional status of Northern Ireland that had largely lost its incendiary power after the GFA and the arrival of devolved government.[34] Mediating the 'constitutional question' was a key tenet of the GFA and the subsequent institutions established after 1998.[35] Northern Ireland's devolved political institutions were based on a form of consociational democracy that has been at the centre of scholarly debates on Northern Ireland since they were established in 1999.[36] The Brexit negotiations potentially further complicate the constitutional question and the stability of Northern Ireland's devolved settlement.[37]

In terms of relations within Northern Ireland, if there is a visible border or any infrastructure pertaining to the territorial demarcation of the UK on the one side and Ireland/EU on the other, the challenges facing the efforts to restore devolved government in the region will increase significantly.[38] The possibility of a visible border alongside the broader Brexit context has also placed political reunification back onto the agenda as a realistic possibility in the medium term and has led to repeated calls from Sinn Féin for a border poll to be held. Sinn Féin MEP Martina Anderson made the point that a traumatic Brexit could advance the objective of Irish unity:

> There is growing support for Irish unity across Ireland and the prospect of Brexit and a hard border has led many more people to realise that unity makes sense. I welcome the fact that Irish unity is now being discussed like never before both at home in Ireland and across Europe.[39]

While this has been resolutely resisted by the UK government, a traumatic exit from the EU in the context of a poor deal or no deal at all (with no transition period and a more chaotic political and economic environment in Ireland) will further energise this option beyond Sinn Féin and gain traction within the nationalist communities in both parts of Ireland. The longer-term political implication of a visible border appearing is likely to be further degrading of the UK/Ireland political relationship. The Anglo-Irish political relationship is at its lowest point in a generation and if there are disagreements over responsibility for the policing of a border, the relationship is likely to deteriorate further. The knock-on political implication of that is further political instability within Northern Ireland – as a partnership approach between London and Dublin has been hard-wired into the peace process since its inception.

Friction over the frictionless border

In the early phases of the Brexit negotiations there was an over-whelming consensus across the UK political spectrum that the Common Travel Area in Ireland that allowed free movement of people between Northern Ireland and the Irish Republic must be preserved. Before Brexit, the CTA was a little-known bilateral deal established between the UK and the Irish Free State in the early years of partition. Dating back to 1922, the CTA established the right of citizens within it (including those in the Isle of Man and

Channel Islands) to travel freely without the need for any passport controls or checks.

The CTA demonstrates that despite developing into completely separate sovereign states, the UK and Ireland have always had a 'special relationship' in terms of free movement between them. In addition, citizens of Ireland currently enjoy preferential entry status to other Europeans entering the UK in that they have permanent immigration rights to remain in the UK immediately from the date when they take up 'ordinary residence' in the UK. To a large extent this is a legal hangover from Britain's colonial past as, although it left Ireland politically, it did so incrementally. It has not fully disentangled itself legally, and Irish citizens enjoy more rights within the UK than those from other EU countries, including eligibility for British citizenship. These bilateral arrangements guaranteeing common travel within and between Britain and Ireland have been an article of faith for several generations and suggest that in some recess of the British mind Britain has never fully left Ireland.[40]

The CTA was an integral part of Theresa May's Lancaster House speech in January 2017 – her first significant statement of the UK government's vision for Britain outside the European Union:

> We cannot forget that, as we leave, the United Kingdom will share a land border with the EU, and maintaining that Common Travel Area with the Republic of Ireland will be an important priority for the UK in the talks ahead. There has been a Common Travel Area between the UK and the Republic of Ireland for many years. Indeed, it was formed before either of our 2 countries were members of the European Union. And the family ties and bonds of affection that unite our 2 countries mean that there will always be a special relationship between us. So we will work to deliver a practical solution that allows the maintenance of the Common Travel Area with the Republic, while protecting the integrity of the United Kingdom's immigration system. Nobody wants to return to the borders of the past, so we will make it a priority to deliver a practical solution as soon as we can.[41]

At a superficial level, this looks very conciliatory and certainly the tone of this part of May's speech was reassuring for those concerned about the implications of Brexit for the Irish border and for free movement within Ireland. On closer inspection, however, there were no guarantees provided here and the language was aspirational in terms of what the UK government would *like* to see happen – rather than any commitments about what it would do. Of course nobody 'wanted' any return to the borders of the past – but that was not quite the same as saying that they would not get them. This aspirational rhetoric was to become emblematic of UK government attitudes towards the Irish border issue for the next two years in the Brexit negotiations.

The Conservative Party manifesto for the 2017 General Election provided another textbook case of a policy agenda that was strong on aspiration but weak on its detailed application. Again there was a commitment to the CTA but there were crucial caveats to the ambitions expressed: 'We will maintain the Common Travel Area and maintain as frictionless a border as possible for people, goods and services between Northern Ireland and the Republic of Ireland.'[42] Again, while the commitment to the CTA was here and due reference made to the 'frictionless border', the phrasing was everything. What did 'as frictionless a border as possible' mean exactly? It could mean anything from a totally invisible border to one where there was a substantial level of friction – unfortunate though that may be. Such phrasing tied the government to little of substance and was designed to prevent it from being boxed in over the final arrangements.

Technology as the answer to the border conundrum

There have been several attempts to overcome the 'Irish border problem' by looking to technology and electronic customs surveillance to provide a means of avoiding new physical infrastructure in order to minimise or even eradicate any visible border. Brexit supporters often suggested that talk of physical infrastructure and long delays and armed security guards at the border was part of a campaign to 'weaponise' the border issue by Remain supporters opposed to Brexit, popularly dubbed 'Project Fear'. The potential of technology such as pre-approval of goods via electronic and pre-approval agreements, number-plate recognition for vehicles crossing the border and cameras on the border to facilitate monitoring and toll-road payments, was seen as the answer by many Brexiteers.

This approach became known as 'maximum facilitation' or 'max fac' for short, and lay at the heart of British government attempts to square the circle of how to avoid having a hard border in Ireland while maintaining its red lines of leaving the customs union and single market after Brexit. The government held an emergency cabinet summit at Chequers in July 2018 in an attempt to thrash out an agreed position on a way forward that could be put to the EU. The max-fac model was central to this, with a plan for a 'Common rulebook on goods, prior authorisations for goods in highly regulated sectors and a 'facilitated customs arrangement', where the UK would apply EU tariffs on products exported to the EU but apply its own tariffs for goods within the UK. The basic logic of this was to avoid, or at least vastly reduce, the need for border checks in Ireland due to variable rules over tariffs and trade.

However, the White Paper that resulted from this meeting owed more to the civil war in the Conservative Party than it did to the negotiation process itself.[13] The White Paper attempted to transform the Backstop by getting out in front of it via a free trade area guaranteeing 'continued frictionless access' for trade between the UK and EU. The EU reacted coolly to this idea and subsequently made it clear that the White Paper was not sufficiently legally binding in its commitments to the Backstop. The EU was unconvinced that a common rulebook could be developed on goods or that there could be a facilitated customs arrangement devised on the basis described or the creation of 'smart borders' to the degree that would replace the need for a conventional border. Thus a legally enforceable backstop was needed.

This position was also derived from the fact that it was felt that the technology required did not yet exist and no other international border of the complexity that would characterise the Irish border after Brexit operated in this way. So from the EU and Ireland's standpoint the max fac and the smart border ideas, while potentially interesting, provided no security or guarantee that they could be delivered to resolve the border problem.

That did not stop advocates of Brexit arguing that such technology was where the solution to the border conundrum was to be found. Some Brexiteers went further, claiming that the reluctance of the EU and Ireland seriously to consider technological solutions as alternatives to the Backstop, demonstrated their political opposition to the Brexit project and their desire to thwart the democratic wishes of the British people to leave the EU. Former Northern Ireland Secretary of State Owen Patterson maintained that solutions already existed if there was good will on all sides to look for them:

> There is a currency border, now a euro–sterling border, there is a VAT border, an income tax border, a corporation tax border. No-one has ever said that this has been a problem. This thing is a complete myth. No-one wants a physical border, neither the North or the South. Even in the Brexit referendum campaign, we made it clear there are electronic measures existing that can be made to work if there is a will on both sides of the border.[44]

The idea of a max-fac solution was leaned upon by Brexiteers in the hope that this would sidestep the need for a legally binding backstop, to ensure that a border did not re-emerge in Ireland after the UK left the EU. While he was Brexit Secretary, David Davis claimed that using technology would lessen the need for physical checks at the Irish border. When it was pointed out to him that such capacity did not yet exist anywhere in the world, Davis responded by saying, 'You can't just say we haven't done it anywhere else: we haven't attempted to do it anywhere else.'[45] This was a weak position that did not gain much traction with the EU, who preferred more evidence-based analysis as a foundation for policy-making rather than Davis's 'suck it and see' approach.

In a characteristically inflammatory intervention to this issue, Boris Johnson – while still Foreign Secretary – ridiculed the threat of a hard border in Ireland after Brexit, citing the domestic comparison of collecting toll charges between different boroughs in London. Speaking on BBC Radio 4's morning flagship programme, *Today*, the former mayor of London suggested that 'all sorts of things' could be done to avoid a hard border:

> We think that we can have very efficient facilitation systems to make sure that there's no need for a hard border, excessive checks at the frontier between Northern Ireland and the Republic. ... There's no border between Islington or Camden and Westminster ... but when I was mayor of London we anaesthetically [sic] and invisibly took hundreds of millions of pounds from the accounts of people travelling between those two boroughs without any need for border checks whatever. ... It's a very relevant comparison because there's all sorts of scope for pre-booking, electronic checks, all sorts of things that you can do to obviate the need for a hard border to allow us to come out of the customs union, take back control of our trade policy and do trade deals.[46]

Even by Johnson's low standards this was a crass intervention that did little to help government negotiating policy and only served to further antagonise his Irish and European partners. Within the Brexit-supporting constituency, however – especially within the Conservative Party and the DUP – the technology argument was seen as a viable option and one that they felt had not been fully explored by the EU. Sammy Wilson, the DUP's Brexit spokesperson, responding to Johnson's comment, pointed out that there was already cooperation taking place between the UK and Ireland via technology to mediate different taxation arrangements between the two countries:

> [T]here's a different tax regime in Northern Ireland than the Irish Republic – VAT, excise duty is different – yet billions of pounds worth of goods cross that border, taxes are paid and not a lorry is stopped to check the goods because through virtual methods, through IT, through electronic invoicing, those taxes are collected by both the Irish government and the British government.[47]

There were useful contributions made on the potential of technology to mitigate a hard border and avoid the need for a backstop, notably from former Swedish customs officer and researcher Lars Karlsson, who authored a report for the European Parliament in late 2017. Karlsson argued that 'smart borders' – such as those existing between Sweden and Norway – could reduce, though not eliminate, the need for physical border checks.[48] This was a serious attempt to square the Brexit border circle, but the parallel made with Norway and Sweden was imprecise in a crucial way. While Norway is outside the EU, it is in the single market and thus respects EU freedom of movement rules – which the UK was intending to move away from after Brexit as set out in the 2018 Withdrawal Agreement.

Karlsson's findings were nevertheless seized upon by UK Brexiteers in the House of Commons, many of whom belonged to the right-wing European Research Group. The ERG also adhered to the notion that technology provided the answer to the Backstop and to the Irish border problem. The ERG came forward with what it called 'a unique solution' in its report *A Better Deal and a Better Future*, published in January 2019, which continued to suggest that the Backstop could be replaced and a hard border in Ireland avoided. *A Better Deal* put forward an amendment to the Withdrawal Agreement that had been agreed between the UK government and the EU but had failed to pass a vote in the House of Commons by 230 votes on 15 January:

> The Government will immediately table legal text to amend the Withdrawal Agreement to replace the backstop with a permanent solution capable of delivering an invisible and compliant border in Ireland under either WTO [World Trade Organisation] rules or an FTA [free trade agreement], using administrative procedures and current technology. No new infrastructure or checks at the border will be required, in accordance with the commitments given by the EU and by the government of the Republic of Ireland.[49]

The key idea of this 'unique solution' was not to hope for future advances in technology – which was clearly gaining little traction with the EU – but to rely on existing technology and rules, and at the same time move the physical checks needed away from the territorial border. So there would be inspections and checks and surveillance and delays – just not at the physical border itself. The phrase that no infrastructure or checks would be required 'at the border' certainly does not equate to a 'frictionless border' and is rather deflating as a solution to the Brexit border conundrum. As Katy Hayward summed up – the max-fac option is predicated on the very thing that the Backstop was trying to avoid – the return of a hard border in Ireland, however sensitively it was operated:

> Maximum facilitation can do no more than its name suggests – facilitate customs procedures. It cannot end the need for customs checks. In fact, it relies upon them. The more hidden the technology monitoring a customs border is, the greater the need for surveillance and data capture. Movements, transactions and communications across the Irish border are a precious part of everyday life for so many in Ireland, north and south. To gather data on such movements, transactions and communications for the purpose of enforcing a customs border that no one in Northern Ireland wishes to see is hardly a viable (let alone democratic) solution.[50]

While the debate surrounding technical solutions to the hard border circulated during the negotiations, the prospect was finally and bluntly terminated by the EU's deputy chief negotiator, Sabine Weyand, who made it very clear in January 2019 that the EU did not accept the viability of technology as a sufficiently robust solution to avoid the need for a hard border in Ireland after Brexit: 'We looked at every border on this Earth, every border the EU has with a third country – there's simply no way you can do away with checks and controls. The negotiators have not been able to explain them to us and that's not their fault; it's because they don't exist.'[51] Despite Weyand's clear guidance that max fac would not be considered by the EU, it remained a necessary illusion for many Brexiteers. They continued to argue that the paradox could be overcome where the CTA could be maintained and no hard borders imposed after the UK left the customs union and single market.

The Backstop

As unionists, we believe that this fundamentally undermines the principle of consent [within the GFA] … This is our problem with the Backstop and we have been consistent with that all the way through … we have had a consistent message right from when the Withdrawal Agreement and the Backstop came out to say: 'Look – we must have a deal. We [the UUP] can't do a no deal; regardless of what happens there has to be a deal. But it can't be this deal, because it fundamentally undermines the constitutional settlement of the United Kingdom.'

Steve Aiken MLA, UUP[52]

Unionists fear that Brexit is going to result in Northern Ireland being treated differently from the rest of the UK – an existential fear that is hard-wired into their political background. The legally binding Backstop became the focal point for this fear and associated suspicion that the Irish border was being weaponised by nationalists for other reasons – namely to progress their desire for constitutional change and Irish political reunification. Sammy Wilson, Brexit spokesperson for the DUP, was consistently one of the most trenchant in believing that the Irish border was not an irresolvable puzzle:

> The fact of the matter is the border is not an issue, the Irish Govern-ment has made it quite clear in the event of a no deal they will not be putting any border checks along the border, so why can they not do the same in the event of a deal which has Northern Ireland out of the customs union and the single market, as we would be in the case of a no deal.[53]

The unionist view was that the Irish border could be mediated via technology, favoured trading status and good will between Ireland and the UK, as outlined above. However, it had been clear from the outset that there were no credible technological solutions to the Irish border issue after Brexit. It was also clear by 2018 that there was a stalemate in the negotiations, with inertia and division at the UK end. The lack of a means of reconciling the UK govern-ment's stated Brexit policy, of leaving the EU customs union and single market and the rules of the European Court of Justice, on the one hand, while maintaining the CTA and frictionless Irish border on the other, resulted in what is popularly known as the 'Backstop'. Ironically, this was devised by the UK government itself in discussion with the EU in 2017 and went into the initial draft agreement between the EU and UK in December 2017. It is shorthand for a legally binding clause that would become operational in the absence of a comprehensive trade agreement between the UK and EU that harmonised rules to the point that there was full regulatory alignment between the UK and EU. In the scenario of a comprehensive trade deal, the rules would be harmonised over tariffs and trade and the movement of people between the UK and EU – and crucially therefore between Northern Ireland and the Irish Republic, making the Irish border immaterial to the trading of goods and services and the movement of people. However, the Backstop was inserted as an insurance policy in the event that this agreement did not occur by the end of the anticipated transition phase after Brexit on 31 December 2020. If a comprehensive trade deal was not concluded by this or any revised date, then the Backstop would become operational and would ensure that the UK adhered to EU standards and rules until such a time as this was replaced with a comprehensive deal. It was thus an insurance policy initially agreed by Theresa May and her government in December 2017 – until it moved from being a *political* device that could be wriggled out of, to a *legally binding* clause that would be mandatory and enforceable.

The fact that the UK government disavowed the Backstop once it was translated into law demonstrated to Ireland and the EU how necessary it actually was. It became the sticking point in the entire Brexit negotiation between the UK and the EU and a source of much tension between the political actors on all sides.

By 2018 it had become a stalemate between the EU and the UK, recognised by all parties to the negotiation. The UK's position had shifted, from agreeing to the Backstop in December 2017, to agreeing *a* backstop but not *the* Backstop as defined by the EU, to agreeing a revised version of the Backstop that appeared in the Withdrawal Agreement in November 2018, to eventually opposing their own agreement in the House of Commons and going back to Brussels in February 2019 to ask for changes to be made to the Withdrawal Agreement that would provide 'alternative arrangements' to the Backstop outside its legally binding obligations.

The alternative arrangements sought were of unknown provenance and led Irish Taoiseach Leo Varadkar to say, 'I think the events in London and the instability in British politics in recent weeks demonstrates exactly why we need a legal guarantee and a solution that is operable, that we know will work and will last.'[54] Varadkar's rather terse reading of British government difficulties might have received more attention from the UK media had it not been for what Donald Tusk had to say at the same press conference. The European Council President let rip with a diplomatic broadside at the UK and thinly veiled anger at the state of the Brexit process so close to the UK's exit date from the EU: 'I've been wondering what a special place in hell looks like for people who promoted Brexit without even a sketch of a plan how to carry it out safely.'[55] This exploded across the UK and international media and while technically he was criticising those who had campaigned for Brexit and not had a credible plan to deliver it, it was taken as a criticism of Brexiteers within the UK government.

In April 2018, the EU's lead negotiator, Michel Barnier, had put it bluntly during a speech in Dundalk, a town located on the Irish border. He underlined that the EU understood not simply the economic arguments for the Backstop, but also the political and historical ones in the context of the peace process in Northern Ireland. Indeed, his speech arguably demonstrated greater empathy for the region, its people and their recent violent history than was evident from the British Prime Minister, her Brexit Secretary David Davis, or her government.

> In 1999, when I became the EU Commissioner for regional policy – in charge of the PEACE programme – the Good Friday Agreement had just been signed. Some check-points and controls were still visible on the border, waiting to be fully dismantled. In May last year, when I returned to the border region at Lough Egish, County Monaghan, there was no physical border to be seen. But, over the last 20 years, the Good Friday Agreement has meant – of course – far more than just removing customs and physical barriers. It removed borders on maps but also in minds. The Good Friday Agreement created wide-ranging cooperation between North and South, and between communities.
>
> … The consequences of Brexit should not and must not lead to the return of a hard border, neither on maps nor in minds. … To be clear: without a backstop, there can be no Withdrawal Agreement. This is an EU issue, not only an Irish issue.[56]

These arguments could just as easily have come from a speech given by the Irish Taoiseach or a member of his government (and in fact these same points had been made many times by Irish politicians on other occasions), demonstrating the synchronicity between Ireland and the EU on the issue.[57]

All roads towards a Brexit deal between the EU and the UK led to a legally enforceable backstop. Even Theresa May herself admitted this when her back was against the wall in the House of Commons in November 2018: '[T]here is no alternative deal that honours our commitments to Northern Ireland which does not involve this insurance policy. ... Put simply, there is no deal that comes without a backstop, and without a backstop there is no deal.'[58]

However, after the New Year Theresa May – without apology – unbelievably proceeded to vote against her own policy by supporting the Brady Amendment[59] on 29 January and committing herself to replacing the Backstop with as yet unspecified 'alternative arrangements'. While this bought her some time, it left Ireland and the rest of the EU feeling that a legally enforceable backstop was essential, given the inconsistency, vacillation and lack of commitment of the UK to it. It looked to many Irish observers as if the British Prime Minister and her government saw the Good Friday Agreement and the peace process as secondary to the survival of the government and the Conservative Party. It posed a tough question: Could the Irish peace process actually survive Brexit?

6

Brexit and the Good Friday Agreement

I have a starting point that says the DUP want there to be a hard border – that it is in their political DNA to want as much separation [as possible] between North and South. I worked in government here with DUP ministers and I know they tried to suffocate, strangle, all the cross-border bodies [established under the GFA] … and the DUP philosophy, mission, is to stymie, block, obstruct any cross-border cooperation. Therefore it's really logical that they should move from that position to back Brexit … because a soft or hard Brexit creates a hard border in Ireland [and] creates obstacles to cross-border cooperation.

Máirtín Ó Muilleoir MLA, Sinn Féin[1]

I believe that the Brexit negotiations have had some role in the situation which has led us to have no local Government for nearly 1000 days now. I would emphasise it is not the only issue since I believe that Sinn Féin would prefer not to have an Assembly and to destabilise Northern Ireland and therefore under no circumstances would they be going back into the Assembly. Brexit has been a further excuse for them because they do not wish to have any part in the arrangements which would be put in place after we leave the EU but the other major reasons are their unwillingness to face up to how to deal with their terrorist past and also, since they have the finance portfolio, how they deal with the difficult budgetary issues which the Assembly would face.

Sammy Wilson MP, DUP[2]

[People] want somebody to make a decision – but they want good governance. … But the problem is that is overlapped with the fear factor. 'You need to vote for us, or you'll get them uns.' The number of people who've said to me, 'I'd love to vote for the UUP because you've got all these [good] people – but I need to vote DUP to keep Sinn Féin out.' … that is a driving factor and it's a classic parasitic arrangement. … and Brexit has added to that because everyone has been politicised to a large degree by Brexit and by the enormous amount of media coverage of it. Some people have switched off, but in the background, people are politicised about it one way or another because people listen to their fears.

Steve Aiken MLA, UUP[3]

It is not an exaggeration to say that Brexit presented the biggest crisis for both parts of Ireland since the island was partitioned by Britain in 1921. The key reasons relate to its implications for the Irish border and the integrity of the Belfast/Good Friday Agreement and peace process more broadly. The prospect of the re-emergence of a hard physical border resulting from a policy agenda driven by a British government in London, which directly contravened the democratically expressed wishes of those in Northern Ireland, was anathema for many of those who supported the GFA.

10 April 2018 marked the twentieth anniversary of the Agreement. This multiparty negotiation, which resulted from two years of formal talks, involved ten political parties in Northern Ireland, the British and Irish governments and included the support and involvement of senior mediators, including the White House administration of President Bill Clinton. A formal agreement was endorsed by the two sovereign parliaments in Ireland and the United Kingdom, lodged as an international treaty between the two states and was passed by dual referendums in Northern Ireland and the Irish Republic with overwhelming majorities. It has lasted for twenty years but, at the same time, the devolved power-sharing institutions that resulted from it have been plagued by instability, political inertia and a chronic lack of collective coherence.[4]

Despite its many flaws the GFA has been widely seen as ending the violent political conflict in Northern Ireland and providing an embryonic model for future governance in the region. In terms of politically motivated violence, the reality is more complex than the headlines would suggest. While fatalities have been vastly reduced and the infrastructure of the paramilitary organisations and British military presence are greatly diminished, levels of structural segregation, ethnonational sectarianism and community friction remain high in Northern Ireland.[5] There are more rather than fewer 'peace walls' in Belfast erected to keep people apart, while over 90% of children continue to be educated in religiously segregated schools. It has been, therefore, a reluctant peace over the last twenty years,[6] where old animosities have been parked rather than resolved with institutions that have proved incapable of transforming the underlying ethnonational divisions between the British identity of unionists and the Irish identity of nationalists.[7] The devolved institutions were restored in January 2020 following three years of suspension. Their collapse in January 2017 was the result of an increasingly dysfunctional relationship between the main political parties, with Sinn Féin and the DUP having a particularly fractious relationship. While the political institutions were brought back to life in 2020, what the DUP and Sinn Féin have in common that might translate into a coherent programme for government, remains unclear. Reflecting on the impact of Brexit on political stability in Northern Ireland, DUP Brexit spokesperson Sammy Wilson was pessimistic about the future of devolution in the region in part because of the gulf between his party and Sinn Féin, which was likely to remain the largest nationalist party in the region:

> I think that [it] is going to be very difficult for the DUP and Sinn Féin to agree any programme for Government, not only because of Brexit, but because of the difficult budgetary issues facing Northern Ireland and of Sinn Féin's unwillingness to introduce any budget cuts, even though we do have a block grant which is now reduced

in real terms and we have public services which are in dire need of reform.[8]

As a consequence, while politicians, the media and academics all marked the twentieth anniversary of the Good Friday Agreement, most pointed to its survival and future potential rather than its record of achievement. The anniversary was celebrated in April 2018 by politicians from around the world, including several of its main architects, with President Bill Clinton, Senator George Mitchell, Bertie Ahern, Tony Blair and other notable figures from the period attending conferences in Belfast and elsewhere. Clinton's message was a hopeful one but cast the GFA and its institutions as fragile and requiring further compromise from politicians and their supporters for peace to be fully realised: 'voters have to stop punishing people who make those compromises. And start rewarding them.'[9] The leader of the SDLP, Colum Eastwood, commented when giving evidence to the Northern Ireland Affairs Committee on 21 February 2018, 'the Good Friday Agreement is recognised as a contrivance – but so is Northern Ireland'.[10] Academic learned societies such as the Political Studies Association (PSA) ran podcasts and commissioned blog pieces from numerous academic specialists on the legacy of the GFA,[11] and broadcast and print media around the world also marked the occasion. A large number of these contributions considered Brexit, and the negative implications this could have for the Irish border and the peace process in Northern Ireland more broadly.[12] A former Irish ambassador spoke of his concern to write up his reflections on the Good Friday Agreement while it still had a shelf life as in his view, Brexit was suffocating it. It was still the 'gold standard' reference point in the peace process, but he suggested that this would not last forever if Brexit continued to hollow out Anglo-Irish relations and the interparty relationship in Northern Ireland.[13]

The Brexit meteor crashed into the already unstable political fabric of Northern Ireland in a way that unearthed questions that had been submerged since the GFA was finalised in 1998. Chief among those was the constitutional question and the accepted wisdoms woven into the political and legal fabric of the GFA. Is Northern Ireland *different* from the rest of the UK? Can the people who live there legitimately claim self-determination? Can people in Northern Ireland really be defined as Irish as well as British if that is their wish – as set out in the GFA? Perhaps most pointedly, will the UK abide by the promises it made at several points during the peace process to recognise (and legislate for) changing Northern Ireland's constitutional status as part of the UK and assist it in reuniting politically with the rest of the island of Ireland if a majority of people demonstrate such a desire? Brexit raised concerns about this for Irish nationalists on both sides of the border given Theresa May's declarations about the 'people' having decided and her lack of recognition of the fact that on the Brexit issue, the people of Northern Ireland had spoken also – and their democratically expressed wish had been ignored by the UK government.[14] Thus, despite the warm words of commitment to the GFA and to the importance of Northern Ireland's bespoke political institutions – when it came to Brexit the devolved arrangements apparently counted for little.

This was crucially important for Northern Ireland because the GFA was built on the 'consent' principle, where Irish nationalists were required to accept that the political status of the region would not change until a majority of the electorate demonstrated their consent for such change.[15] The Irish Republic, meanwhile, reformed Articles 2 and 3 of its constitution via a referendum in 1998 to reflect the consent principle and to water down its constitutional claim to Northern Ireland.[16] More fundamentally, the 'consent principle' has been front and centre of the peace process since the early 1990s and is written clearly into the GFA: 'it would be wrong to make any change in the status of Northern Ireland save with the consent of a majority of its people'.[17] However, Brexit potentially tears that consent principle apart, and since the Brexit vote, Northern

Ireland's 'consent' has been studiously ignored by the British government and actively disavowed by unionists, who had previously been adamant about its importance in the negotiated settlement. The border provides the physical and existential manifestation of that consent principle and any re-emergence of a physical border if/when Brexit formally takes place will further undermine the devolved political structures in Northern Ireland and jeopardise the broader peace process.[18]

The GFA was of course more than just a set of political institutions within Northern Ireland, it also institutionalised a new Anglo-Irish relationship – explicitly in terms of Strand Three arrangements but also implicitly, to the extent that both the British and Irish governments were connected as co-guarantors and joint custodians of the 1998 Agreement.[19] Brexit disrupted the Anglo-Irish relationship to a significant degree and this had a knock-on effect on the political situation in Northern Ireland and the power-sharing institutions that were established after the GFA.[20] The strained Anglo-Irish relationship produced by the difficult Brexit negotiations from 2017 to 2019 also created a sense of uncertainty about the future of the GFA and the UK's commitment to it.[21] This was fuelled by UK politicians at times suggesting that it might be time to revisit or update the GFA and that it could not have a veto over the need to deliver on the government's Brexit ambitions. In February 2018, Labour MP Kate Hoey intimated that the GFA was no longer 'sustainable', triggering concerns that some British politicians were using Brexit to damage the Agreement. Hoey, a keen Brexit supporter, suggested that the GFA was no longer a sustainable political model for Northern Ireland:

> I think there is a need for a cold rational look at the Belfast agreement. Even if a settlement had been agreed a few days ago there is nothing to stop Sinn Féin or the DUP finding something else to walk out about in a few months. Mandatory coalition is not sustainable in the long term.[22]

Hoey's remarks were echoed by other leading Brexit supporters around the same time, notably former Secretary of State for Northern Ireland Owen Patterson, another member of the pro-Brexit European Research Group. The fact that Patterson, who had been Northern Ireland Secretary from 2010 to 2012, was seen to be prioritising Brexit over the future of the GFA led many Irish nationalists to question the commitment of the UK to the Agreement, the devolved institutions and the peace process itself. Hoey's comments were condemned by her own Labour Party branch, which asserted its continuing commitment to the GFA and Northern Ireland peace process.[23] Several critics made the connection between Hoey's remarks and her Brexit aspirations, with former Labour leader and Prime Minister Tony Blair being particularly direct in his criticism: 'There are politicians prepared to sacrifice the Good Friday Agreement on the altar of Brexit and declare that the peace agreed in Northern Ireland is not, really, worth having anyway. This is irresponsibility that is frankly sickening.'[24] Others, such as Irish Foreign Minister Simon Coveney, called Hoey's remarks 'reckless' and claimed that they could undermine the foundations of the fragile peace in Northern Ireland.[25] Such forthright condemnation of a UK politician by the Irish government was indicative of the state of the wider Anglo-Irish relationship as a result of the Brexit negotiations, and the frustration and irritation within Ireland at the UK's inability to develop and deliver a coherent negotiating position. Such remarks would have been very unlikely before Brexit, when episodes of megaphone diplomacy were rare.[26] Social media platforms (Twitter in particular) became the forum for such recrimination across the political classes as well as the wider population. It was Twitter that Coveney used to send a direct tweet to Hoey, Tory MEP Dan Hannan and Owen Patterson, accusing them of political irresponsibility in their attacks on the GFA. 'Talking down [the] Good Friday Agreement because it raises serious and genuine questions of those pursuing Brexit is not only irresponsible but reckless and potentially undermines the foundations of a fragile peace process in Northern Ireland that should never be taken for granted.'[27]

As the next chapter demonstrates, Brexit pushed Anglo-Irish relations to breaking point and arguably to a low not experienced since the disastrous relationship between Eamon de Valera and Winston Churchill during the Second World War in the early 1940s.

Concern at the attempt by Brexit-supporting politicians in the UK to attack the GFA was shared by others within Irish nationalism, with SDLP leader Colum Eastwood referring to Hoey's remarks during a testy exchange at the Northern Ireland Affairs Committee hearing in the House of Commons. Hoey was a member of this committee, and when he appeared as an expert witness before it Eastwood declared, 'I, for one, will not have the Good Friday Agreement torn up just to facilitate a very awkward negotiation that's going on between the United Kingdom and the European Commission.'[28] Given the febrile political atmosphere, any mention of the GFA and Brexit in the same context was bound to lead to accusations and counter-accusations of malice and bad faith, and this was undoubtedly the case during 2018 and 2019. There was certainly more heat than light on display and very little detailed analytical attention was given to how exactly Brexit did relate to the GFA in terms of its institutions and not least to the European dimension contained within it.

The European dimension of the GFA

Europe was entwined with the Good Friday Agreement in a manner that was one of its least controversial or difficult elements back in 1998. It is ironic that references to the European Union within the text of the GFA received relatively little attention at the time and were largely unproblematic aspects of it. Now, however, they are seen by some as trapping the UK in European glue, while others cherish them as fundamental anchor points to the Agreement, its political institutions and the peace process generally.

Before looking at the extent to which the EU is woven into the GFA, it is worth addressing why it is important at all. The EU (and the EEC that preceded it) has had a long-standing involvement in Northern Ireland politically, economically and culturally. It has also acted as a bridge between Ireland and the UK, allowing the two countries to meet and providing considerable financial resources for Northern Ireland prior to, during and after the political conflict there from the 1970s to the 2000s.[29] Both the UK and Ireland entered the EEC at the same time in 1973. Before that point there had been a degree of political frost between the two over events in Northern Ireland and little sense of common purpose. However, EEC membership provided opportunities for the politicians and civil servants to get to know each other, build trust networks and a sense of common purpose that would prove vital in the early stages of the peace process in the 1990s. Issues could be discussed in the margins of European Summits away from the glare of the media in a way that provided some continuity of conversation between the two countries.[30] When there were the inevitable disagreements, these could increasingly be contained internally, rather than result in megaphone diplomacy or public allegations of bad faith.[31] The EEC/EU also stood as a physical manifestation of how the political union of European nations could help to provide common interests between them and offered a stark contrast between the end of the twentieth century and its earlier decades. This point was regularly made by former SDLP leader and architect of the peace process, John Hume. When he was jointly awarded the Nobel Peace Prize in 1998 with David Trimble (leader of the UUP), Hume invoked the EU as a key player in peacebuilding during his lifetime.

> In my own work for peace, I was very strongly inspired by my European experience. I always tell this story, and I do so because

it is so simple yet so profound and so applicable to conflict resolution anywhere in the world. On my first visit to Strasbourg in 1979 as a member of the European Parliament, I went for a walk across the bridge from Strasbourg to Kehl. Strasbourg is in France. Kehl is in Germany. They are very close. I stopped in the middle of the bridge and I meditated. There is Germany. There is France. If I had stood on this bridge 30 years ago after the end of the second world war when 25 million people lay dead across our continent for the second time in this century and if I had said: 'Don't worry. In 30 years' time we will all be together in a new Europe, our conflicts and wars will be ended and we will be working together in our common interests,' I would have been sent to a psychiatrist. But it has happened and it is now clear that the European Union is the best example in the history of the world of conflict resolution and it is the duty of everyone, particularly those who live in areas of conflict to study how it was done and to apply its principles to their own conflict resolution.[32]

Hume often referred to the European dimension as a key to unlocking the identity politics within Northern Ireland's contested ethnonational dispute – so much so that his critics dubbed it as his 'single-transferable speech'. Hume knew a thing or two about political communication – primarily that repetition of a simple message over time was the key to getting it heard: 'I learnt as a schoolteacher that even with the cleverest pupils you have to say what's on your mind at least 20 times. I have always done this in politics.'[33]

While it might not be clear from the modern media coverage of Northern Ireland, Hume was arguably the key to the peace process in Ireland. It was Hume who acted as intermediary between Dublin, Washington and London to make the case that militant republicanism was willing and able to take a political path out of violence. It was Hume who took immense personal and political risks to talk to Sinn Féin, against the wishes of many senior colleagues in his party to make the case for a non-violent route to achieve political ends. It was Hume who worked with key Irish-Americans

such as Ted Kennedy, Tip O'Neill and eventually President Bill
Clinton, to take risks for peace (such as granting Sinn Féin president
Gerry Adams a visa to visit the US before the Provisional IRA had
announced a ceasefire in 1994).[34] Hume had been an MEP as well
as a Westminster MP and he took his understanding of European
politics into his attempts to build political agreement in Ireland.
George Mitchell, former chair of the multiparty talks that resulted
in the GFA in 1998, went so far as to say; 'I believe the talks would
never have occurred had there not been a European Union.'[35]

Europe also committed a vast amount of resources in support
of peace and stability in Northern Ireland, colloquially known as
the Peace Funds. It is not by accident that the EU negotiation with
the UK has put the GFA in Northern Ireland at the centre of its
priorities. A former EU Commissioner for the Peace Programme in
Northern Ireland was one Michel Barnier, who was Commissioner
for Regional Policy. In this role, Barnier led the second Programme
for Peace and Reconciliation in Northern Ireland that pumped over
€500 million of EU structural funds into the region for economic
regeneration and cross-border cooperation.[36] If all of this has
been forgotten by the UK, it certainly has not by Barnier – or
by Ireland. This points again to two things. Firstly, politicians in
Great Britain have really failed to understand the importance of
how Northern Ireland politics have evolved within a European
context, more closely than they have with the rest of the UK.
Secondly, the British political mind simply lacks a rudimentary
understanding or appreciation of the extent to which the EU has
been a key asset to political stability in Northern Ireland. The
EU effectively subsidised peacebuilding activity in this part of the
UK for a generation, but this seems not to have percolated into
the political consciousness of British politicians trying to negotiate
their way out of EU membership.

It is also worth noting that the EU contribution to peace in
Northern Ireland is not an historical artefact that has understandably
slipped the attention of busy politicians in Westminster. It is still

ongoing, and the government that is ultimately responsible for the region (and the Treasury) will be very aware that two EU programmes, INTEREG and PEACE IV, collectively contribute around £470 million per annum into Northern Ireland, 85% of which is bankrolled by the EU. So the EU remains a major peacebuilder in Northern Ireland and has invested economically and politically in the GFA and peace process from the outset. This significant EU contribution was called into question by Brexit and the subsequent negotiations between the UK and the EU. Would this funding continue after Brexit if there was a no-deal outcome? There was close to zero attention given to this EU role by the UK government or by pro-Brexit groups in the UK.

Those working in the EU on cross-community initiatives on the Irish border were more tuned in to the benefits this was having and to the dangers that Brexit posed for the continuation of this peacebuilding activity. A report from the European Parliament concluded in 2018, rather magnanimously, that this funding should be continued irrespective of how the Brexit negotiations concluded – even in the event of a no-deal outcome, so important was it for peace and stability in Northern Ireland: '[P]ost-2020, without prejudice to the ongoing EU–UK negotiations, EU support for territorial cooperation, especially regarding cross-border and cross-community projects, should be continued.'[37]

That this report was endorsed overwhelmingly by the European Parliament (565 votes in favour and only 51 against) speaks to the empathy within the EU and its governing structures for Northern Ireland's recent political history and for the future of its hard-won peace process. It was also evidence that the European Parliament and the vast majority of MEPs saw Northern Ireland and the EU funding that has gone into it as an EU success story and an example of how cohesion funding could work in providing support for EU member states.

The silence from the UK said more about its attitudes towards the EU and Northern Ireland than it did about the MEPs who supported it. Indeed, in June 2018, an opinion poll found that two-thirds of Brexit supporters would rather leave the customs union than avoid a hard border in Ireland, and six out of ten of them 'would not mind either way' if Northern Ireland voted to leave the UK.[38] In part such statistics demonstrate the frustrations that accompanied the Brexit negotiations, not least the legitimate aspirations of those who supported Brexit. From their perspective, they had voted for Brexit in the 2016 referendum and their democratically expressed wishes were being thwarted by Remainiacs, the EU, the hapless leadership of their government – and by the grit in the oyster that was Northern Ireland.

Does Brexit breach the 'terms' of the GFA?

Unsurprisingly, supporters and opponents of Brexit take different views on whether the UK's departure from the EU actually breaches the terms of the GFA or the agreements entered into by the UK government in 1998. Those who are against Brexit have used a variety of arguments to claim that it breaches the terms of the GFA and its subsequent iterations. Brexiteers meanwhile contend that there is nothing contained within the text of the GFA that requires the UK (or Northern Ireland) to remain within the EU. Furthermore, there is no explicit requirement specified in the GFA or subsequent negotiated agreements in 2006 or 2014 that there cannot be a hard border in Ireland. The argument here was that the phrase 'hard border' was not in the GFA – nor for that matter was the CTA or a 'frictionless border' mentioned within its hallowed text. All that was said was that there would be a normalising of the border between Ireland and Northern Ireland, not that it would evaporate entirely. This is true in literal terms, but it is not true in political terms.

This supports the meteor theory put forward in Chapter 2. Such phrases are missing because Brexit hit the GFA and wider peace process like a meteor, knocking the EU-shaped front teeth out of the GFA on impact in a manner not envisaged in the mid-1990s, when the border was seen as a binary legal entity between Ireland and the UK. Normalising the border referred to demilitarising it, taking down the army watchtowers, opening roads in Ireland that had been closed by the British for security reasons, reducing surveillance of the border and those travelling across it and returning the territory to civilian use.[39] But those were simpler times when both the UK and Ireland were in the EU single market and customs union together and thus harmonised over trade, tariffs and travel. To argue that a hard border was acceptable because the GFA makes no mention of a frictionless border in Ireland within its text was a spurious claim by Brexit supporters peddled across their own echo chambers, but with little credibility beyond that.'

The opponents of Brexit suggest that the UK is legally tied to the EU via the GFA and cannot simply withdraw unilaterally from its legal obligations. In the technical legal sense this is correct as it has been pointed out that the UK, as a member of the EU when the GFA was signed in 1998, needed and received the EU's implicit approval to make a political agreement with another EU member state, Ireland.[40] But it is difficult to see how the terms of the GFA can be adhered to after the UK's departure from the European Union. For one thing, the GFA refers to the joint EU membership of both countries (Ireland and the UK), so having the UK defaulting from the EU is a formal breach of the GFA. More importantly, many of the structures set out within the GFA and subsequently established, such as the North South Ministerial Council (Strand Two), obliged it to consider the EU dimension to all matters that it considered:

> This provision is inevitable, because any agreements between EU Member States must comply with EU obligations. It is duly mirrored in UK legislation relating to the second section of the Belfast Agreement: for example the Northern Ireland Act of 1998 requires that any secondary legislation issued by the Legislative Assembly must comply with EU law.[41]

In this analysis there would be a need to comply with pockets of EU law in Northern Ireland even after the rest of the UK left the EU. Of course the UK could choose to align itself with EU law in these respects, but to do this it would have to ditch its 'Brexit means Brexit' mantra and red line that all of the UK would be leaving the EU on the same terms. The UK will also face significant legal wrinkles in trying to negotiate any future deal with Ireland as it would be doing so as a non-member state, and there are likely to be additional requirements placed on Ireland by the EU over its making a unilateral agreement with a third country.

It is in the human rights dimension that the EU's role within the GFA can be most clearly seen.[42] Both the UK and Ireland agreed in a binding international treaty to incorporate the European Convention on Human Rights (ECHR) into Northern Ireland law, providing guarantees for those who live there over EU human rights standards, including the right to 'direct access to the courts, and remedies for breach of the Convention, including power for the courts to overrule Assembly legislation on grounds of inconsistency'.[43] This commitment to complete alignment with the ECHR was underwritten and enshrined in UK legislation with the 1998 UK Human Rights Act.[44] Even should the UK try to wriggle out of such undertakings after Brexit, it are likely to be held to the spirit of the legislation by Ireland and other European partners with whom they will want to have some form of relationship after their formal departure from the EU. Ireland, for its part, already has more than one eye on UK intentions in this regard and made that clear even before the Brexit referendum took place in 2016. Ireland's former foreign minister, Charlie Flanagan, made his government's position on the centrality of EU and the ECHR clear in 2015 prior to the Brexit vote:

> The protection of human rights in Northern Ireland law, predicated on the European Convention of Human Rights, is one of the key principles underpinning the Agreement. ... Protecting the human rights aspects of the Good Friday Agreement is not only a shared

responsibility between the two Governments in terms of the welfare of the people of Northern Ireland but is also an obligation on them as parties to the international treaty.[45]

Civil society groups in Northern Ireland also highlighted the importance of EU legal standards especially over human rights issues as the Brexit negotiations moved forwards. The Northern Ireland Council for Voluntary Action (NICVA), an umbrella organisation for the voluntary and community sector in Northern Ireland, made this point explicitly in a paper published in July 2017: 'The all-island legal framework that shared EU membership provides on the island of Ireland is also incredibly important to protecting continued peace and stability in NI'.[46]

Certainly the fingerprints of the EU can be seen across the text of the GFA and are integral to many of the political institutions established on the basis of the 1998 Agreement. These prints were both implicit and explicit. The implicit dimension related to the fact that the consent of people in Northern Ireland for any constitutional change to the status quo was placed at the centre of the GFA. The British and Irish governments signed up in the Declaration of Support to the GFA to: '(i) recognise the legitimacy of whatever choice is freely exercised by a majority of the people of Northern Ireland with regard to its status, whether they prefer to continue to support the Union with Great Britain or a sovereign united Ireland'.[47] Arguably, however, Brexit unilaterally changes the status of Northern Ireland against its declared wishes, removing it from the EU, and thus breaches the consent principle at the heart of the Agreement. The EU was part of that status quo infrastructure, and as Northern Ireland had voted to remain within it in 2016, there is a case to be made that the UK is defaulting on its side of the deal.

More explicitly, the GFA incorporated a series of rights and safeguards within and across its proposed mechanisms and operations. Many of these are inextricably linked to legal norms, practices and guarantees established by the EU and its affiliated institutions. In this sense the EU was mainstreamed into the GFA and bound up with it through a series of interconnected legal layers. Some of these are connected to EU legal guarantees while others are not; however, the GFA needs to be understood as an integrated agreement and an international treaty that is binding in its entirety – not an agreement with numerous detachable sections or elements to it.

One of the key legal elements established by the GFA was the right of people born in Northern Ireland (and their legal partners and children) to choose to have Irish citizenship and/or British citizenship. The following passage in the Declaration of Support provides an explicit undertaking of nationality rights that was a key dimension for nationalists in terms of recognising their legitimate aspirations to national identity:

> [It is] the birthright of all the people of Northern Ireland to identify themselves and be accepted as Irish or British, or both, as they may so choose, and accordingly confirm that their right to hold both British and Irish citizenship is accepted by both Governments and would not be affected by any future change in the status of Northern Ireland.[48]

Brexit was a game-changer in that respect as it potentially altered the status of Northern Ireland by removing it from the EU and also the right of those living within it to have access to the EU single market, customs union and legal protections enshrined by EU membership. This definition of the right to dual citizenship that would not be affected by any change to the status of Northern Ireland took some of the heat out of the ethnonational dispute between unionists and nationalists over the constitutional position of Northern Ireland as being a binary zero-sum option between being British or being Irish. Here national identity became an opt-in concept and the GFA gave a right for everyone in Northern Ireland to have an Irish passport and define their nationality as Irish (though they could also define their identity as both Irish and

British), while unionists were at liberty to self-define as British (or to also have a British-Irish or Irish nationality). While the rights to dual citizenship enshrined in the GFA were located within UK law rather than EU law, this was one legal strand of a wider set of legal guarantees that could not easily be disentangled from one another.

Beyond citizenship rights, the GFA was also bound up with an array of EU labour and human rights legal norms, uncontroversial when the GFA was negotiated and agreed in 1998, but problematic after Brexit, when the UK would be potentially beyond EU legal authority and responsibility.[49] The GFA states explicitly in paragraph 26 that the ECHR would act as a guarantor of human rights standards for primary legislation passed by any consequent devolved Assembly in Northern Ireland: 'The Assembly will have authority to pass primary legislation for Northern Ireland in devolved areas, subject to: (a) the ECHR and any Bill of Rights for Northern Ireland supplementing it which, if the courts found to be breached, would render the relevant legislation null and void.'[50]

This provided the ECHR and thus by extension the EU with arbitration-type powers over the legality of any primary legislation passed in Northern Ireland. Removing the UK from the EU raises a question about whether this aspect of the GFA still holds, or whether the UK will abide by the rulings of the ECHR within Northern Ireland if it refuses to do so in the rest of the United Kingdom.

The GFA Declaration of Support meanwhile, accepted and endorsed by both the UK and Irish governments, made it clear that all legislation passed by the Northern Ireland Assembly would be checked for its compatibility with EU standards and would 'provide that key decisions and legislation are proofed to ensure that they do not infringe the ECHR and any Bill of Rights for Northern Ireland'.[51] In this sense the EU acted as a legal arbiter within the GFA political infrastructure – in part because of the historical and well-grounded insecurities within Northern Ireland concerning the role of the criminal justice system. It provided a third-party legal dimension to communities that did not fully trust national legal instruments. Legal scholars demonstrated how Brexit potentially unpicked the legal infrastructure on which the GFA was founded, with Christopher McCrudden arguing:

> The following range of rights will all potentially be affected: EU-underpinned rights, particularly those specifically mentioned in the GFA (such as equality rights); fundamental rights deriving directly from EU membership, including those in the EU Charter of Fundamental Rights; labour and employment rights deriving from EU law; and the right to an effective judicial remedy.[52]

While supporters of Brexit argued that these legal dimensions did not undermine the fabric of the GFA, critics focused on the extent to which it damaged the internal legal integrity of the Agreement as an integrated set of legal rights and obligations. It would certainly seem to mean that unless the UK takes action after Brexit to align Northern Ireland legally with EU regulations and standards, then the political dimensions of the GFA will be affected. For one thing, assuming the devolved institutions are re-established in Northern Ireland and endure, the absence of EU law from the workings of those institutions will materially affect the competences of those bodies – allowing them greater authority and political interpretation over areas that remain contentious within Northern Ireland. As McCrudden said: 'Brexit has the potential, therefore, to reshape devolved government, by both increasing the powers of devolved institutions in some respects, and decreasing their powers in others, in both cases adding to the political difficulties of forming and maintaining devolved government in Northern Ireland.'[53]

The wider dimension here is a political one and owes more to the nature of the Brexit negotiations than to the text of the GFA and the legal obligations contained within it. It relates to a lack of trust between the Irish and British governments and many of those who live in Ireland and the UK. The Brexit negotiations have been characterised by delay, confusion, broken deadlines and mutual recrimination between the UK on the one side and Ireland/EU on the other. The UK government would give verbal guarantees of its intentions one day, but would seem to change or complicate its position the next day. So while the UK committed itself to ensuring that the legal obligations enshrined within the GFA would be honoured, it was less clear how cast-iron such assurances were or whether these could be relied upon into the future: 'Thus, although the current administration may commit to retain EU legal standards, future administrations will be under no obligation to do so and there would be nothing to prevent equality and human rights protections currently derived from, or supported by, EU law being eroded over time.'[54]

In a speech given to a university audience in Cork in 2019, the SDLP's former Brexit spokesperson Claire Hanna provided a political perspective on the role of the EU within the context of the GFA. Commenting on the 1998 Agreement's three-stranded structure (relations within Northern Ireland, within the island of Ireland and between Ireland and Great Britain), Hanna cast the EU as an additional indirect strand, that added value to the other three:

> For all the vitality of the three-stranded approach, I consider there to be a fourth unwritten GFA strand. The European dimension, a passion of [John] Hume's, was baked in, though not explicitly … that to spare the blushes of the then Eurosceptic SF and Unionist parties. The EU provided a backdrop of ambiguity, for dialling down the focus on national allegiance, sovereignty, borders, identity. Outside of trade, environmental and rights degradation, it is the core tragedy of Brexit that each of those issues has been thrown back into the centre of our everyday discourse, making our uphill boulder push even harder.[55]

Brexit, however, did not just revive ethnonational political dynamics in Northern Ireland, it also had clear impacts on the political parties themselves in Northern Ireland – and those within them – not least Hanna herself.

Brexit and reshaping of the political parties in Northern Ireland

While Brexit presented challenges for the legal framework of the GFA it also produced a new series of questions for political parties in Northern Ireland and senior figures within them.[56]

On the nationalist side, as has been made clear in previous chapters, it connected Sinn Féin more explicitly to the 'consent principle' at the heart of the GFA and peace process. Not that the party was not already comfortable with that – it certainly was by the time of the 2016 referendum. However, the result of that vote and the subsequent three-year negotiations on UK withdrawal from the EU was that Sinn Féin framed the consent principle more directly as an article of faith for the party. Of course 56% of the Northern Ireland electorate had voted to remain within the EU so Sinn Féin saw the ignoring of this by the UK as an example of British/English dominance over Irish democratic wishes. It also used it to campaign for a border poll over Irish reunification, catered for within the terms of the GFA but so far denied to it by the UK Secretary of State (who is the individual charged with making that decision). Former Sinn Féin finance minister in the Northern Ireland Executive, Máirtín Ó Muilleoir, was unequivocal in this view:

If Brexit goes ahead in the way envisaged by the DUP and Brexiteers then you have effectively binned the Good Friday Agreement and that just can't be countenanced by Europe, by the US, by the Irish government, by Northern nationalists and by anyone who believes in peace and democracy on this island. … It's an absolute rupture, from the Good Friday Agreement to say that a majority [of people] here voted to remain, in the most important referendum in our lifetimes, since the Good Friday Agreement certainly, and the DUP say 'no it doesn't matter, we're going to force you out [of the EU] anyway'.[57]

The positions taken by Sinn Féin and the SDLP on Brexit were that they wanted Northern Ireland to be given some form of opt-out or special designated status after the UK left the EU. This was primarily focused on avoiding the need for a hard border in Ireland after Brexit as well as respecting the consent principle within the GFA. Behind the specific appeal for 'special status', unionists felt there was also a more traditional nationalist agenda – namely to mark Northern Ireland out as different from the rest of the UK and annexe it in administrative if not cultural terms from 'the mainland'.

Brexit also created some more concrete issues for both political parties in terms of their approach to the devolved institutions at Stormont and broader political strategy. Sinn Féin hardened its position towards the restoration of the devolved institutions at Stormont and focused on lobbying outside of those institutions, around its Brexit position and other policy concerns. After the UK General Election in 2017, Sinn Féin also faced increased scrutiny over its abstentionist policy towards the Westminster parliament. The election resulted in a minority Conservative government, propped up by a confidence-and-supply agreement with Sinn Féin's main political opponents, the DUP. Sinn Féin returned seven MPs to the House of Commons who could have exerted significant influence on the Brexit negotiations and protected what it saw as attacks to the integrity of the Good Friday Agreement. The absence of these seven MPs from key votes in the House of Commons was questioned by the media in Britain and used by the SDLP (who won no seats at the 2017 General Election) to argue that Sinn Féin was failing in its duty to represent its constituents when the GFA and Northern Ireland's future was at stake. No one within main-stream republican circles shared such an analysis, however, and virtually no one within the Sinn Féin voter base suggested that it should take up its seats after the 2017 election.

Brexit had a more fundamental impact on the SDLP. The smaller nationalist party had been in crisis for some time – haemorrhaging political leaders and steadily losing its share of the vote within the nationalist electorate, to the point where it returned no MPs for the first time in living memory in the 2017 Westminster election. This was partly a consequence of the first-past-the-post electoral system that made it more difficult for the smaller parties to secure enough votes to win a parliamentary seat. Regardless of the electoral system, however, the general decline in the SDLP vote was accelerated by Brexit and raised an uncomfortable question for the party. What was the SDLP for? This was partly a question of practical political strategy – but it was also an existential one. The party that John Hume led in the 1980s and 1990s was defined by its support for constitutional nationalism, its disavowal of violence for political ends and its commitment to Europe and social democratic values.

In 2019 the SDLP crisis over its strategic direction came to a head with the decision to align itself with Fianna Fáil in the Irish Republic. This decision split opinion in the party, with some seeing it as a threat to the social democratic ethos of John Hume and a narrower 'green' form of nationalism that would result in the SDLP's absorption by its Southern partner. The decision to form an alliance with Fianna Fáil led directly to South Belfast MLA Claire Hanna's resignation as Brexit spokesperson, though she continued to represent the SDLP as an MLA in South Belfast. In her resignation letter following a party meeting in February 2019, Hanna made her opposition clear: 'I remain unconvinced that an exclusive partnership with Fianna Fáil is the right vehicle with which to deliver the non-sectarian, transparent and social democratic new Ireland I believe in.'[58] Hanna was widely regarded as one of the brightest political talents in the SDLP – and in Northern Ireland political life – and the sort of human capital that the party could ill afford to lose in its current parlous state. The decision to select Hanna as parliamentary candidate for South Belfast in the 2019 General Election suggests that the SDLP was aware of this too. Hanna's victory in South Belfast, along with SDLP leader Colum Eastwood's success in Foyle in the December 2019 General Election was a major boost for the SDLP and its profile. The party's decision to re-enter the Northern Ireland Executive when it was restored in January 2020 – rather than go into opposition in the Assembly – leaves an open question over the direction of nationalism in Northern Ireland in the coming years. For the remaining period of the Assembly's mandate, which is due to end in 2022, the SDLP needs to establish itself as an alternative to its larger Sinn Féin rival, but to do so within an Executive that will implicate it in collective decisions with Sinn Féin. The danger is that it will not be able to establish an alternative political agenda and will look to the nationalist electorate like a pale imitation of its larger rival.

Unionists were having their own political dramas as a result of Brexit. Perhaps the most obvious one was within the DUP – the largest unionist party in Northern Ireland. The DUP won ten seats in the 2017 Westminster General Election, wiping out its smaller unionist rival the UUP and with only independent unionist Lady Sylvia Hermon as an alternative unionist voice in the House of Commons. The DUP took various positions in parliament at different times, voting for Theresa May in a vote of No Confidence called by the Labour Party opposition in December 2018, but crucially voting against the Withdrawal Agreement repeatedly when the government tabled it in the House of Commons at the end of 2018 and in 2019.

While this tweaking of the Tory tail went down well among the DUP's core supporters and demonstrated its relative superiority to its smaller UUP rival, it created its own challenges for the party. Most directly, it made the DUP complicit in propping up a minority government which was incapable of delivering a coherent Brexit policy that maintained a frictionless border in Ireland. In 2019 the DUP found itself badly exposed over its opposition to the Withdrawal Agreement as erstwhile supporters in the farming and business sectors peeled off from its position and advocated acceptance of Theresa May's deal. The Ulster Farmers' Union, Confederation of British Industries (CBI) and other leading groups within civil society in Northern Ireland made it clear that they did not support the DUP's position and urged them to avoid a no-deal Brexit. Some republicans viewed this as a shift in the status quo, with potential implications for the constitutional position of Northern Ireland. Ó Muilleoir later said:

> [It] is unprecedented in my lifetime that twenty-one business groups have united around one political position [in opposition to no-deal]. What I would say is that whatever way Brexit goes – and it's very true if it's a harder Brexit, that the only way back into Europe, the only way to have full European citizenship, is a united Ireland.[59]

By March 2019 over fifty business organisations were publicly arguing in favour of the Withdrawal Agreement, such was their fear of a no-deal alternative.[60]

For these groups, including Ulster Bank and Queen's University Belfast, avoiding a hard Brexit and a border on the island of Ireland was more important than the Backstop issue that would see Northern Ireland being treated differently to the rest of the UK in terms of border regulations. John Manley, political correspondent of the *Irish News*, raised this as a significant new dynamic within Northern Ireland politics and evidence that the normal rules of political gravity no longer applied as clearly as they once did:

> Before Christmas [2018] the divergence between the business community and farmers and the DUP was hugely significant I believe. …I'm no friend of the Ulster Farmer's Union, … but they took an agnostic position on Brexit beforehand, even though there were warnings … and now they are having to reap what they sowed in many ways.[61]

Glyn Roberts, CEO of Retail Northern Ireland, suggested that the main focus of the manufacturing sector and business more broadly, was to minimise the damage of Brexit, with a no-deal scenario being the most destructive.

For us a [Brexit] deal is very much based on remaining in the customs union and the single market, because I don't see all these fantastic trade deals that are there. Whether we get that I don't know, but [we would favour] as soft a Brexit as it possible. ... Hindsight is a wonderful thing, but we've been consistent in our view that Brexit was a mistake. There's no good Brexit, there's only damage limitation.[62]

The DUP's Brexit spokesperson Sammy Wilson was characteristically dismissive of the role of these civil society groups and their attempts to intervene in the political debate concerning the impact of a no-deal Brexit on Northern Ireland. His perspective was that the DUP was not squeezed by those voices outside the party who argued that a no-deal outcome would inflict significant damage to the Northern Ireland economy or political stability in the region:

The question of a no deal has not been a difficult issue for us. We have always believed that a deal was possible and have argued that with the right Prime Minister and determination that a deal could be achieved. The fact that we had a Prime Minister who probably wanted the United Kingdom tied to the EU meant that there was never any real kickback against the EU in the arguments that were made during the negotiations. One of the reasons why we believed a no deal had to be kept on the table so that if Theresa May was not prepared to walk away from the negotiations, whoever succeeded her could. Of course many of the interest groups that you have mentioned ... have sought to stir fears about a no deal, fears which I believe were unfounded and thankfully there is plenty of evidence that the predictions that were made by the remain camp in the past have been nonsense and it is one of the reasons why I believe many people do not even listen to the siren voices of the Ulster Farmers' Union, the CBI and other groups who are unashamedly pro-remain anyhow and one would only expect them to oppose a no deal.[63]

Brexit, allied with the absence of devolved institutions in Belfast, also changed the Northern Ireland political geography significantly. After the 2017 General Election the DUP found itself with a bloc of ten MPs at the epicentre of political debate in the UK and a larger number of MLAs in Northern Ireland waiting to become members of an Assembly that was not operational and a government that would not exist for over two years. As a result, the axis of attention moved from Belfast to London and with it some degree of political authority moved away from Arlene Foster, former First Minister in Northern Ireland and leader of the DUP, and towards Nigel Dodds, leader of the DUP group at Westminster.

The UUP could only watch the leverage exerted by the DUP with envy. Like the SDLP it had had a succession of leaders since the heady days of the GFA in 1998 when it could boast of being the largest party in Northern Ireland. The party had experienced a steady decline since that point, being overtaken by the DUP as the largest unionist party in 2003 and, like the SDLP, it too failed to win any seats at the 2017 General Election. As one seasoned journalist recollected in 2019 – 'The UUP is all over the place unfortunately ... they used to be the party of business, but the DUP have stolen their clothes.'[64]

Steve Aiken, the UUP's Brexit spokesperson [before he was elected as leader of the party in November 2019], remarked on the way in which the party's fortunes had changed since the GFA in 1998 and how history was being rewritten to depict the DUP rather than the UUP as the party that had delivered the peace agreement:

> The speed with which [David] Trimble is being air-brushed out of the narrative is unbelievable. I went to a conference in Boston ... and George Mitchell started off, and it was all 'John Hume this, John Hume that'. And I was the first panellist and someone asked 'what would you like to say about John Hume?' And I said 'two words – David Trimble'.[65]

While it officially supported Remain in the 2016 referendum, the UUP has taken a similar line to the DUP during the Brexit negotiations. It opposed the Withdrawal Agreement on the same basis as the DUP, due to the Backstop treating Northern Ireland differently to the rest of the UK in terms of border checks. This protected the UUP in one respect, preventing it from being damaged by ethnic outbidding and cast by its main unionist rival as being soft on the Union. However, it also prevented the UUP from isolating the DUP as the facilitator of a hard Brexit, which had limited support within Northern Ireland, and for keeping a government in office that might deliver such a damaging outcome. So the UUP aligned itself with the DUP on Brexit and had a much lower profile than its main unionist rival during the entire negotiation period.

Irish government analysis of Brexit and the GFA

In line with most nationalist opinion in Northern Ireland, the Irish government placed the Good Friday Agreement at the centre of its response to the Brexit negotiations and lobbied intensively for the EU also to maintain the integrity of the GFA as a key priority in its negotiations with the UK over its withdrawal from the EU. The Irish government had highlighted the risk to the GFA posed by a Brexit vote back in 2014 in its 'National Risk Assessment' document that flagged the dangers to Ireland's economic and political relationship with the UK if the latter left the EU.[66]

The diplomatic temperature of these demands to protect the GFA and prevent the return of a hard border in Ireland went up a few degrees when Leo Varadkar replaced Enda Kenny as Taoiseach in 2017. However, this owed more to the fact that UK negotiations were stalling with the EU in 2017–18 and a no-deal outcome was becoming more likely, than to a deliberate strategy by Varadkar to take a tougher line on Brexit than his predecessor. Irrespective of this, the Irish government became increasingly publicly agitated by the UK negotiating position during 2018 and the implications of this for the GFA and peace process in Northern Ireland. As a result the political relationship between the two countries became more fraught as the negotiations developed during 2018 and into 2019.

The Irish government developed a 'Brexit Contingency Plan' that was based on four pillars:

1. Intensive engagement with the EU and EU Member States.
2. Contact and consultation with Northern Ireland.
3. Bilateral engagement with the UK.
4. Mitigating effects of Brexit at the domestic level (for example, by using budgetary measures to 'Brexit-proof' the economy).[67]

This seems like a sensible plan under the circumstances, and the first pillar of the strategy has been conducted very successfully. The second pillar has perhaps understandably found greater traction within the nationalist community in Northern Ireland than across unionism. This was certainly true after Leo Varadkar became Taoiseach and Simon Coveney replaced Charlie Flanagan as foreign minister. As the negotiations moved into 2018 and 2019 (and as the UK government fragmented over its Brexit policy), unionists felt that the Irish government was using the Irish Backstop within the Withdrawal Agreement to boost its own internal popularity in the Irish Republic.[68] While the success of the fourth pillar is yet to be tested, the third is probably the one that has been most challenged over the three years from 2016 to 2019. Although successive Irish governments have maintained contact with the UK it has not been an easy relationship. Telling one of your best friends that they are wrong or that they need to change course is never easy – and the Anglo-Irish relationship is some way off BFF status given the troubled history between the two countries. The impact on Northern Ireland and the GFA lay at the centre of this, and as the negotiations developed, Ireland's insistence on legal guarantees (which became the Backstop in the Withdrawal Agreement) over ensuring there would be no hard border in Ireland after Brexit, became the focal point for strained diplomatic relations between the two countries.

The Irish government felt that its British counterpart was not sufficiently prepared to ensure a frictionless border in Ireland in signing up without hesitation to the Backstop element of the Withdrawal Agreement. Brexiteers within the UK, on the other hand, including several leading members of the UK government, felt that the Irish government was 'weaponising' the GFA and the border issue in an attempt to thwart the UK negotiating a deal with the EU.

It is to those strained Anglo-Irish relations, which were so fundamental to the peace process and had made such huge advances since the 1990s, that we must now turn our attention. The two governments were co-guarantors of the GFA and the peace process and their bipartisan relationship was the cement that held it together. Brexit has strained the Anglo-Irish relationship to the point that it is breaking peace in Northern Ireland.

7

From partners to rivals: Anglo-Irish relations after Brexit

[Ireland] is the tail that wags the dog on this and we need to make sure we can do more to build that goodwill in Ireland and build their confidence.

Sajid Javid, UK Home Secretary/candidate for Conservative
Party leader and UK prime minister, 2019[1]

We have opened ourselves to perpetual political blackmail. We have wrapped a suicide vest around the British constitution – and handed the detonator to Michel Barnier.

Boris Johnson, former UK Foreign and Commonwealth
Secretary/candidate for Conservative Party leader and
UK prime minister, 2019[2]

These quotes from senior members of the UK government are just two examples that epitomise the sensitivity surrounding Anglo-Irish relations in recent years. The response in Ireland to both comments across the main political parties and wider public reaction on social media platforms was mostly critical. Comments of this nature became a regular drip-feed during 2018 and 2019 as the Brexit negotiations limped forwards. Many of these comments were either directed at the EU or more commonly at the fractured government and Conservative Party which was at war with itself over how (or even whether) it should leave the EU. The regular diet of poorly received comments from British politicians unnerved policy actors and the wider population in Ireland who interpreted such remarks as evidence of either benign neglect or malign intent. They degraded a relationship – which had reached new levels of warmth and confidence over recent years – to a point where suspicion, frustration and anger became more common traits.

Brexit was the fundamental cause of a more tense atmosphere that has prevailed since the 2016 referendum. There were other factors involved such as personal chemistry between the politicians in Britain and Ireland also playing its part. Theresa May, for instance, did not apparently hit it off with her counterparts in Ireland. Irish journalist and doyen of Brexit-watchers Tony Connelly provided an insight into these relationships when reflecting on Theresa May's resignation announcement in May 2019. The former Prime Minister, he suggested, exhibited little empathy or understanding for Ireland or Europe during her efforts to deliver Brexit:

> 'She didn't have any intuitive feel for the Irish issue,' says one senior British official who worked closely with her. 'None whatever. There was no understanding at the heart of Number 10. There was no even-handedness.' … Mrs May appeared to say all the right things. There should be no return to a hard border, the Common Travel Area should be maintained, and so on. But she would not say how. Nor was there any of the warmth that [Enda] Kenny and David Cameron had enjoyed.[3]

Another Irish journalist, Fintan O'Toole, was typically more withering in his assessment of Theresa May and her inability to persuade her negotiating partners or even her own colleagues to back her Brexit plans:

> The Tories tried to build a personality cult around a woman who doesn't have much of a personality. … The vicar's daughter was woefully miscast as the Robespierre of the Brexit revolution, the embodiment of the British popular will sending saboteurs to the guillotine. She is awkward, wooden, and, as it turned out, prone to panic and indecision under pressure.[4]

These personality dynamics were symptoms of a bigger issue – namely that Brexit suddenly set the UK and Ireland on different journeys to separate destinations (Ireland within the EU single market and customs union and the UK beyond it) when previously they had both been EU member states with similar economic regulatory frameworks and longer-term national interests within the EU. What was compatible on 23 June 2016 suddenly became less so on 24 June and the difficult negotiations since that point have only served to define the interests of the two countries as distinct, rather than overlapping.

At a headline level, the fact that Ireland was going to remain within the EU and that the UK was going to lie beyond it was always going to present challenges. With good will on both sides it would have required skilled statecraft to navigate this shock to the political and economic systems of both countries. In truth, both of these attributes have been lacking on the part of the UK, though Ireland can reasonably claim to have done what it could to coax the British government towards a deal with the EU. Nationalist and unionist opinion is divided on this point, unsurprisingly, with the former tending to see Dublin as doing what it could, given the constitutional proprieties, and viewing the UK as veering between political cynicism and ineptitude. Former SDLP Brexit spokesperson Claire Hanna believed that the Irish government of Leo Varadkar and that of his predecessor Enda Kenny did as much as they could do to maintain good relations with the UK and try to establish an agreed and amicable way forwards.

> I don't really think you could fault the Irish government and particularly anybody with any insight into Irish politics knows that Fine Gael aren't a 'republican' government and aren't an expansionist government in that respect. And I don't see how you could possibly have handled the UK in any different way. And I think they are correct to show some comfort and leadership to Northern nationalists but I think they haven't overstepped the boundary there.[5]

Unionists generally agree with nationalists on the British ineptitude point, but are firmly of the view that the Irish government
have played politics with Brexit – 'Leo and Simon putting on the
green jersey'[6] to curry favour within their domestic electorate. This
is certainly heartfelt among many unionists, but not everyone will
be convinced by the effort to portray the Fine Gael-led government
as an administration that was using Brexit in order to facilitate the
strengthening of Irish nationalist sentiment. Fine Gael has historically
been the least 'green' in the political sense of that colour – the
party of Garret FitzGerald who brokered the Anglo-Irish Agreement
with Margaret Thatcher in 1985 and established a de facto acceptance of Northern Ireland's constitutional integrity regardless of
the wording of the Irish constitution.[7] In more pejorative terms
Fine Gael has been seen by republicans as a party of 'West Brits',
partitionists and right-wing monetarists in Thatcher's image.
Varadkar was of course a much more complex, progressive, cosmopolitan and multi-faceted leader, but anyone trying to paint him
as an Irish nationalist who was weaponising Brexit for ulterior
motives would struggle to convince any apart from core unionist
opinion. Claire Hanna's view was that criticism of Irish government
intransigence over the Backstop within the Withdrawal Agreement
and its role generally in requiring legal assurances on free movement
of goods and people within Ireland was part of a wider blame
narrative around Brexit: 'So when it fails, it is not because it is an
inherently bad idea. It's because of Brussels, or the Remainers, or
the Irish.'[8] Whatever the underpinning reasons, what is clear is
that the relationship between Ireland and the UK has soured
considerably at the political level since 2016 and that Brexit is the
primary cause of that decline.

Ireland and the UK are close neighbours and will continue
being so regardless of the shape that Brexit eventually takes. Political,
economic and cultural relationships might become more complex
once the UK leaves the EU, but they will persevere one way or
another due to the proximity of the two countries, their economic

ties and their shared history. However, the relationship between Britain and Ireland is a complex one, frequently violent and rooted in British colonial decline. Northern Ireland is a symptom of that difficult relationship, as it was created as a direct result of a power struggle between the two countries and the retreat of empire in the early twentieth century. Anglo-Irish relations have waxed and waned between love and hate, friendship and resentment. They have been tempestuous but also vital to political stability in both countries and to peaceful relations between them. The relationship has moved broadly consistently from one of war and bitterness to peace and partnership – and it became a vital foundation for the peace process in Northern Ireland in the 1990s.[9]

It is important to outline some of the twists and turns in the Anglo-Irish relationship in order to understand why Brexit presents such a challenge to relations between the UK and Ireland and in turn why a degraded Anglo-Irish relationship is 'breaking peace' in Ireland.

A troubled past

Northern Ireland media columnist and former communications director of the UUP Alex Kane once wrote, 'the past is always in front of us in Northern Ireland'.[10] It is certainly true that the relationship between the UK and Ireland has never been a straightforward one, not least because the former tried to colonise and subjugate the latter several centuries ago and more recently (merely one century ago) the latter fought and won a violent struggle for independence from its larger and more powerful neighbour. To put it more directly: it is a difficult relationship because for some Irish nationalists who continue to hanker after a thirty-two-county republic, Britain is still occupying part of their country – the 'Fourth Green Field' of Northern Ireland, which is still 'in bondage', in the words of Tommy Makem's 1967 folk song.[11] This song is an Irish nationalist allegory that connects English misdeeds with Irish suffering, political repression and resistance. It finishes with the suggestion that the one field left in bondage (Northern Ireland) will 'bloom once again' in the future.[12]

In historical terms, Ireland and Britain were bound together by their geographical proximity but also forced together by what divided them, not least by conflicting versions of the Christian religion from the sixteenth century onwards. Ireland was a Catholic country – well before its independence from the UK in the twentieth century – while Britain became a Protestant country after the Reformation. Religious differences were of course themselves bound up with politics, economics and the search for power and security. In case this seems like a throwback to a bygone age with little contemporary relevance, the British monarch remains the Defender of the Faith and this has historically been a key pillar of unionist loyalty. The UK constitution is nested within a feudal system led by the monarch – a facet of British democracy that was thrown into sharp relief when Boris Johnson asked the Queen to prorogue parliament in September 2019 in his pursuit of his own Brexit strategy. While casual observers might not always appreciate the significance of the monarch's role as Defender of the Faith and head of UK armed forces, these are central components of unionist iconography. While the DUP has secularised in recent years, under the leadership of Rev. Ian Paisley from the party's formation in the 1960s the Protestantism of the British monarch was a fundamental principle of commitment to the Union and loyalty to the state. Unionists are loyal to the Crown – rather than to the government of the day, a fact underlined by former unionist leader Edward Carson during the Home Rule crisis at the beginning of the twentieth century. Carson, a member of the British cabinet, formed and armed a militia to resist the UK government's Home Rule policy.[13]

Although it is an historical leap forwards, unionists have frequently separated out their loyalty to the Crown and the Union from their loyalty to the UK government.[14] In 1985, Carson was again invoked by unionists in their resistance to the Anglo-Irish Agreement and again by the DUP in its initial opposition to the Good Friday Agreement in 1998. In the context of Brexit it is much easier to understand the position of the DUP on the Irish Backstop element of the Withdrawal Agreement within this historical perspective. For them the Backstop was yet another example of British government perfidy, the sort of expediency demonstrated by Lloyd George in 1912 during the Home Rule crisis, Winston Churchill during the Second World War when he tried to use Northern Ireland to get Irish Free State support for the war effort, Margaret Thatcher when she signed the Anglo-Irish Agreement in 1985 and by Theresa May in 2017–19. To the casual observer in Great Britain, the DUP's seeming obsession about being treated differently from the rest of the UK via the Backstop within the Withdrawal Agreement might have appeared near-pathological bloody-mindedness. However, to the DUP and its supporters, it was part of an historical and political continuum, when it was important to resist a government policy that in their mind threatened the Union and their position within it.

Back in the sixteenth and seventeenth centuries, religion itself became a key divider between the dominant and the dominated sections of society in Ireland, linked to attempts by the Protestant English state to colonise and Anglicise Catholic Ireland. Ireland had resources such as land that could be given in reward for service by the English Crown to its soldiers. Ireland was also a potential security threat to Britain as a launch pad for foreign invasions from Spain and France, and its adherence to Catholicism increased this threat considerably. In this sense, Ireland was a security issue for England, a weak spot that, despite its small size, had the potential to destabilise England politically. The modern parallel with Ireland today is obvious – only this time it is not Spain or France alone that present the problem, but twenty-six other EU member states that together with Ireland have so far brought down two prime ministers and counting.

As a result of the English belief that Ireland was a 'problem' in security terms, resources were confiscated from the 'native' Catholic population during the seventeenth century and given to the newer Protestant community. This was done in a number of ways through a combination of bribery and force, as the English Crown attempted to colonise and control Ireland and thereby enhance its own political and territorial security. The picture was a complicated and uneven one, but there was an inexorable and enormous transfer of land ownership between 1641 and 1703. Catholic ownership fell from around 60% to just 14%, following William's victory over James II and the subsequent 'Act of Settlement'. By the 1750s the figure for Catholic land ownership is estimated to have fallen to around 5%.[15]

Irrespective of their motives for doing so, the English were the architects of a policy designed to subjugate the majority of the Irish population to a degree that has left its mark on both countries. Even within our shared language its traces can be found. For instance, the phrase 'beyond the pale' is part of our shared vernacular, to indicate that someone or something is outside the boundaries of decency or acceptability. To be 'beyond the pale' was to be contemptible, uncivilised and beyond the scope of control. This common contemporary idiom comes directly from the Anglo-Irish relationship, as the Pale referred to a strip of land in Ireland within the security control of the English government. By the fifteenth century this was centred around Dublin. It was the zone of English authority, a safe haven for those loyal to the Crown and the seat of English power in Ireland.

The Irish Famine of 1845–49 represented another low point in the Anglo-Irish relationship. The famine was crucial to the future political history of Ireland for a number of reasons. The resulting exodus from Ireland in the middle of the nineteenth century sowed the seeds of the Irish diaspora, which today is believed to number some 70 million people. While the depth of this ethnic inheritance needs to be treated with caution, large numbers of Irish emigrants went to the United States and Britain and maintained a sense of Irish identity. Given that Ireland's population before 1845 was around 8–9 million, the numbers involved represent a massive social dislocation, and the population to this day has not recovered to pre-famine levels, currently standing at under 7 million in the Irish Republic and Northern Ireland combined.

Over 1 million people left Ireland between 1845 and 1851 and a further 2 million in the subsequent twenty years. Even when the famine was over, the high level of emigration continued, and in the following sixty years an additional 6 million left. The prime destination of the emigrants was overwhelmingly the United States, with approximately 80% choosing to go there.[16] This exodus provided the raw material for the establishment of ethnic networks that remain today, some of which are now lobbying over Brexit and trying to ensure that if the GFA is compromised as a result of a no-deal outcome, the US Congress will block a US trade deal with the UK in retaliation.

More immediately, the famine period left a lasting and visceral grievance within Catholic Ireland against the predominantly Protestant landlord class and against the British in particular, who were seen as callous and vindictive in their treatment of those who starved to death. The Irish Famine might seem like a long time ago to many people in England and not particularly relevant to Brexit or contemporary Anglo-Irish relations. However, for many people in Ireland (and across its diaspora), the past intersects with the present on a regular basis. The famine (like the Home Rule crisis for unionists) is an ever-present part of the political psyche – not an historical artefact that comes and goes.

The Irish nationalist desire for self-government grew from the mid-nineteenth century and evolved into the Home Rule movement.[17] It is difficult to overstate the importance of the 'Home Rule' issue in the development of politics in Ireland in the late nineteenth and early twentieth centuries. It dominated the Anglo-Irish relationship for over fifty years and it also indirectly reframed the British political system: the powers of the House of Lords were curbed in the collateral damage. The 'death by a thousand cuts' nature of the Home Rule policy saw British politicians vacillating between opposition and support for it over a forty-year period, while it took three attempts for legislation to pass through parliament between 1880 to 1914, only to be postponed for another six years by the onset of the First World War. Unionists were left embittered and split by the experience, while the delay in the granting of Home Rule breathed new life into militant republicanism. The period taught unionists to be distrustful of the British government and brought the gun into Irish politics on both unionist and nationalist sides.

The parallel with the Brexit process is clear. Both issues have been massively divisive and dominated the political atmosphere; both led to paralysis within the British parliament and were defined by political pragmatism, with government policy flip-flopping over support and opposition for Home Rule depending on the parliamentary arithmetic. Both were defined by the balance of power at Westminster with the Irish Parliamentary Party playing a similar role in its leverage over the Liberal Party to the role that the DUP had with the Conservative Party over Brexit until Boris Johnson cut them loose after he became prime minister in 2019. Both actions were of course also hugely delayed.

Despite the years that separate these momentous events, Anglo-Irish relations exist on a hair trigger, and the Brexit negotiations have tripped the mechanism for both nationalists and unionists on numerous occasions. The controversy over the Withdrawal Agreement and in particular the aspect popularly known as the 'Irish Backstop' is emblematic of this historical insecurity. The unionist fear was that symbolically this treats Northern Ireland as a special case within the UK – rather than an integral part of it – more like the Falklands than Folkestone. And unionists were acutely aware that today's Gibraltar can become tomorrow's Hong Kong, so they have always been hyper-sensitive about the political symbolism of the special treatment for Northern Ireland implied within the Withdrawal Agreement.

Anglo-Irish relations and the Northern Ireland peace process

While the relationship between Ireland and Britain has not been an easy one, over time it became cordial, even close, and over Northern Ireland in particular it became bipartisan, empathetic and crucial in the journey out of political violence towards dialogue and negotiation in the 1990s.

This phase in Anglo-Irish relations can be traced to the mid-1980s with the signing of the Anglo-Irish Agreement by Irish Taoiseach Garret FitzGerald and British Prime Minister Margaret Thatcher in November 1985. Although it had numerous setbacks, this was a watershed moment in the political relationship between the two countries as they moved from rivals to partners in their approach to the political violence in Northern Ireland. This evolved to the point where the two governments worked together to promote multiparty negotiations in the 1990s and to the Good Friday Agreement in 1998.[18]

The European Union was crucial to the emergence of the Anglo-Irish Agreement in 1985 and to the later developments in the 1990s. The two countries' common membership of the EU provided a forum for them to meet and discuss security and political challenges in Northern Ireland without having to set up specific bilateral meetings – which would inevitably have been politically contentious within the unionist community. As Paul Arthur describes it:

> The European context has reinforced Anglo-Irish contacts through frequent meetings of the respective foreign ministers (and of prime ministers on the margins) as well as, of course, officials. An Irish official on the staff of the European Commission has commented that 'the effects of common United Kingdom and Irish membership of the community and particularly their attitudes to the emerging

community are so great that Anglo-Irish relations can hardly usefully be discussed except in that context.'[19]

EU Summits provided low-key and ready-made opportunities for the civil servants from both countries and the political leaders to get to know each other, iron out misunderstandings and follow up on issues where there was real disagreement between them. The EU and EEC that preceded it was keen to encourage the two countries but was conscious of the need not to interfere politically in Northern Ireland too. There was a recognition of the potential for economic support to evolve into a more direct peacebuilding role in Northern Ireland, and incremental efforts to move in that direction took place via a number of EU initiatives to promote bilateral talks between the UK and Ireland.[20] In essence, the EU regarded Northern Ireland as central to the European mission of reducing violent conflict and enhancing stability within its zone of influence. Although Northern Ireland was formally part of the UK, it was defined as being distinct within the UK for the purposes of economic support (it was defined as being a priority region for EU structural fund assistance for instance).[21]

The EEC publicly supported the 1985 Anglo-Irish Agreement and pledged money to provide political and economic support to it.[22] In the more contemporary context of the Brexit negotiations, and the concern over the Backstop dimension of the Withdrawal Agreement, no one was objecting to Northern Ireland been treated as a special case when it came to money. The two things are not the same, of course: one is about economics and the other is about politics and the constitutional position. There is nonetheless an overlap in the recognition of Northern Ireland's unique circumstances. Northern Ireland was defined as having 'Objective 1 Status' within the European Structural Funds. As Mary C. Murphy points out, this classification was normally reserved for regions that fell below 75% of the average per capita GDP within the EU – which Northern Ireland did not: 'Although Northern Ireland's GDP per capita was above this ceiling throughout the period, the region nevertheless qualified for this assistance on the basis of the so-called "special circumstances" pertaining to the region. This was a reference to the impact of the conflict on Northern Ireland's socio-economic position.'[23] This special status seems to have been forgotten during the discussions over the significance of the Backstop for the constitutional integrity of the Union.

Through the combination of economic support and the provision of its 'good offices' to successive UK and Irish governments, it is certainly true to say that the European Union made a major contribution to Anglo-Irish relations. It oiled the diplomatic wheels between the two countries and facilitated their improving relationship, as evidenced in European support for the Anglo-Irish Agreement in 1985, and its endorsement of the Good Friday Agreement in 1998.

By this point, a level of soft power had been established between the two governments and their respective civil servants, forged in the fires of political initiatives in the preceding eighteen years, when John Major succeeded Margaret Thatcher in 1990 as Conservative Party leader and prime minister. Within Irish nationalism Thatcher was widely reviled as a monster who had watched without mercy as ten republicans died on hunger strike in 1981. While the Anglo-Irish Agreement in 1985 improved the diplomatic relationship with Dublin temporarily, it became internally fractious as Thatcher seemed interested only in the security dimensions of the Agreement and became frustrated at the lack of extradition of suspected IRA members from the Irish Republic to the UK.[24] John Major had none of this baggage, being a pragmatist rather than ideologue, which offered a fresh start for Anglo-Irish relations and for progress in Northern Ireland. The UK and Ireland inched their way towards convening inclusive negotiations during the first half of the 1990s. In part they were pressurised into a joint approach by to the rising scale of violence in Northern Ireland during the early 1990s – and the need to demonstrate that they were in control and had a democratic political alternative to offer. By 1993 the momentum had swung away from the Anglo-Irish relationship to heightened violence in Northern Ireland with the Shankill Road bomb and Greysteel shootings in October/November 1993. Twenty-three people were killed in the space of a week, the television news was filled with condemnations, funerals, grieving relatives and a pervading sense of dread and hopelessness that things were getting worse rather than better.

Also by 1993 it had become public knowledge that SDLP leader John Hume and Sinn Féin president Gerry Adams had been holding face-to-face meetings periodically since 1988, mediated by Catholic priest Fr Alec Reid at Clonard Monastery in Belfast. These discussions took place without the knowledge of London or Dublin (or many others within the SDLP or Sinn Féin) and became known as the Hume/Adams talks. The two leaders reportedly exchanged documents and referred to their discussions as the 'Irish Peace Initiative'.[25] This frightened the unionist community into thinking that political change was imminent and that the British government was in cahoots with what they began referring to as the 'Pan-Nationalist Front'. They were not, and John Major and his Irish counterpart became frustrated that others were setting the political agenda.

In another parallel with the Brexit period, in 1993 Major led a government that was chronically divided over Europe and, as time went on, he increasingly needed the support of unionist MPs in the House of Commons. The Irish government, SDLP and the Provisional IRA were very aware of Major's position and this complicated the Anglo-Irish relationship. In the end it boiled down to whether the Irish side could trust the British to act in good faith over key declarations such as Secretary of State Peter Brooke's announcement in November 1990 that the UK had 'no selfish strategic or economic interest' in Northern Ireland.[26] This statement had become a foundation for the gradual shift in militant republican thinking and across more mainstream Irish nationalist opinion:

that the UK might be prepared to consider constitutional change. The ability to trust also relied on the British side believing that Irish Taoiseach Albert Reynolds was equally committed to securing a ceasefire from the IRA and improving the security situation, without pushing the UK towards an overtly nationalist agenda. A bad-tempered Anglo-Irish summit took place in Dublin, where both Major and Reynolds haggled over the terms of a joint statement.

> They shouted and they swore at one another (Major banging his fist on the table and breaking his pencil in frustration, Reynolds threatening to walk out before lunch had even been served). However, their frank exchanges seemed to have a cathartic effect as the two sides eventually calmed down and came to the conclusion that they could move forwards together. When asked afterwards for a summary of the meeting Reynolds told a colleague: 'Well, he chewed the bollocks off me, but I took a few lumps out of him.'[27]

The point here in the context of Brexit is that such disagreements took place in private rather than in the public gaze during the 1990s, and during the Blair years relations with Dublin were warmer still; disagreements were kept away from the cameras and a united front was usually put on public display.

The idea that members of the cabinet would disavow their own government policy, or suggest that the Irish were a tail wagging the British dog, would have been unthinkable before Brexit. Since 2016 the drip-feed about Irish government mendacity over the Backstop element of the Withdrawal Agreement has been exacerbated by the feuding within the Conservative Party and its frustration born out of its own political ineptitude. Boris Johnson's comment at the beginning of this chapter that the Backstop (and wider Withdrawal Agreement) represented a suicide vest around the British constitution was perhaps the most vivid example of this form of Anglo-bombast between the two countries. As is typical of Johnson (as with President Trump), his comments divided opinion – but got people talking about him. His former colleague at the Foreign

Office Alan Duncan said the remarks were 'disgusting' and, perhaps rather prematurely, announced Johnson's political demise: 'I'm sorry, but this is the political end of Boris Johnson. If it isn't now, I will make sure it is later.'[28]

Trust between London and Dublin in the good faith of the other had been the lifeblood of the peace process. It got both sides through difficult periods and was crucial to the establishment of the paramilitary ceasefires in 1994 and the signing of the GFA in 1998. That trust has ebbed away since the Brexit referendum result in 2016 and it is 'breaking peace' in Northern Ireland.

Anglo-Irish relations before Brexit

Just a few years ago, how different everything looked. Before Brexit had emerged as a serious issue, Anglo-Irish relations were at an historic highpoint. At the political level, the UK and Ireland had successfully wrangled a peace process in the 1990s, and a succession of politicians from both countries had put their collective shoulders to the wheel and turned it, to a cacophony of international applause and celebration. Prime ministers and other politicians from both countries took huge risks with their core supporters (and one another) in order to further the peace process and political agreement within Northern Ireland. Albert Reynolds supported Gerry Adams being given visas to the United States despite strong opposition from the UK. The late Mo Mowlam (Northern Ireland Secretary of State during the multiparty talks in 1997–98) visited loyalist prisoners in the Maze, to ask them to continue with their support for the talks – an action taken on her own initiative without getting Prime Minister Tony Blair's prior approval.[29] Blair himself took a political risk by engaging in direct talks with Sinn Féin shortly after becoming prime minister in 1997 – to the consternation of the unionist community and even to his own senior allies such as Peter Mandelson.

Without the foundation of trust and mutual recognition of one another's good faith – built up over a thirty-year period from the

Anglo-Irish Agreement in 1985 until Cameron's kamikaze Brexit run in 2015 – the GFA would probably have had a significantly shorter lifespan.

The improving Anglo-Irish relationship was visible in a broader social context as well as in the formal political sphere, not least in the sporting arena, when Ireland hosted England in the Six Nations rugby tournament in February 2007. This was no ordinary game and was invested with huge political and historical significance as it was to be played in Croke Park due to renovation work being carried out at Irish rugby's home stadium, known then as Lansdowne Road – rebadged now as the Aviva Stadium. Croke Park was the home of the Gaelic Athletic Association (GAA), a sporting body steeped in Irish nationalism. As ever, the occasion was overlaid with historical resonance. British soldiers had entered Croke Park in 1920 during a GAA game between Dublin and Tipperary and shot indiscriminately into the crowd, killing fourteen people, yet in 2007 the English National Anthem 'God Save the Queen' rang out loud and proud as both teams lined up.[30] Given the history it was quite something that this took place with minimal protests. It was emblematic of improving Anglo-Irish relations and would have been impossible without political agreement in Northern Ireland and the security that went along with that.

The existence of the GFA and stability provided by devolved government in Northern Ireland allowed other things to happen. They provided a degree of space within the political system for conflict parties to move a little from their ethnocentric positions. The warmth in Anglo-Irish relations and political stability in Northern Ireland allowed the Queen to visit the Irish Republic in a way that would not have been feasible during the political conflict. This four-day event on 17–20 June 2011 was hugely symbolic and the first time that a serving British monarch had visited independent Ireland. The visit would not have taken place without the GFA and was widely seen as a Rubicon-crossing for both countries in dealing with their troubled past.

The Queen laid a wreath and bowed her head at the Garden of Remembrance in Dublin at the graves of the old IRA who had fought against Britain for Irish independence in the early twentieth century. She gave a keynote speech which attempted to draw a line under the past and mark a new beginning between the two countries. Irish President Mary MacAleese pointed to a positive future for both countries: '[A] new future, a future very, very different from the past, on very different terms from the past – and I think the visit will send the message that we are, both jurisdictions, determined to make the future a much, much better place.'[31] These words seemed entirely appropriate at the time but they ring a little hollow now after three years of difficult Brexit negotiations and recrimination between the two countries over who is responsible for the crisis that has resulted.

Anglo-Irish relations after Brexit

Let me also make one thing absolutely clear – Ireland will be on the EU side of the table when the negotiations begin.

Taoiseach Enda Kenny, February 2017[32]

I am a little bit concerned that some people in London seem to think that because the House of Commons failed to ratify that [Withdrawal] agreement that automatically means they are going to get a better one. ... That is a terrible political miscalculation.

Taoiseach Leo Varadkar, June 2019[33]

The Irish government sought to calm nerves in its initial response to the outcome of the 2016 referendum. The following day, Irish Taoiseach Enda Kenny issued a series of holding statements, while pointing out that no instant changes to people's lives or to business arrangements would take place in the short term. The implications of the result would thus 'require careful consideration' by the Irish government as an urgent priority but there would 'be no immediate change to the free flow of people, of goods and of services between our islands'.[34] In contrast to its UK counterpart, the Irish government quickly rebooted after the referendum to intensify its lobbying activities within the EU in Brussels and its charm offensive across key EU member states.[35]

While the first reaction from Dublin following the referendum was a containment strategy, to avoid panic in the economy and buy time to adjust to the new Brexit reality, there was a noticeable hardening of the Irish government's public position as the negotiations progressed – or, more accurately, as time progressed, as the negotiations got nowhere for a considerable time. Also, the minority administration of Leo Varadkar that led Ireland when the Brexit process moved into its latter stages in 2018 and 2019 took a more forceful line in response to the UK negotiating position than under his predecessor Enda Kenny. In May 2018, the Taoiseach outlined the uncompromising timeline that would be acceptable to Ireland:

> By June we need to see substantial progress as the tánaiste [Varadkar's deputy, Simon Coveney] and I have said on many occasions. The European council will review progress in June. The deadline of course for the withdrawal agreement is October, but if we are not making real and substantial progress by June then we need to seriously question whether we're going to have a withdrawal agreement at all.[36]

As outlined above, Brexiteers and the main unionist parties in Northern Ireland interpreted this hardening as an unnecessary and cynical attempt by the Irish government to use Brexit to boost its domestic support. Nationalists in Northern Ireland viewed it in much more benign terms – as a result of UK ineptitude in its handling of the negotiations and a response to what was assumed to be a hard deadline of 29 March 2019 when the UK was scheduled to leave the EU.

Irish political nerves were shredded due mainly to the chaos within the UK negotiating team, the inability of the UK for most of the period to define a clear Brexit strategy that was capable of meeting its own rhetorical commitments to the Common Travel

Area and to keeping a hard border out of Ireland. It became increasingly clear that UK Brexit policy was dominated by a civil war within the UK government that was itself a symptom of divisions within the Tory Party that had destroyed previous UK Prime Minister David Cameron and John Major before him. By the mid-1990s, Major, like May, was beholden to unionist MPs at Westminster for his political survival. As Major's frail administration drifted towards its inevitable electoral defeat at the 1997 General Election, it shared another trait with Theresa May's administration. It became an untrustworthy negotiating partner, a government incapable of acting in good faith, a government unable to sell a deal even if it could reach an internal consensus for one. This lack of trust infected the peace process in the mid-1990s and was one of the reasons why the Provisional IRA ceasefire broke down in February 1996. The conclusion reached by the IRA was that Major was not motivated to act as an 'honest broker' because his government was being held hostage by unionists in parliament and he needed their support for political survival. The parallel with May's reliance on the DUP after the 2017 General Election is striking – though in her case it was DUP votes that kept her life-support machine bleeping.

Weak negotiators are bad negotiators, and while it is *desirable* that there is a personal rapport established between the sides involved in a negotiation, it is *essential* that they believe that any agreements that are made can be sold and delivered by all parties to those negotiations. By the time of the 2017 UK General Election, when Theresa May's government lost its majority and returned to power in a confidence-and-supply agreement with the DUP, it was clear that her government could not deliver a Brexit policy that was capable of negotiating the UK's exit from the EU while protecting political and economic interests in Ireland – principally stability in Northern Ireland and the integrity of the GFA.

Perhaps the most emblematic evidence for this UK incapacity was provided on 4 December 2017, when a breakthrough was reached between the UK and EU on the Irish border issue and a press conference speedily arranged between Prime Minister May and Jean-Claude Juncker, President of the European Commission. As described above in Chapter 5, during lunch, Theresa May put a call through to DUP leader Arlene Foster, who informed her that the DUP would not support the deal and would vote against it. To be fair to Foster and her party, they had been entirely consistent about their 'blood-red' line – that Northern Ireland had to leave the EU in same way as the rest of the UK. May misunderstood the importance of this principle to the DUP and continued to do so over the next two years. She had to return to the dinner table after her phone call and tell Juncker than the deal was off and returned to the UK empty handed. While she scrabbled around to see what could be done to placate the DUP, her critics were unforgiving about her mismanagement of the whole fiasco.

The episode provides an excellent case study of how not to negotiate. Start with a weak leader and a divided party, add a confused set of core objectives, agree to a text that you are not in a position to deliver on, reach an agreement with your main opponents and raise their expectations that you are primed to conclude a deal on those terms, then abandon your position at the last minute, leaving your negotiating partners dangling.

Irish Taoiseach Leo Varadkar reacted curtly to the diplomatic shambles that unfolded in December 2017 and made the unvarnished point that it was difficult to expedite a negotiating process if the other party could not be relied upon to hold its own end of the deal together: 'The responsibility of any prime minister is to ensure that they can follow through on agreements that they make and we are surprised and disappointed that they haven't been able to.'[37]

Irish diplomacy maintained a polite but firm line with the UK to the effect that the aspirations to maintain the CTA and ensure the absence of a border in Ireland after Brexit were laudable – but that such commitments needed legal certainty. This was combined with a consistent message that it was the EU that was negotiating with the UK – not Ireland, or any of the other twenty-six member states. This was certainly the formal position but it seemed clear that the EU and member states put a lot of store by what Ireland said with respect to the integrity of the GFA and the need for a legally binding backstop to ensure that a hard border would not be needed in Ireland. The demand for a legally enforceable guarantee became a matter of faith for Ireland and the EU as the negotiations progressed – in part because it was clear that the UK seemed unable to abide by the commitments that it made. This became obvious once the Backstop issue moved from being a political to a legal agreement. While many Brexiteers felt that the EU and Irish government were being too rigid over their demands for a legally enforceable guarantee, the more the UK looked for alternative arrangements to the Backstop that did not need to be legally binding, the more it entrenched the view in Brussels and Dublin that any agreement needed to be legally watertight.

Theresa May was duly stretched on a rack made of her own red lines and the incompatibility of these lines with her commitments to avoiding a border in Ireland. As a result she tacked politically from one day to the next, telling people what they wanted to hear and saying whatever she needed to in order to survive. Yet she ended up in an impossible trilemma – where she made promises in three incompatible directions.

A solution would either disappoint the Brexiteers (if the UK essentially remained in the single market or customs union), the unionists in Northern Ireland (if a border was placed in the Irish Sea) or Irish nationalist opinion (if there was any semblance of a north–south border). It was all bound to come tumbling down on May due to the central incompatibilities of her Brexit policy – like the denouement of a bedroom farce, when everyone who has been walking through doors and just missing each other finally all come through together and realise the colossal misunderstanding that caused so much comedy. Sadly for Theresa May, at the end of her Brexit run, there were only tears and the cold realisation of her own failure.

By early 2019 the UK government began eating itself alive in full public view, to the horror of those in Ireland and the EU who were desperately trying to negotiate a deal and help the poor victim of auto-cannibalism from consuming itself. By the beginning of 2019 the UK government had entered a zombie phase; such was the weakness and the deadlock within it that no faction had the capacity to prevail in terms of setting a direction on Brexit and specifically on the Withdrawal Agreement, and so political coherence could not be established and decisions could not be made.

Theresa May's government limped on from January to June 2019 in this state, unable to recover, but unable to die a natural death either. In normal political times, Theresa May would have been likely to resign or have been pushed out of power before she dramatically announced her resignation in June, but Brexit had produced some extraordinary political dynamics in the UK and the normal principles of political gravity were suspended. By the spring of 2019 collective cabinet responsibility had largely gone, the Prime Minister's authority had crumbled, both in parliament and in her government, and the UK became politically rudderless. Ministers felt at liberty to abstain or even vote against their own government and not resign. Famously in the case of Brexit Secretary Stephen Barclay, he advocated the extension of Article 50 at the dispatch box in the House of Commons in a key debate in February 2019 and urged his parliamentary colleagues to 'act in the national interest', then promptly voted against his own motion – while staying in his job. The Prime Minister seemed unable to sack, or publicly censure, her cabinet colleagues for indiscipline, and her own MPs felt able to call publicly for her to resign. When Theresa May did eventually sack a member of her cabinet, the story had something of a 'man bites dog' element to it, so blunted was her authority. Gavin Williamson, the upwardly mobile Defence Secretary, was dismissed for allegedly leaking a cabinet discussion linked to the security dimensions of Chinese company Huawei being given the contract for the next phase of the UK's 5G mobile phone development. Williamson, the former chief whip, who had been central to the negotiation of the confidence-and-supply deal with the DUP, strenuously denied the allegation that he had been the source of the leak.[38] May's anti-Midas touch was so all-encompassing by this stage that she could not even sack him properly – doing so on the eve of the local council elections and ensuring that the headlines when people went to the polls were negative ones about government division and strife rather than positive stories about Tory candidates' plans for the local area.

Ireland watched this descent of the UK government into incoherent futility with a mixture of frustration, concern and pity. But at times the frustration on the UK side reminded people in Ireland that its parlous position could result in some baser political instincts rising to the surface of political debate.

Noises off

Theresa May's memoirs of her time as prime minister should be well worth reading if she can bear to write them (it would require her to revisit a painful litany of failure and humiliation). In truth she was a poor leader, lacking in empathy or the ability to communicate and develop a soft power relationship that could convince people to support her.

Back in December 2018, former cabinet minister Priti Patel came under sustained attack from a number of sides within Ireland and Britain for suggesting that the UK could make more of the difficulties Ireland would face in a no-deal Brexit scenario as a way of leveraging a better deal. Commenting on a leaked UK government report that suggested Ireland's GDP would drop by 7% and that Irish trade in perishable goods would be hit particularly hard in a no-deal Brexit outcome, Patel said: 'This paper appears to show the Government was well aware Ireland will face significant issues in a no-deal scenario. Why hasn't this been pressed home during the negotiations? There is still time to go back to Brussels and get a better deal.'[39] While she did not explicitly refer to food, the febrile atmosphere between the UK and Ireland caused by the Brexit negotiations led many to connect this to the Irish Famine of 1845–49 when over 1 million people starved to death in Ireland and another several million emigrated. The whiff of UK politicians exploiting economic hardships in Ireland for political gain triggered memories of the past that are hard-wired into the Irish political psyche, even though they are largely invisible to people in GB. Sinn Féin MP Chris Hazzard connected Patel's remarks to the famine and claimed it was indicative of the malign intent of those within the Brexit project and their disregard for the negative impact it would have in Ireland. Her comment, he said:

> exposes the Brexiteer attitude to Ireland as nothing more than a colonial irritant whose rights really shouldn't be taken into account. … They know the history of the Irish famine and Britain's role in it, and the very fact that they would seek to inject that into the Brexit debate is crass and offensive … The Tories couldn't care less about the impact of their reckless Brexit agenda on the people and economy of Ireland. We are simply collateral damage.[40]

Hazzard was not alone in this reading of Patel's remarks and similar sentiments were expressed within the SDLP and by commentators across the Irish Republic as well as her political critics in Great Britain. Stewart MacDonald, the SNP MP, attacked Patel for her willingness to threaten Ireland with food shortages in light of its historical experience: 'It's a particularly cruel and historically illiterate type that would think to threaten a friendly neighbouring country that saw 1 million of its citizens die as a result of famine – and a further 1 million to emigrate – with modern-day food shortages. A deeply ugly side of Brexit.'[41]

While she did not actually refer to the Irish Famine or even to food shortages per se, it was the motivation behind Patel's remarks and link to perishable goods (food being the main one) that gave them their political traction. The episode provides a small vignette of the decline in Anglo-Irish relations that Brexit had produced since 2016. But it also indicates why it is impossible to understand the impact of Brexit on Anglo-Irish relations without some knowledge of the historical lens through which the contemporary relationship is being played out. Patel herself comes from the British-Indian community, so it is even more surprising that she should have displayed such a tin ear to the echoes of Britain's colonial past, given Britain's historical relationship with that part of its former empire.

Previously, such a remark would have been brushed off as individual aberration, a crass and ignorant intervention, but nothing more. But the Brexit negotiations had sucked political trust out of the Anglo-Irish relationship to a remarkable degree since 2106, to the point where the comment had a more powerful impact. There was a feeling that Patel spoke for a sizeable proportion of Brexiteers and in policy terms demonstrated yet again why the UK's word on its post-Brexit intentions over the Irish border could not be relied upon. Both the EU negotiators and the Irish government became increasingly frustrated by the UK's shifting position on Brexit and its tendency to use aspirational language that fell some way short of its actions. This obviously came to a head over the Backstop aspect of the Withdrawal Agreement between the UK government and the EU – which remained unratified by the House of Commons.

It was a toxic mix as the negotiations moved forwards and the UK and Irish governments became weaker. While Varadkar is portrayed in the UK media as a smooth and confident politician with an able deputy in Foreign Minister Simon Coveney, in reality they led a minority government like their British counterpart Theresa May. One key difference, however, was that Varadkar had over-whelming support in Ireland for his position on the Backstop and the need for a legally binding guarantee on arrangements relating to the Irish border.

The Anglo-Irish relationship has not yet deteriorated to the level of Winston Churchill's often frosty interaction with his Irish counterpart Eamon de Valera in the 1940s, but there is clear concern about the direction of travel and that Brexit has been a catalyst for a significant deterioration. In April 2019, Ireland's ambassador to Great Britain, Adrian O'Neill, took the unusual step of writing an open letter to the *Spectator* magazine to complain about the tone of its coverage of Ireland over recent years. The *Spectator* is located firmly on the right of the political spectrum (a previous editor was Boris Johnson) but it is an influential publication that can drive the news agenda in the UK, along with similar periodicals such as the *Economist* and the *New Statesman*. O'Neill is an urbane, intelligent and cultured diplomat, Ireland's top representative in the UK and the voice of the Irish government in Britain. For him to intervene so publicly was a highly undiplomatic move – regardless of the eloquence with which he made his point. While his complaint to the editor focused on one particular article that had suggested that Ireland should rejoin the British Commonwealth after Brexit, he alluded to a more systemic anti-Irish sentiment within the UK.

> I am not unduly thin skinned but, over the last couple of years, the prevailing tone and tenor of most *Spectator* articles relating to Ireland have been snide and hostile – Robert Hardman's polemical piece about Ireland's observer status at La Francophonie being an egregious example. … Brexit has undeniably placed some pressure on British–Irish relations. Nevertheless most British people I meet understand the rationale underlying the Irish Government approach to Brexit, a policy which enjoys cross-party support in our parliament and across public opinion in Ireland. In a minority of cases criticism of that approach here has lapsed into an anti-Irish sentiment which we all hoped had been consigned to the past.[42]

This intervention was not a solo run by Ambassador O'Neill or written in anger or without careful consideration of its impact and implications. The fact that he felt obliged to write it demonstrates the extent to which relations had declined since the Brexit negotiations began.

In terms of how the Anglo-Irish relationship develops from this point onwards, it depends largely on a number of factors within UK politics. A deal and an orderly Brexit with a lengthy transition period is likely to prove the least damaging option, with at least some time to work through the economic impacts of the UK's departure. A no-deal Brexit, and a more compressed timeline to make adjustments at political and economic levels – with the obvious implications for the Irish border, the GFA, and political stability in Northern Ireland – is more likely to degrade the Anglo-Irish relationship further. A no-deal outcome remains a possibility at the end of 2020 regardless of the passing of the Withdrawal Agreement Bill and the UK's formal departure from the EU on 31 January.

Any Brexit is likely to do damage because it recalibrates the political and economic interests of the two countries. Like two ocean liners that have been sailing in parallel on their long European journey, one of them is now slowly deviating. At the moment this is barely perceptible, as countries (like ocean liners) take some time to turn around. Over time, however, the two ships are likely to move apart from one another quite considerably. The problem with this is that Northern Ireland sits like a little tug boat between them, with ropes across to each of the larger sister ships. At the risk of strangling this nautical metaphor, this is fine so long as both of the larger ships move in parallel; once they begin to diverge, however, the ropes stabilising the tug boat will be stretched to breaking point and will eventually rip off and destabilise the smaller boat. Brexit will inevitably cause HMS GB to change its direction over time and this is likely to damage the prospects for political stability in Northern Ireland.

Aside from the UK not being able to present itself as a non-partisan co-guarantor of the GFA and wider peace process in Northern Ireland, a more distant Anglo-Irish relationship is likely to prevail. This is likely to make it more difficult for any future problems within Northern Ireland's devolved institutions to be assisted by a bipartisan approach from the two governments. A resumption of the Anglo-Irish relationship prior to the entry of Britain and Ireland into the EEC in 1973 is more likely in the medium term: a formal, arm's-length relationship, without the soft power capacity that existed at the height of the peace process.

This is not good news for either country, but is particularly worrying for those who believe what is patently obvious – Brexit is 'breaking peace' in Northern Ireland.

Epilogue: Brexit – do or die?

When I first started planning this book and for most of the time I spent writing it, I envisaged the *Breaking peace* title as a question. Having come to the end of writing, my punctuation has changed and it has moved from being a question to a statement. Brexit is breaking peace in Northern Ireland and this is already happening – irrespective of where the Brexit train finally stops in the years ahead. The final denouement will certainly be a crucial moment for the UK, its European neighbours and both parts of Ireland, but the journey to this point has given life to Brexit in terms of traumatising the political debate in Northern Ireland and the people who live there.

I am writing this just after the 31 October deadline for a Brexit deal between the UK and the EU, which itself was an extension of the original 29 March date when the UK was scheduled to have formally left the European Union. The temperature rose significantly after Boris Johnson succeeded Theresa May as prime minister in the summer of 2019; his 'Brexit do or die' mantra stretched the UK constitution to breaking point, stress-testing the separation of powers between the executive, the legislature, the courts and even the role of the monarch within the UK's political system. In the end Johnson was not able to 'do Brexit' by 31 October as he had promised – though he was able to claim that he had renegotiated a deal with the European Union by the deadline but was thwarted by opponents in parliament.

The Johnson denouement

With some predictability, Boris Johnson was victorious in the Conservative leadership race in July 2019, beating his cabinet colleague Jeremy Hunt comfortably and thus, like his predecessor, he automatically became prime minister of the UK. While he thanked Theresa May for her service to the country, it was clear from the outset that he was going to try to bulldoze his way to a renegotiated Brexit deal that eliminated the Irish border Backstop roadblock.

He deployed four main tactics to do this. Firstly using the 'gift' of his personality, a charm offensive that was simultaneously optimistic and belligerent, and this was the tone set as early as his acceptance speech as Tory Party leader on 23 July when posing himself a rhetorical question about the chances of getting a Brexit deal with the EU and leaving by the planned date of 31 October:

> I think we know we can do it and the people of this country are trusting us to do it and we know that we will do it. ... We are going to get Brexit done on 31 October, we are going to take advantage of all the opportunities that it will bring in a new spirit of can-do. And we are once again going to believe in ourselves and what we can do and like some slumbering giant we are going to rise and ping off the guy ropes of self-doubt and negativity.[1]

His second tactic was ruthless control over his parliamentary party, his government and especially his cabinet, which was treated with a distain that would have made Margaret Thatcher blanche. Opposition to his Brexit policy and its ambitious timeline was fiercely eradicated by his chief adviser Dominic Cummings, the mastermind of the Vote Leave campaign in 2016. Johnson's approach was outlined the day he took over as prime minister in a speech that was simultaneously outcome focused while also full of his trademark convivial-sounding bluster.

> The doubters, the doomsters, the gloomsters – they are going to get it wrong again. The people who bet against Britain are going to lose their shirts because we are going to restore trust in our democracy and we are going to fulfil the repeated promises of parliament to the people and come out of the EU on October 31. No ifs or buts and we will do a new deal, a better deal that will maximise the opportunities of Brexit while allowing us to develop a new and exciting partnership with the rest of Europe.[2]

Johnson's third tactic was to play hardball with his European colleagues in Brussels over the necessity of reopening the Withdrawal Agreement and removing its Backstop element or face the UK leaving the EU without a deal. While claiming in September 2019, on his first visit to Dublin as prime minister, that a no-deal Brexit would amount to a 'failure of statecraft',[3] he gave the impression of spending more time preparing for a no-deal outcome than of presenting detailed alternative proposals that would be legally enforceable, as requested by his negotiating partners in Brussels. Johnson used Cummings as his political attack-dog, creating the impression that – as he said himself – he would 'rather be dead in a ditch' than request an extension to Brexit beyond the scheduled exit date of 31 October 2019.[4]

As relations between Leavers and Remainers hit rock bottom within the UK parliament and outside it, Johnson seemed prepared to push the UK constitution to breaking point, by proroguing parliament and withdrawing the Tory whip from twenty-one Conservative Party MPs who voted with the opposition in an attempt to prevent the UK from leaving the EU without a deal on 31 October. This effort to discipline his MPs who voted for what became known as the Benn Act risked destroying not only his own government but also the Conservative Party itself, as stalwarts of the party such as former Chancellors Ken Clarke and Philip

Hammond, former Attorney General Dominic Grieve and the grandson of Winston Churchill, Nicolas Soames, were all summarily relieved of their membership of a party that they had served with distinction for many decades. The Speaker of the House of Commons, meanwhile, was effectively marched out of the chamber against his will on 10 September, declaring the decision to prorogue parliament to be 'an act of Executive fiat'.[5]

At a stroke, Johnson had plunged his government into crisis with a minority of over forty – making it difficult to pass legislation or deliver on other aspects of the government's legislative programme. His attempt to prorogue parliament in September 2019 even dragged the Queen into politics. Gina Miller's legal case was unanimously supported by the eleven-judge Supreme Court panel, in effect humiliating Johnson and his government for making the Queen give Royal Assent to a Bill that was unlawful. After a three-day hearing, the Supreme Court quashed the legislation and in a withering verdict, Lady Hale, president of the court, declared that it was as if it had never happened:

> This court has … concluded that the prime minister's advice to Her Majesty [to suspend parliament] was unlawful, void and of no effect. This means that the order in council to which it led was also unlawful, void and of no effect [and] should be quashed. This means that when the royal commissioners walked into the House of Lords [to prorogue parliament] it was as if they walked in with a blank sheet of paper. The prorogation was also void and of no effect. Parliament has not been prorogued. … Unless there is some parliamentary rule of which we are unaware, they can take immediate steps to enable each house to meet as soon as possible.[6]

Despite this episode – or perhaps because of it – with the Benn Act requiring him legally to ask Brussels for an extension to Article 50 if he was unable to reach a deal with the EU before the scheduled European Summit on 17 October, Johnson deployed his fourth and final tactic. This amounted to conceding the very thing that he had previously said no government could ever do, namely allowing Northern Ireland to have different customs arrangements from the rest of the UK and accepting a border in the Irish Sea between Great Britain and Northern Ireland. In his desperation for a deal with the EU, Johnson had finally decided to cut the unionists loose and try to win over enough support at Westminster to ratify the deal, even without the support of the DUP.

Meeting with Varadkar

It seemed unlikely that Johnson's government would be able to reach a deal with the Brussels negotiators and the other twenty-seven members of the European Union before the October deadline. However, to his credit, Johnson did, as he had said he would, renegotiate Theresa May's Withdrawal Agreement with the EU, get rid of the Irish border Backstop and line up a mechanism to enable the UK to leave the EU as foretold on 31 October 2019. Viewed through one lens it seemed to be a diplomatic triumph for Johnson that he managed this. However, it was hardly a masterstroke, as he did it by effectively caving in to the position that the EU had outlined since the negotiations had begun. There would not be a hard border in Ireland and the integrity of the single market and the Good Friday Agreement were sacrosanct. A last-ditch meeting with Irish Taoiseach Leo Varadkar at a hotel outside Liverpool on 10 October saw a palpable change in tone, which signalled to the EU that Johnson had changed his position and that final negotiations in 'the tunnel' could produce a deal:

> I think sometimes at this point in negotiations and discussions, the less said the better. But what I can say is that I had a very good meeting today with the prime minister and our teams together – very positive and very promising. I am now absolutely convinced that both Ireland and Britain want there to be an agreement. ... I do see a pathway towards an agreement in the coming weeks.[7]

Johnson had signed up to most of Theresa May's Withdrawal Agreement, which he had condemned months earlier. He had managed to replace the Backstop with a solution that would effectively leave Northern Ireland aligned with the EU in terms of customs regulations and he had signed up to a permanent situation of a border in the Irish Sea that recognised the unique circumstances of Northern Ireland. In effect, this would mean that Northern Ireland would not be leaving the EU on the same terms as the rest of the United Kingdom, as previously advertised. Proving that a year is a long time in politics, Johnson did in 2019 precisely what he said 'no British government could or should' ever do, when speaking to the DUP conference less than twelve months earlier.[8]

The Prime Minister had effectively thrown his DUP allies under the proverbial bus, much to their anguish and anger. Unsurprisingly the DUP quickly found itself abandoned by erstwhile Tory allies at Westminster, including the self-styled 'Spartans' within the European Research Group who had previously been at one with their DUP colleagues over Theresa May's version of the Withdrawal Agreement. The ancient fears of unionists had been realised once again as they felt their loyalty to the UK was being thrown back in their faces when it was expedient for the government to do so – as it had been after the Anglo-Irish Agreement in 1985, after the prorogation of the majority-rule Stormont parliament in 1972 and during the Home Rule crisis at the beginning of the twentieth century.

The Withdrawal Agreement Bill

Johnson had his deal, so it was back to the process of getting it ratified through parliament, with the House of Commons being recalled to sit on a Saturday for the first time since 1982, when Argentina invaded the Falkland Islands. Dubbed Super Saturday by the English media, when there would at last be a final yes/no decision on the Brexit deal, it turned out in classic Brexit form to be anything but. An amendment by former Tory MP Oliver Letwin was passed by 322 votes to 30, withholding parliamentary approval for the deal until the full Withdrawal Agreement Bill had been debated and passed by parliament. Under the terms of the Benn Act the Prime Minister was thus legally obliged to request an extension to Brexit from the European Union – which he begrudgingly did. It was not Brexit do or die after all.

So yet again the Brexit deadline was missed. Johnson, like May before him, seemed incapable of getting a Brexit deal ratified in the UK parliament while everyone blamed one another for the political inertia that continued to define the UK. 31 October 2019 came and went and at the end of it the UK was still in the EU, to a mix of relief and exasperation on the part of the other twenty-seven EU countries. The Brexit alarm clock was reset to 31 January 2020, an extension to the extension, and the main parties in the UK voted to have a General Election on 12 December 2019 – the first winter election in the UK since 1923.

At the time of writing (October 2019), the election campaign has barely got going – but it will undoubtedly be seen as the Brexit election, as this issue was the reason that it was called in the first place and it has been Brexit that has torn the political fabric of the UK apart since the 2017 election.

A number of scenarios are conceivable after the dust settles on the 12 December election result. If the Conservative Party wins a reasonable majority within the House of Commons, it is likely that the existing deal negotiated by Johnson and the EU will finally be ratified in the UK parliament and the UK will leave the EU on or before 31 January 2020. If Labour manages to confound the opinion polls and form a government, it is likely that it will try to negotiate a deal quickly that keeps the UK closer to the EU – what is popularly called Brexit In Name Only – and will put that to a confirmatory referendum, including the possibility of revoking

Article 50 and remaining within the EU. The outcome of such a referendum is difficult to predict, but it is likely that if Brexit was revoked there would be continued political unrest in the UK from those who voted Leave in 2016.

If the result of the 12 December election is another hung parliament, then we are likely to face further political convulsions within UK politics – with a no-deal hard Brexit remaining a possible outcome. As this book has demonstrated, in all of these scenarios, Northern Ireland is unlikely to feature as the most important dimension of the political equation for whatever government is in power – though it is probable that a non-Tory administration would take fewer risks with the peace process than the current regime led by Boris Johnson.

Conclusion

The final irony, perhaps, is that while I was writing the book I had thought for most of the time that my *Breaking peace* title was just a reference to Northern Ireland. But, as the political atmosphere became increasingly febrile, encouraged and enabled by Boris Johnson both before and after he became prime minister, it could equally be applied to Great Britain – certainly if the eventual outcome leads to a no-deal scenario. The implications of a no-deal Brexit are stark for everyone, and, if the government's own planning documents are to be believed, there is an expectation of significant economic pain as well as social dislocation and public disorder in the short to medium term within Britain. Brexit is breaking peace in Northern Ireland but it may also result in the breakdown of the social fabric in Britain too.

The visceral sectarianism that is seen periodically in Northern Ireland, especially at times of heightened political uncertainty, is now commonplace within Great Britain over the Brexit issue. Shouts of 'traitor' (and worse) are now frequent around the Palace of Westminster, as politicians and judges are seen as thwarting 'the will of the people' by some Brexiteers. This has caused trauma within the political system in Britain, with a number of prominent women MPs in particular being the subject of death threats and in need of police protection just to enter the House of Commons, while angry mobs hound them on the way in. This has been the fate of politicians on both sides of the Brexit debate, but the vitriol that has been released into the political bloodstream in Britain is arguably 'breaking peace' in the metropolitan centre, as well as in Northern Ireland.

Of course much depends on the final destination for Brexit and whether the prospective deal over Northern Ireland develops in a way that assuages fears over the Irish border, its nature, location and political significance for both the nationalist and unionist communities.

But the story of how we got here should provide a salutary tale for policy practitioners and especially for potential negotiators, whatever happens. I hope that this account of how we have almost reached Brexit base camp will help us to frame and understand the next phases of the slow process of the UK disentangling itself from its membership of the European Union.

It is imperative that lessons are learned by all parties concerned, for political stability to be advanced in Northern Ireland and to avoid Brexit 'breaking peace' there. One such lesson is to think carefully about how a binary political tool such as a referendum can help to resolve a complex and multi-faceted issue such as the UK's membership of the European Union. Another is that holding a referendum is easy – but dealing with the political implications of the result can be much harder to manage.

While there are several potential scenarios for the future direction of Brexit, some broader themes are more certain at this point. Firstly, irrespective of any future twists and turns of the Brexit negotiations, the UK will still have to formulate an economic and political relationship with the EU after Brexit, as Europe will remain a vital trading partner and in geographical proximity to Britain.

Secondly, the UK will need to prepare itself for a lengthy period where it reformulates a new relationship with the EU, which could take a decade or longer to develop. The idea of a 'clean Brexit' is a misnomer; irrespective of when and how the amputation of the UK from the EU is carried out, post-operative care will be needed for some time afterwards, whether or not there is a deal over the terms of the operation. Finally, Northern Ireland will remain geographically, politically, economically, legally and culturally connected to the UK and Ireland, though the precise balance might change over time, if the constitutional responsibility for this part of the UK moves from Britain to Ireland in future years. Political stability in the region will always depend on how it is nested within the UK/Ireland axis and a bipartisan approach from both countries is likely to remain crucial to maintaining political and economic stability in Northern Ireland and to avoid Brexit breaking peace, with the obvious implications that would result for everyone living across 'these islands'.

The final word should perhaps be given not to an Irish or a British person but to a Frenchman, who warned his fellow Europeans two generations ago that the United Kingdom was not equipped to function as an effective member of the European family. His words seem both prescient and ominous as we await the next stages of what has been an attritional Brexit story:

> England in effect is insular, she is maritime, she is linked through her interactions, her markets and her supply lines to the most diverse and often the most distant countries; she pursues essentially industrial and commercial activities, and only slight agricultural ones. She has, in all her doings, very marked and very original habits and traditions.[9]

These remarks by Charles de Gaulle in 1963 were to justify France's unwillingness to support the UK's application for admission into the EEC. De Gaulle famously said 'Non', in part because he was worried that the British would become dysfunctional and insurgent members of the European team and damage the great post-war European project for those at the centre of it. He defined this as an English rather than British condition, linked to a colonial mentality that rendered the country unable to make peace with its post-imperial status.

Over half a century later – it looks as if he was right.

Acknowledgements

Three decades ago when I was an undergraduate student at university, I was not interested in Europe and I avoided modules on it like the plague, as they seemed full of dry process on its institutions and seemingly tedious arguments over fishing and farming. Occasionally it would get interesting when, for instance, the late Rev. Ian Paisley denounced Pope John Paul II as 'the antichrist' in the European Parliament in 1988, but otherwise Europe seemed a rather dull topic of study. What a difference thirty-plus years can make as it is hard to think of a more febrile area of political analysis today.

During the course of writing the book I have reflected on how blasé I used to be about the role of the European Union within Northern Ireland prior to Brexit and how important it has been to political stability, economic regeneration, and peace and reconciliation over the last forty years. On the day of the in/out referendum on UK membership of the EU on 23 June 2016, I was travelling to Belfast for a workshop I had organised on the future of devolution in Northern Ireland with my close colleague Professor Neophytos Loizides. We had carefully designed the day-long event but were worried about the after-lunch session on the impact of Brexit on devolved government and whether there would be much to say as it was odds-on to be a 'Remain' victory. We need not have worried as that issue dominated the event on 24 June among all of the participants and has continued to do so. There was an added electricity in the room as if a political meteor had just landed upon the body politic.

There are numerous people I need to thank who have helped to shape my thinking or given me advice during the writing process. I would especially like to thank those who provided on-the-record interviews on the themes within the book, including Steve Aiken MLA, Brexit spokesperson of the UUP, prior to becoming leader of the Party; Claire Hanna MP, former Brexit spokesperson for the SDLP; Stephen Farry MP, Brexit spokesperson for the Alliance Party; Alex Kane, journalist and commentator; Ben Lowry, deputy editor of the *Belfast News Letter*; Máirtín Ó Muilleoir, former Sinn Féin finance minister; John Manley, political correspondent *Irish News*; Glyn Roberts, CEO of Retail Northern Ireland; Peter Sheridan, CEO Co-Operation Ireland; and Sammy Wilson, Brexit spokesperson for the DUP. I am indebted to all of those who generously gave up their time to be interviewed for the book and for sharing their insights and expertise on the themes within it.

I also owe a debt of gratitude to colleagues in the Political Studies Association, the largest and oldest professional association of political scientists in the UK and also to colleagues in the Political Studies Association of Ireland (PSAI). Both associations took a leading role in advocating the need for evidence-based expertise in the Brexit debate and also provided funding support for a number of initiatives that I was lucky enough to participate in. I would especially like to thank Professor Angie Wilson, chair of the PSA, who I worked closely with in my capacity as vice-chair as well as the other trustees and the fantastic PSA staff team.

Other scholars I would like to thank who have helped along the way include Professor Yvonne Galligan, Dr Katy Hayward, Professor Cathy Gormley-Heenan, Professor Anand Menon, Dr Mary C. Murphy, Dr Kathryn Simpson, Professor Simon Usherwood, Professor John Garry, Dr Muiris MacCarthaigh, Professor Nicola McEwen, Professor John O'Brennan, Dr Etain Tannam and Professor David Phinnemore.

Acknowledgements

I would also like to thank my academic colleagues and students at the University of Kent, where I have worked for the past eight years. My colleagues within the Conflict Analysis Research Centre (CARC) as well as colleagues in the School of Politics and International Relations at Kent have provided a rich and rewarding environment to work in. In particular I would like to thank Dr Nadine Ansorg, Dr Yaniv Voller, Professor Hugh Miall, Dr Harmonie Toros, Professor Adrian Pabst and Professor Richard Whitman for their friendship and collegiality. During the last two years I have been very lucky to have worked in CARC with Professor Neophytos Loizides, Dr Edward Morgan-Jones and Dr Laura Sudulich on a project funded by the United States Institute for Peace (USIP) that focuses on citizen preferences in the design of effective peace settlements. This project developed a pioneering conjoint methodology and applied it to issues such as Brexit, border arrangements and the future of the peace process in Northern Ireland. This has been an amazingly rich research collaboration and many of the themes and arguments at the centre of this book emanate directly from that project. I would like to thank my three collaborators for their patience when discussing the complex methodology of these surveys with me as I stared blankly back at them and I am grateful to the USIP also for funding the research of which this is in part a product.

The book is dedicated to my two favourite Irish and European citizens, my partner Professor Rosaleen Duffy and my son Oisín. Both of them have shown heroic patience as this book has gestated over the last eighteen months and have my undying love and gratitude. I would also like to thank my parents, Gerry and Roisin Cochrane, who have always provided a sounding board when I went 'home', where Brexit was always the main topic of conversation during family gatherings.

Finally – though less romantically, I would like to thank the anonymous reviewers who provided constructive feedback on both the initial proposal and on the finished manuscript and who helped me to think about its structure and the robustness of the arguments within it. I also want to thank Tony Mason for his initial interest in the project while he was at MUP and my editor at MUP, Jon de Peyer, for his guidance and advice in seeing the book through to publication. They, along with those colleagues listed above, have helped to shape my thinking on the main arguments put forward, but of course I alone am responsible for all errors of fact, judgement and interpretation within its pages.

Brexit has been a frustrating journey for everyone – and writing about it has at times been like chasing shadows. Writing about such an unstable and unpredictable political environment has been challenging and on occasions stressful. I contracted shingles the day after I delivered the draft manuscript, which seemed like an appropriate metaphor for Brexit, with random unsightly sores, unexpected shooting pains hitting me without warning and an almost overwhelming sense of fatigue. I hope in this sense at least, the book is less painful to read than it was to write.

Notes

Introduction

1 Máirtín Ó Muilleoir MLA, Sinn Féin, interview with author, 19 April 2019.

2 Sammy Wilson MP, DUP Brexit spokesperson, personal communication with author, 1 October 2019.

3 Steve Aiken MLA, UUP Brexit spokesperson, interview with author, 24 April 2019.

4 Ben Lowry, deputy editor, *Belfast News Letter*, interviewed by author, 23 April 2019.

5 This line was quoted by deputy First Minister Seamus Mallon in a speech welcoming President Bill Clinton to Northern Ireland on 3 September 1998 and was spoken by Maya Angelou herself when she delivered her 'Inaugural Poem' at President Clinton's Inauguration in Washington on 20 January 1993. For Mallon's address, see http://cain.ulst.ac.uk/events/peace/docs/sm3998.htm (accessed 8 January 2020).

6 *Irish Times*, 'Full text of speech by Queen Elizabeth II', *Irish Times*, 18 May 2011, www.irishtimes.com/news/full-text-of-speech-by-queen-elizabeth-ii-1.876770 (accessed 27 January 2020).

7 Appropriately, given the political divisions in Northern Ireland, unionists and nationalists tend to call the 1998 Multi-Party Agreement by different names, the former preferring Belfast Agreement and the latter the Good Friday Agreement. The deal was reached on 10 April 1998 – which was Good Friday – but some unionists want to remove its Easter connotations given the significance of that in Irish republican mythology with the 1916 Easter Rising. This book mainly sticks to GFA or Good Friday Agreement for the sake of consistency.

8 Phinnemore D. & McGowan, L., 'After the EU referendum: establishing the best outcome for Northern Ireland', briefing paper, Centre for Democracy and Peace Building, Belfast August 2016, p. 46.

9 While 'Ireland' is the correct term constitutionally, the legal description 'Republic of Ireland' and the 'Irish Republic' are also used to avoid confusion when referring to Ireland and Northern Ireland in sequence.

10 See Cochrane, F., *Northern Ireland: The Reluctant Peace*, New Haven, Yale University Press, 2013; McGarry, J. & O'Leary, B., 'Consociational theory, Northern Ireland's conflict, and its agreement. Part 2: What critics of consociation can learn from Northern Ireland', *Government and Opposition*, 41:2 (2006), 249–77. Tonge, J., *Comparative Peace Processes*, Cambridge, Polity, 2014.

11 See Taylor, R., 'The injustice of a consociational solution to the Northern Ireland problem', in Taylor, R. (ed.), *Consociational Theory: McGarry and O'Leary and the Northern Ireland Conflict*, Abingdon, Routledge, 2009; McCrudden, C., McGarry, J. O'Leary, B. & Schwartz, A., 'Why Northern Ireland's institutions need stability', *Government and Opposition*, 51:1 (2016), 30–58.

12 Arthur, P., 'The British–Irish relationship: confusion, complexity and (ultimately) consensus', in O'Dochartaigh, N., Hayward, K. & Meehan, E. (eds), *Dynamics of Political Change in Ireland Making and Breaking a Divided Island*, London, Routledge, 2017; McEvoy, J., *The Politics of Northern Ireland*, Edinburgh, Edinburgh University Press, 2008; Murphy, M., *Northern Ireland and the European Union: The Dynamics of a Changing Relationship*, Manchester, Manchester University Press, 2014.

13 Hogan, P., 'Now is the time to cut our ties with Brexiting Britain', *Irish Times*, 9 January 2017.

14 'No Deal' was the popularly used term to refer to the UK's departure from the European Union without any agreement in place with the EU over its future relationship, including tariffs and trade and free movement of people. It also meant no agreement over the border in Ireland and how the free movement of goods and people and free trade could continue while also protecting the single European market given the land border between a member state, Ireland, and a non-member state, the UK.

15 The Backstop was shorthand for a legally binding clause that would come into force in the absence of a comprehensive trade agreement between the UK and EU that harmonised rules to the point where there was full regulatory alignment between the UK and EU in a manner that maintained the largely invisible status of the Irish border. The Backstop would only become operational after the transition period had elapsed and if a comprehensive trade deal was not in place.

16 O'Rourke, K., *A Short History of Brexit: From Brentry to Backstop*, London, Penguin, 2018.

17 See, for instance, Coulter, C. & Nagle, A. (eds), *Ireland under Austerity: Neoliberal Crisis, Neoliberal Solutions*, Manchester, Manchester University Press, 2015; Ó Riain, S., *The Rise and Fall of Ireland's Celtic Tiger: Liberalism, Boom and Bust*, Cambridge, Cambridge University Press, 2014.

1 Brexit and Northern Ireland: hardening positions during the referendum

1 Claire Hanna, former SDLP Brexit Spokesperson, interviewed by author, 23 April 2019.

2 At this stage it was referred to as the in/out referendum rather than by the B word, which only really came into popular usage after the referendum result and the in/out title became redundant, having been answered on 23 June 2016. Brexit was a portmanteau word for Britain and Exit – hence BREXIT. While often used in uppercase this becomes distracting in the text and has since been reduced to Brexit in common usage. For the purposes of linguistic convenience Brexit will be used across the book most of the time, regardless of this chronology.

3 Fine Gael, *Fine Gael General Election Manifesto 2016 – Let's Keep the Recovery Going*, Dublin, Fine Gael, 2016, p. 93.

4 Fine Gael, *Fine Gael General Election Manifesto 2016*, p. 92.

5 Sinn Féin, *Ard Fheis '16*, Dublin, 22–23 April 2016, pp. 12–13.

6 Hanna, interviewed by author.

7 Lowry, interviewed by author.

8 McGuinness, M., 'Foreword', in Sinn Féin, *Better with Sinn Féin Níos fearr le Sinn Féin: Sinn Féin Manifesto, Assembly Election 2016*, Belfast, 2016, p. 4.

9 SDLP, *Build a Better Future: 2016 Assembly Election Manifesto*, SDLP, Belfast, 2016, p. 8.

10 UUP, *#MakeitWork: 2016 Assembly Election Manifesto*, UUP, Belfast, 2016, p. 5.

11 Aiken, interviewed by author.

12 Simpson, K., 'The model EU citizen? Explaining Irish attitudes towards the EU', *Political Insight*, 9:1 (2018), 16–19. See also: Simpson, K. & Loveless, M. 'Another chance? Concerns about inequality, support for the European Union and further European integration', *Journal for European Public Policy*, 24:7 (2017), 1069–89. For an excellent analysis of Ireland's broader political relationship with the EU, see Laffan, B. & O'Mahony, J., *Ireland and the European Union*, Houndmills, Palgrave Macmillan, 2008.

13 Tonge, J., 'Plus ça change? The 2066 devolved elections in the UK, *Political Insight*, 7 (2016), 12–16, p. 15.

14 Tonge, 'Plus ça change?', p. 14.

15 Aiken, interviewed by author.

16 Green Party in Northern Ireland, *A Zero Waste Strategy for Northern Ireland: The Green Party Manifesto for the Northern Ireland Assembly Elections 2016*, Belfast, 2016, www.greenpartyni.org//wp-content/uploads/2016/04/GreenParty_Manifesto_2016-for-email.pdf (accessed 8 January 2020).

Notes

17 Green Party in Northern Ireland, *Green Party Manifesto, 2017 Westminster Election: #PuttingYouFirst*, Belfast, 2017, www.greenpartyni.org/wp-content/uploads/2017/05/GPNI-Manifesto-2017.pdf (accessed 8 January 2020).

18 Green Party in Northern Ireland, *#PuttingYouFirst*.

19 TUV, *Manifesto 2016: Straight Talking Principled Politics*, Belfast, TUV, May 2016.

20 TUV, *Manifesto 2016*, p. 3.

21 TUV, *Manifesto 2016*, p. 3.

22 Cowburn, A., 'Theresa May says "Brexit means Brexit" and there will be no attempt to remain inside EU', *Independent*, 11 July 2016.

23 Aiken, interviewed by author.

24 John Manley, political correspondent, *Irish News*, interviewed by author, 25 April 2019.

25 BBC, *Politics Show*, 17 October 2003, http://news.bbc.co.uk/1/hi/programmes/politics_show/3190894.stm (accessed 8 January 2020).

26 UUP, *#MakeItWork: Northern Ireland Assembly Manifesto 2016*, Belfast, UUP, 2016, pp. 5–6.

27 *Belfast Telegraph*, 'DUP confirms it will campaign for Brexit in Leave/Remain referendum', *Belfast Telegraph*, 20 February 2016.

28 Lowry, interviewed by author.

29 Glyn Roberts, CEO, Retail Northern Ireland, interviewed by author, 22 April 2019.

30 Aiken, interviewed by author.

31 This group also became known as 'NI Stronger In'.

32 NI Stronger In Europe website, www.strongerin.co.uk/northern_ireland#WekOiokopzUStM8U.97 (accessed 8 January 2020).

33 Glyn Roberts, vice-chair, NI Stronger IN, 1 June 2016, https://sluggerotoole.com/2016/06/02/competing-visions-the-leave-and-remain-campaigns-present-their-pitch/ (accessed 8 January 2020).

34 Lee Reynolds, regional coordinator, Vote Leave, 1 June 2016, https://sluggerotoole.com/2016/06/02/competing-visions-the-leave-and-remain-campaigns-present-their-pitch/ (accessed 8 January 2020).

35 Reynolds, 1 June 2016.

36 Quoted in Bardon, S., 'Sinn Féin to campaign against Brexit in EU referendum', *Irish Times* 24 December 2015.

37 Bardon, 'Sinn Féin to campaign against Brexit'.

38 *Belfast Telegraph*, 'DUP confirms it will campaign for Brexit'.

39 *Belfast Telegraph*, 'Sinn Féin "campaigning vigorously" for Remain vote in referendum', *Belfast Telegraph*, 3 June 2016.

40 *Belfast Telegraph*, 'Sinn Féin "campaigning vigorously" for Remain vote'.

41 Manley, interviewed by author.

42 McDonald, H., 'Sinn Féin calls for vote on Irish reunification if UK backs Brexit', *Guardian*, 11 March 2016.

43 McHugh, M., 'Sinn Féin calls for Ireland reunification poll if UK votes to leave EU – Do you agree?' *Belfast Telegraph*, 12 March 2016.

44 Eastwood, C., 'Eastwood calls for strong IN campaign', SDLP press release, 20 February 2016.

45 McKeown, L.A., 'Tony Blair and John Major warn a Brexit could threaten peace process during visit to Derry', *Irish News*, 9 June 2016.

46 McKeown, 'Blair and Major warn Brexit could threaten peace'.

47 Stewart, H., 'Tony Blair and John Major: Brexit would close the border', *Guardian*, 9 June 2016.

48 BBC News, 'Major and Blair say an EU exit could split the UK', 9 June 2016.

49 Stewart, 'Blair and Major: Brexit would close the border'.

50 BBC News, 'Major and Blair say an EU exit could split the UK'.

51 Geoghegan, P. & Ramsey, A., 'The dark money that paid for Brexit', *Open Democracy UK*, 15 February 2017.

52 BBC News, 'EU referendum: DUP takes out four-page "Vote Leave EU" ad in British Metro free newspaper', 21 June 2016.

53 Foster, A., 'It is right to vote to leave the EU and to take back control of our future', DUP press release, 17 June 2016 (article was originally published in *Belfast Telegraph* on 17 June 2016).

54 Foster, 'It is right to vote to leave the EU'.

55 McBride, S., 'EU referendum: more UUP councillors backing Brexit', *Belfast News Letter*, 21 June 2016.

56 Quoted in McBride, S., 'UUP grandees urge party's supporters to quit "out of control" EU', *Belfast News Letter*, 17 June 2016.

57 Quoted in McBride, 'UUP grandees urge party's supporters to quit "out of control" EU'.

58 Murphy, M., *Europe and Northern Ireland's Future: Negotiating Brexit's Unique Case*, Newcastle, Agenda Publishing, 2018.

59 Embassy of Ireland, Great Britain, 'Remarks by Ambassador Mulhall, House of Commons, 10 February 2016'.

60 BBC News, 'Brexit "would create serious difficulties for Northern Ireland"', 25 January 2016.

61 *TheJournal.ie*, 'Brexit has the Irish government worried – Here's why', *TheJournal.ie*, 12 June 2016.

62 Kenny, E., 'Why Ireland is so fearful of our closest neighbour leaving the EU', *Guardian*, 20 June 2016.

2 Brexit as meteor theory: external shocks to peace settlements

1 Peter Sheridan, CEO Co-Operation Ireland, interviewed by author, 24 April 2019.

Notes

2 Blair, T., '1998 speech on foreign affairs', *UKPOL*, 15 December 1998.

3 Cochrane, F., 'Chilcot Report: Tony Blair's sad and shameful political epitaph', *The Conversation*, 6 July 2016.

4 Karen Bradley achieved the notable feat of uniting both nationalist and unionist communities in the common belief that she was the worst Secretary of State in living memory. Bradley proved to be especially gaff-prone in her comments towards Northern Ireland – a tone set shortly after her appointment to the role in 2018 when she declared that she hadn't realised that unionists and nationalists voted along ethnonational lines, when she took the job: 'I didn't understand things like when elections are fought, for example, in Northern Ireland – people who are nationalists don't vote for unionist parties and vice versa. So, the parties fight for election within their own community.' See Andersson, J., 'Northern Ireland Secretary Karen Bradley admits she didn't know anything about Northern Irish politics before she became Secretary of State of NI', inews.co.uk, 7 September 2018, https://inews.co.uk/news/politics/northern-ireland-secretary-karen-bradley-didnt-understand-politics/ (accessed 8 January 2020).

5 Associated Press, 'Northern Ireland multi party peace talks update', AP Archive, *YouTube*, 21 July 2015.

6 De Mars, S., Murray, C., O'Donoghue, A. & Warwick, B. *Bordering Two Unions: Northern Ireland and Brexit*, Bristol, Policy Press, 2018.

7 Sheridan, interviewed by author.

8 Alex Kane, journalist and commentator, interviewed by author, 25 April 2019.

9 Manley, interviewed by author.

10 Hayward, K. *Irish Nationalism and European Integration: The Official Redefinition of the Island of Ireland*, Manchester, Manchester University Press, 2009.

11 De Mars, Murray, O'Donoghue & Warwick, *Bordering Two Unions*.

12 Hanna, interviewed by author.

13 Aiken, interviewed by author.

14 Kane, interviewed by author.

15 Aiken, interviewed by author.

16 Hayward, *Irish Nationalism and European Integration*.

17 Hayward, *Irish Nationalism and European Integration*.

18 Hanna, interviewed by author.

19 Stephen Farry, deputy leader and Brexit spokesperson of the Alliance Party, interviewed by author, 26 April 2019.

20 Archer, B., 'Leo Varadkar: UK has got it wrong in Emma DeSouza citizenship case', *Irish News*, 15 May 2019.

21 DeSouza, E., 'It is not up to the UK government to decide whether I'm Irish or not', *Guardian*, 6 May 2019.

22 Farry, interviewed by author.

23　Vayrynen, R., 'To settle or to transform? Perspectives on the resolution of national and international conflicts', in Vayrynen, R. (ed.), *New Directions in Conflict Theory: Conflict Resolution and Conflict Transformation*, London, Sage, 1991, p. 4.

24　See Cochrane, F., *Ending Wars*, Cambridge, Polity, 2008; Kriesberg, L., *Constructive Conflicts: From Escalation to Resolution* (3rd ed.), Lanham, Rowman and Littlefield, 2007; Lederach, J.P., *Preparing for Peace*, New York, Syracuse University Press, 1995; Lederach, J.P. *Building Peace: Sustainable Reconciliation in Divided Societies*, Washington, United States Institute of Peace, 1997. For an econometric perspective on the link between structure and agency in civil war, see Collier, P. & Hoeffler, A., 'Greed and grievance in civil war', *World Bank Policy Research Working Paper*, Washington, 2002. See also Berdal, M., 'Beyond greed and grievance – and not too soon …', *Review of International Studies*, 31 (2005), 687–98; Keen, D., 'Incentives and disincentives for violence', in Berdal, M. & Malone, D. (eds), *Greed and Grievance: Economic Agendas in Civil Wars*, Boulder, Lynne Rienner, 2000, pp. 19–43.

25　See for instance Ramsbotham, O., Woodhouse, T. & Miall H., *Contemporary Conflict Resolution* (4th ed.), Cambridge, Polity, 2015; Reimann, C., 'Assessing the state of the art in conflict transformation', in *Berghof Handbook*, Berlin, Berghof Research Centre for Constructive Conflict Management, 2003; Rupesinghe, K., *Conflict Transformation*, New York, St Martin's Press, 1995; Stedman, S.J., 'Spoiler problems in peace processes', *International Security*, 22:2 (1997), 5–53.

26　Reimann, 'Assessing the state of the art in conflict transformation', p. 13.

27　Wehr, P., *Conflict Regulation*, Boulder, Westview, 1979; Burton, J., *Conflict: Resolution and Prevention*, New York, St Martin's Press, 1990; Ramsbotham, O., Woodhouse, T. & Miall, H., *Contemporary Conflict Resolution* (3rd ed.), Cambridge, Polity, 2011, pp. 89–93.

28　Miall, H., 'Conflict transformation: a multi-dimensional task', in *Berghof Handbook*, Berlin, Berghof Research Centre for Constructive Conflict Management, 2004, p. 6.

29　Ó Muilleoir, interviewed by author.

30　Cochrane, F., Loizides, N. & Bodson, T., *Mediating Powersharing: Devolution and Consociationalism in Deeply Divided Societies*, Abingdon, Routledge, 2018. There are a number of nuances here that explain unionist approaches to power-sharing with nationalists, but the broad point remains that *some* unionists were able to accept in the 1990s policy options that were unacceptable to many others during the 1970s (1973/74 in particular).

31　Simpson, C., 'Michel Barnier joins Leo Varadkar and Simon Coveney at rugby match', *Irish News*, 11 March 2019.

32　De Mars, Murray, O'Donoghue & Warwick, *Bordering Two Unions*.

33　Arthur, P., *Special Relationships: Britain, Ireland and the Northern Ireland Problem*, Belfast, Blackstaff Press, 2000.

34 Cunningham, C., 'Northern Ireland and the "War on Terror": political perceptions', *Irish Political Studies*, 24:3 (2009), 285–302.

35 *Guardian*, 'IRA arms decommissioned', *Guardian*, 26 September 2005.

36 DUP, *DUP European Election Manifesto 2019*, Belfast, DUP, May 2019.

37 See, for instance, Ramsbotham, Woodhouse, & Miall, *Contemporary Conflict Resolution* (4th ed.).

38 Ramsbotham, Woodhouse & Miall, *Contemporary Conflict Resolution* (4th ed.), pp. 31–2.

39 See Kriesberg, *Constructive Conflicts*; Lederach, *Preparing for Peace*; Lederach, *Building Peace*.

40 See Cochrane, *Ending Wars*; Gurr, T., *People versus States: Minorities at Risk in the New Century*, Washington, United States Institute of Peace, 2000; Lund, M., *Preventing Violent Conflicts*, Washington, United States Institute of Peace, 1996; Holzgrefe, J. & Keohane, R. (eds), *Humanitarian Intervention: Ethical, Legal and Political Dilemmas*, Cambridge, Cambridge University Press, 2003; Bellamy, A., *Responsibility to Protect: The Global Effort to End Mass Atrocities*, Cambridge, Polity, 2009.

41 The Agreement (1998), Belfast, p. 31. https://assets.publishing.service.gov.uk/government/uploads/system/uploads/attachment_data/file/136652/agreement.pdf (accessed 8 January 2020).

42 Cochrane, Loizides & Bodson, *Mediating Powersharing: Devolution and Consociationalism*.

3 Brexit day: the result and the fallout

1 Hanna, interviewed by author.

2 Kane, interviewed by author.

3 Woodcock, A., 'EU Referendum results live: Nigel Farage "concedes defeat" in Brexit vote', *Irish News*, 23 June 2016.

4 YouGov, 'YouGov on the day poll: Remain 52%, Leave 48%', 23 June 2016.

5 BBC News, 'Brexit: David Cameron to quit after UK votes to leave the EU', 24 June 2016.

6 BBC News, 'Brexit: David Cameron to quit'.

7 Boffey, D., 'Is it West Ham? Or is it Villa? Cameron mocked on Twitter as he forgets which team he backs', *Guardian*, 25 April 2015.

8 Woodcock, A., 'Theresa May resigns: PM breaks down as she announces departure amid Brexit gridlock and expected European election wipeout', *Independent*, 24 May 2019.

9 BBC News, 'EU referendum: Scotland backs Remain as UK votes Leave', 24 June 2016.

10 Allen, K., Treanor, J. & Goodley, S., 'Pound slumps to 31 year low following Brexit vote', *Guardian*, 24 June 2016.

11 Davidson, L., Curry, R. & Dean, S., 'Business world reacts to Brexit vote as Britain's EU Commissioner Lord Hill announces resignation', *Telegraph*, 25 June 2016.

12 Connelly, T., *Brexit and Ireland: The Dangers, the Opportunities, and the Inside Story of the Irish Response*, Dublin, Penguin Ireland, 2018, pp. 1–2.

13 Connelly, *Brexit and Ireland*, pp. 1–2.

14 *Telegraph*, 'Nigel Farage: "Dawn is breaking over independent UK"', *Telegraph*, 24 June 2016.

15 Steerpike, 'Sarah Vine reveals the Gove household reaction to Brexit: "you were only supposed to blow the bloody doors off"', *Spectator*, 29 June 2016.

16 https://en.wikiquote.org/wiki/The_Italian_Job_(1969_film) Ironically, given the Brexit context, Michael Caine divulged in 2008 at an event he attended with Boris Johnson – then mayor of London – that an alternative ending to the film had been shot. The alternative ending sees the gang escape in the coach but all the gold falls into the ravine and is picked up by a rival gang of Italian mafia. Alleyne, R., 'At last Michael Caine reveals ending to the Italian Job', *Telegraph*, 28 November, 2008, www.telegraph.co.uk/news/celebritynews/3533647/At-last-Michael-Caine-reveals-ending-to-the-Italian-Job.html (accessed 8 January 2020).

17 Sky News, 'Faisal Islam struggles with Leaver's explanation there is no Brexit plan', 16 January 2017.

18 ITV News, 'Sinn Féin Calls for Referendum on United Ireland', 24 June 2016.

19 ITV News, 'Ulster Unionists call for Executive's plan following EU vote', 24 June 2016.

20 ITV News, 'Sinn Féin calls for referendum on a United Ireland'.

21 Payton, M., 'Ian Paisley Jr urges Northern Irish citizens to apply for Republic of Ireland passports', *Independent*, 25 June 2016.

22 Payton, 'Ian Paisley Jr urges Northern Irish citizens'.

23 Kane, interviewed by author.

24 ITV News, 'Ulster Unionists call for Executive's plan'.

25 BBC News, 'EU referendum: Arlene Foster says Brexit vote offers "opportunities"', 27 June 2016.

26 BBC News, 'EU referendum: Arlene Foster says Brexit vote offers "opportunities"'.

27 Wilson, personal communication with author.

28 BBC News, 'EU Referendum: Arlene Foster says Brexit vote offers "opportunities"'.

29 Foster A., & McGuinness, M., 'Open letter from Arlene Foster and Martin McGuinness', Northern Ireland Executive Office, 10 August 2016, www.executiveoffice-ni.gov.uk/sites/default/files/publications/execoffice/Letter%20to%20PM%20from%20FM%20%26%20dFM.pdf (accessed 8 January 2020).

30 Foster & McGuinness, 'Open letter'.

31 Cooper, C., 'Michael Gove to stand in Tory leadership contest and says "Boris is not a leader"', *Independent*, 30 June 2016.

32 *Independent*, 'Theresa May's Tory leadership launch statement: full text', *Independent*, 30 June 2016..

33 Asthana, A., Mason, R. & Elgot, J., 'Andrea Leadsom pulls out of Conservative leadership race', *Guardian*, 11 July 2016.

34 Stone, J., 'Theresa May officially becomes UK prime minister', *Independent*, 13 July 2016.

35 Thatcher, M., 'Remarks on becoming prime minister (St Francis's prayer)', 4 May 1979.

36 Stone, 'Theresa May officially becomes UK prime minister'.

37 Stone, 'Theresa May officially becomes UK prime minister'.

38 O'Rourke, *A Short History of Brexit*, p. 104.

39 Williamson, C., 'Brexit: Theresa May responds to letter from Arlene Foster and Martin McGuinness', *Belfast Telegraph*, 18 October 2016.

40 Williamson, 'Brexit: Theresa May responds to letter'.

41 Scottish Government, *Scotland's Place in Europe*, Edinburgh, Scottish Government, 2016, p. 26.

42 SDLP, 'Durkan warns fissures are being driven into foundations and bedrock of GFA', 8 December 2016.

43 May, J., 'Read in full: Theresa May's Conservative Conference speech on Brexit', *PoliticsHome*, 2 October 2016.

44 May, 'Read in full: Theresa May's Conservative Conference Speech on Brexit'.

45 The government appealed the High Court decision but was turned down in January 2017, upholding the sovereignty of parliament.

46 Sparrow, A., 'Brexit: government will introduce Article 50 Bill "within days" following Supreme Court ruling as it happened', *Guardian*, 14 February 2018.

47 Sparrow, 'Brexit: government will introduce Article 50 Bill'.

48 May, T., 'The government's negotiating objectives for exiting the EU: PM speech', *Gov.UK*, 17 January 2017.

49 *Telegraph*, 'EU papers react with fury the day after Theresa May's Brexit speech', *Telegraph*, 18 January 2017.

50 *Telegraph*, 'EU papers react with fury'.

51 Foster, P., '"Ready as soon as UK is": how Europe's leaders reacted to Theresa May's Brexit speech', *Telegraph*, 17 January 2017.

52 Foster, "'Ready as soon as UK is'".

53 Foster, "'Ready as soon as UK is'".

54 BBC News, 'Brexit: hard border for island of Ireland says Sinn Féin', 17 January 2017.

55 BBC News, 'Brexit: hard border for island of Ireland', 17 January 2017.

4 The election that changed the course of Brexit: Westminster 2017

1 Lowry, interviewed by author.

2 Manley, interviewed by author.

3 Asthana, A., Mason, R. & Elgot, J., 'Theresa May calls for UK General Election on 8 June', *Guardian*, 18 April 2017.

4 Dallison, P. & Khetani-Shah, S., 'Brexit quotes of 2017', *Politico*, 12 December 2017.

5 Wilson, personal communication with author.

6 Aiken, interviewed by author.

7 McBride, S., 'RHI inquiry: Arlene Foster admits she didn't even read her own "cash for ash" legislation', inews.co.uk, 13 April 2018.

8 *Irish Times*, 'Full text of Martin McGuinness's resignation letter', *Irish Times*, 9 January 2017, www.irishtimes.com/news/politics/full-text-of-martin-mcguinness-s-resignation-letter-1.2930429 (accessed 8 January 2020).

9 Moriarty, G., 'Northern Ireland on election footing as Martin McGuinness resigns as deputy First Minister', *Irish Times*, 9 January 2017.

10 Sinn Féin, *Equality, Respect Integrity: 2017 Assembly Election Manifesto*, Sinn Féin, Dublin, 2017, p. 3.

11 Sinn Féin, *Equality, Respect Integrity*, p. 5.

12 Sinn Féin, *Equality, Respect Integrity*, p. 9.

13 Stone, J., 'Theresa May accuses EU of trying to influence UK election in astonishing attack', *Independent*, 3 May 2017.

14 Stone, 'Theresa May accuses EU of trying to influence UK election'.

15 Stone, J., 'European Commission says it is "too busy" to interfere in UK General Election after Theresa May claim', *Independent*, 4 May 2017.

16 Watts, J., 'Election 2017: Theresa May to put Brexit at heart of campaign again amid shrinking poll lead', *Independent*, 31 May 2017.

17 Conservative Party, *Forward, Together: Our Plan for a Stronger Britain and a Prosperous Future. The Conservative and Unionist Party Manifesto 2017*, London, Conservative Party, 2017.

18 Labour Party, *For the Many Not the Few: The Labour Party Manifesto 2017*, London, Labour, 2017, p. 4.

Notes

19 Labour Party, *For the Many Not the Few*, p. 24.

20 Amber Rudd in BBC News, 'BBC One UK General Election 2017 leaders' debate: the battle for No. 10', *YouTube*, 31 May 2017.

21 Asthana, A. & Mason, R., 'General Election: May falters during challenge over record on public services', *Guardian*, 2 June 2017.

22 McClements, F., 'Mark Durkan: "I regret that only Derry voice in Commons is Gregory Campbell"', *Irish Times*, 13 June 2017.

23 Manley, interviewed by author.

24 Cowley, P. & Kavanaugh, D., *The British General Election of 2017*, Palgrave, London, 2018.

25 Simpson, K., 'General Election 2017: what does this mean for Brexit?' *The Conversation*, 9 June 2017.

26 *Irish Times*, 'Chilling DUP deal raises prospect of change to UK abortion law', *Irish Times*, 10 June 2017.

27 The Westminster parliament passed legislation in July 2019 to bring abortion law in Northern Ireland into line with the rest of the United Kingdom. This was the result of an amendment to a government Bill by Labour MP Stella Creasy. On the same day, Westminster also extended same-sex marriage to Northern Ireland as a result of an amendment introduced by Labour MP Connor McGinn. The new legislation became law in October 2019. Walker, P. & Carroll R., 'MPs vote to extend abortion and same-sex marriage rights in Northern Ireland', *Guardian*, 9 July 2019, www.theguardian.com/uk-news/2019/jul/09/mps-vote-to-extend-same-sex-marriage-to-northern-ireland (accessed 27 January 2020).

28 Hunt, A., 'Theresa May and the DUP deal: what you need to know', BBC News, 26 June 2017.

29 Malnick, E., 'DUP to support minority government after "confidence and supply" deal reached', *Telegraph*, 10 June 2017.

30 May, J., 'In full: Arlene Foster statement on DUP-Conservative confidence and supply deal', *PoliticsHome*, 26 June 2017.

31 Roberts, R., 'Sinn Féin accuses the DUP of "betraying Northern Ireland" by entering into deal to prop up Conservative government', *Independent*, 11 June 2017.

32 BBC News, 'DUP–Tory deal secures extra spending in Northern Ireland', 26 June 2017.

33 Morris, N., 'Tory–DUP "confidence and supply deal" facing legal challenge', inews.co.uk, 9 July 2017.

34 BBC News, ' Tory/DUP deal an outrageous straight bung, Carwyn Jones says', 26 June 2017.

35 Watts, J., 'Theresa May accused of bribing DUP with £1bn deal despite claiming "there is no magic money tree"', *Independent*, 26 June 2017.

36 Kipling, R., 'Ulster', *Morning Post*, 9 April 1912.
37 Wilson, personal communication with author.

5 Aspiration or guarantee? The 'frictionless' border

1   Sheridan, interviewed by author.

2   Aiken, interviewed by author.

3   Under UK General Election rules, Irish citizens resident in GB (like those from Cyprus and Malta) were allowed to vote in the referendum, while other EU citizens were not.

4   Quinn, B., 'Irish prime minister says border controls could return if Britain exits EU', *Guardian*, 29 May 2016.

5   This was sent out in England during April and distributed in Wales, Scotland and Northern Ireland in May after the elections to the devolved assemblies/parliaments had taken place.

6   HM Government, *Why the Government Believes that Voting to Remain in the European Union is the Best Decision for the UK*, EU referendum leaflet, April 2016.

7   Britain Stronger in Europe, '6 reasons you need to vote Remain on June 23rd', *YouTube*, 3 June 2016, www.strongerin.co.uk/#1KyquBoBoxf9B8Fy.97 (accessed 8 January 2020).

8   Britain Stronger in Europe, 'Get the Facts', Britain Stronger in Europe website.

9   Labour In for Britain, YouTube video, 30 November 2015.

10 See Cochrane, *Northern Ireland: The Reluctant Peace*; Gilligan, C., 'Northern Ireland ten years after the Agreement', *Ethnopolitics*, 7:1 (2008), 1–19; McGarry & O'Leary, 'Consociational theory, Northern Ireland's conflict, and its Agreement. Part 2'; Tonge, *Comparative Peace Processes*.

11 Taylor, 'The injustice of a consociational solution'; McCrudden, McGarry, O'Leary & Schwartz, 'Why Northern Ireland institutions need stability'.

12 Arthur, 'The British–Irish relationship'; McEvoy, *The Politics of Northern Ireland*; Murphy, *Northern Ireland and the European Union*.

13 ITV News, 'EU referendum debate', 9 June 2016.

14 Staunton, E., *The Nationalists of Northern Ireland 1918–1973*, Dublin, Columba Press, 2001.

15 Morgan, A. & Purdie, B., *Ireland: Divided Nation, Divided Class*, London, Ink Links, 1980.

16 *Belfast Telegraph*, 'Thatcher misgivings over Anglo-Irish Agreement revealed', *Belfast Telegraph*, 30 December 2015.

17 Northern Ireland Affairs Committee, *The Land Border between Northern Ireland and Ireland: 2nd Report of Session 2017–19*, House of Commons, HC329, 16 March 2018, p. 8.

Notes

18 Hayward, K., *Brexit at the Border: Voices of Local Communities in the Central Border Region of Ireland*, Belfast, Irish Central Border Network and Queen's University Belfast, June 2018, p. 8.

19 Hayward, *Brexit at the Border*, p. 26.

20 Northern Ireland Affairs Committee, *The Land Border between Northern Ireland and Ireland*, p. 7.

21 Government of Ireland, 'Brexit: Ireland's priorities', Dublin (undated), p. 7.

22 Northern Ireland Affairs Committee, *The Land Border between Northern Ireland and Ireland*, p. 7.

23 Connelly, T., 'EU report highlights Brexit effect on north–south cooperation', *RTE News*, 20 June 2019.

24 May, 'The government's negotiating objectives for exiting the EU: PM speech'.

25 BBC News, 'In full: Theresa May's Conservative conference speech 2017', 4 October 2017.

26 Daniel Mulhall, Ireland Ambassador to GB, oral evidence to the House of Lords EU Committee, 27 October 2015.

27 See European Commission, TF50 (2017) 19 – Commission to EU 27, 8 December 2017, p. 8.

28 See European Commission, TF50 (2017) 19 – Commission to EU 27, p. 8.

29 See European Commission, TF50 (2017) 19 – Commission to EU 27, p. 8.

30 Elgot, J., 'Theresa May calls for "red white and blue Brexit"', *Guardian*, 6 December 2016.

31 Northern Ireland Affairs Committee, *The Land Border between Northern Ireland and Ireland*, pp. 7–8.

32 Garry, J., 'House of Lord's European Union Select Committee, witness evidence', 16 January 2018.

33 Garry, J., McNicholl, K., O'Leary, B. & Pow, J., *Northern Ireland and the UK's Exit from the EU: What Do People Think? Evidence from Two Investigations: A Survey and a Deliberative Forum*, UK in a Changing Europe, ESRC Report, May 2018, p. 6.

34 Garry et al., *Northern Ireland and the UK's Exit from the EU*.

35 Cochrane, *Northern Ireland: The Reluctant Peace*; McGarry, J. & O'Leary, B., 'Consociational theory, Northern Ireland's conflict, and its Agreement. Part 1: What consociationalists can learn from Northern Ireland', *Government and Opposition*, 41:1 (2006), 43–63; Tonge, *Comparative Peace Processes*.

36 McCrudden, McGarry, O'Leary & Schwartz, 'Why Northern Ireland's institutions need stability'.

37 McGarry & O'Leary, 'Consociational theory, Northern Ireland's conflict, and its Agreement. Part 1'.

Notes

38 Shirlow, P. & Coulter, C., 'Northern Ireland: 20 years after the cease-fires', *Studies in Conflict and Terrorism*, 37:9 (2014), 713–19.

39 Sinn Féin, 'EU has key role in assisting transition to Irish unity – Anderson', 28 April 2017.

40 O'Toole, F., *Heroic Failure: Brexit and the Politics of Pain*, London, Head of Zeus, 2018, pp. 88–9.

41 May, 'The government's negotiating objectives for exiting the EU: PM speech'.

42 Conservative Party, *Forward, Together*.

43 Allen, N., Consterdine, E., Cochrane, F., Salter, J-P. & Garcia, M., 'Britain's Brexit plan revealed: experts react', *The Conversation*, 12 July 2018.

44 Smith, O., 'Brexiteer slams "myth" of Irish border chaos as part of anti-Brexit "blackmail"', *Daily Express*, 26 November 2017.

45 David Davis speaking on *The Andrew Marr Show*, BBC, 25 March 2018, quoted in *TheJournal.ie*, 'David Davis: "Irish border can be solved by a whole load of new technology"', 25 March 2018.

46 BBC News, 'Boris Johnson likens Irish border challenge to congestion charge', 27 February 2018.

47 BBC News, 'Boris Johnson likens Irish border challenge to congestion charge'.

48 Karlsson, L., *Smart Borders 2.0: Avoiding a Hard Border on the Island of Ireland for Customs Control and the Free Movement of Persons*, AFCO Committee European Parliament, PE 596828-November 2017.

49 European Research Group, *A Better Deal and a Better Future*, 19 January 2019, pp. 4–5.

50 Hayward, K., 'Can technology and "max fac" solve the Irish border question? Expert explains', *The Conversation*, 23 May 2018.

51 Rankin, J. & Boffey, D., 'Risk of no-deal Brexit "very high", says key EU negotiator', *Guardian*, 28 January 2019.

52 Aiken, interviewed by author.

53 Wilson, personal communication with author.

54 Murphy, J. & Cecil, N., 'Donald Tusk slams Brexit saying there's a "special place in hell" for people who promoted Leave without a plan', *Evening Standard*, 6 February 2019.

55 Kentish, B., 'EU Council president savages Brexit campaigners who failed to plan for departure: "Special place in hell"', *Independent*, 6 February 2019.

56 European Commission, 'Speech by Michel Barnier at the All-Island Civic Dialogue', European Commission press release, speech delivered at Dundalk, 30 April 2018.

57 O'Rourke, *A Short History of Brexit*, pp. 223–4.

58 Elgot, J. & Walker, P., 'Theresa May tells MPs: no Brexit deal comes without a backstop', *Guardian*, 26 November 2018.

59 The Brady Amendment to the Withdrawal Agreement was named after Sir Graham Brady, then chair of the Conservative Party's 1922 Committee. This was passed in the House of Commons on 29 January 2019 (and supported by the Prime Minister herself). It authorised the UK government to try to reopen negotiations with Brussels and replace the Backstop with 'alternative arrangements' (as yet unspecified) that could command the support of the House of Commons.

6 Brexit and the Good Friday Agreement

1 Ó Muilleoir, interviewed by author.
2 Wilson, personal communication with author.
3 Aiken, interviewed by author.
4 Braniff, M. & Whiting, S., 'Deep impact: the fiction of a smooth Brexit for Northern Ireland', *Juncture*, 23:4 (2017), 249–53.
5 Wilson, R., *Northern Ireland Peace Monitoring Report, Number 4*, Belfast, Community Relations Council, September 2016, pp. 117–20.
6 Cochrane, *Northern Ireland: The Reluctant Peace*.
7 Braniff & Whiting, 'Deep impact'.
8 Wilson, private communication with author.
9 Know, K.B., 'Compromise is not a dirty word – Bill Clinton delivers keynote speech to mark 20th anniversary of Good Friday Agreement', *Independent.ie*, 9 April 2018.
10 Eastwood, C., 'Northern Ireland Affairs Committee: devolution and democracy in Northern Ireland, witness evidence', 21 February 2018.
11 Political Studies Association, '20 years of the Good Friday Agreement', 10 April 2018.
12 Castle, S., 'With Good Friday Agreement under threat, voters urged to "stand up"', *New York Times*, 9 April 2018.
13 Former Irish ambassador, in private conversation with author, 26 February 2019.
14 Murphy, *Europe and Northern Ireland's Future*, p. 87.
15 Carmichael, P. & Knox, C., 'Devolution, governance and the peace process', *Terrorism and Political Violence*, 16:3 (2004), 593–621; Gilligan, 'Northern Ireland ten years after the Agreement'; McEvoy, *The Politics of Northern Ireland*; Murphy, *Europe and Northern Ireland's Future*; O'Kane, E., 'To cajole or compel? The use of incentives and penalties in Northern Ireland's peace process', *Dynamics of Asymmetric Conflict*, 4:3 (2011), 272–84; Todd, J., 'The effectiveness of the agreement: international conditions and contexts', in O'Dochartaigh, N., Meehan, E. & Hayward K. (eds), *Dynamics of Political Change in Ireland: Making and Breaking a Divided Island*, Abingdon, Routledge, 2017.

16 Nineteenth Amendment of the Constitution Act, 1998, www. irishstatutebook.ie/eli/1998/ca/19/schedule/enacted/en/html#sched-parti (accessed 8 January 2020).

17 The Agreement 1 (iii).

18 Murphy, *Europe and Northern Ireland's Future*, p. 87.

19 O Beacháin, D., *From Partition to Brexit: The Irish Government and Northern Ireland*, Manchester, Manchester University Press, 2018.

20 Humphreys, R., *Beyond the Border: The Good Friday Agreement and Irish Unity after Brexit*, Dublin, Merrion Press, 2018.

21 Braniff & Whiting, 'Deep impact'.

22 Wearmouth, R., 'Good Friday Agreement "not sustainable" says Brexiteer Kate Hoey', *Huffington Post*, 19 February 2018.

23 Schofield, K., 'Kate Hoey condemned by her own Labour branch for attacking the Good Friday Agreement', *PoliticsHome*, 23 February 2018.

24 Schofield, 'Kate Hoey condemned by her own Labour branch'.

25 BBC News, 'Brexiteers branded "reckless" over NI peace process', 20 February 2018.

26 O Beacháin, *From Partition to Brexit*.

27 BBC News, 'Brexiteers branded "reckless" over NI peace process'.

28 O'Carroll, L., 'Kate Hoey accused of putting Brexit before peace', *Guardian*, 21 February 2018.

29 Murphy, *Europe and Northern Ireland's Future*, pp. 10–11.

30 Arthur, *Special Relationships*.

31 O Beacháin, *From Partition to Brexit*.

32 Hume, J., 'John Hume Nobel Lecture', Oslo, 10 December 1998.

33 Minihan, M., 'John Hume's single-transferable speech', *Irish Times*, 30 December 2015.

34 Arthur, *Special Relationships*; Cochrane, *Northern Ireland: The Reluctant Peace*.

35 McGowen, M., 'Remembering John Hume's key role in NI's Good Friday Agreement', *Metro Eireann*, 15 April 2018.

36 McGowen, 'Remembering John Hume's key role'.

37 Stone, J., 'Brexit: Northern Ireland should keep EU funding to support peace process, European Parliament says', *Independent*, 11 September 2018.

38 Cochrane, F., 'Most Brexit voters feel a hard border in Northern Ireland would be worth it to leave the customs union – we shouldn't be surprised', *Independent*, 24 June 2018.

39 O'Rourke, *A Short History of Brexit*, p. 228.

40 Schiek, D., 'What does the 23 June mean for Northern Ireland specifically? Legal perspectives no 2: peace', Queen's Policy Engagement, 17 June 2016.

41 Schiek, 'What does the 23 June mean for Northern Ireland specifically?'

42 Smith, A., McWilliams, M. & Yarnell, P., 'Does every cloud have a silver lining? Brexit, repeal of the Human Rights Act and the Northern Ireland Bill of Rights', *Fordham International Law Journal*, 40:1 (2016).

43 Institute of International and European Affairs, 'Brexit, the Good Friday Agreement and the European Convention on Human Rights', 9 January 2017.

44 Institute of International and European Affairs, 'Brexit, the Good Friday Agreement and the European Convention on Human Rights'.

45 Institute of International and European Affairs, 'Brexit, the Good Friday Agreement and the European Convention on Human Rights'.

46 Northern Ireland Council for Voluntary Action (NICVA), 'NICVA position paper on Brexit', Belfast, July 2017, p. 3, www.nicva.org/article/nicva-position-paper-on-brexit (accessed 8 January 2020).

47 The Agreement, Declaration of Support, p. 3.

48 The Agreement, Declaration of Support, p. 3.

49 Murphy, *Europe and Northern Ireland's future*, pp. 6–7.

50 The Agreement, Declaration of Support, p. 10, para 26.

51 The Agreement, Declaration of Support, p. 3.

52 McCrudden, C., *The Good Friday Agreement, Brexit, and Rights*, Royal Irish Academy/British Academy October 2017, p. 5.

53 McCrudden, *The Good Friday Agreement, Brexit, and Rights*, p. 6.

54 McCrudden, *The Good Friday Agreement, Brexit, and Rights*, p. 11.

55 Hanna, C., 'Picking up the pieces – restoring relationships after Brexit', Jean Monnet Lecture Series, University College Cork, 27 March 2019.

56 Murphy, *Europe and Northern Ireland's Future*, pp. 130–5.

57 Ó Muilleoir, interviewed by author.

58 Edwards, M., 'Claire Hanna resigns SDLP whip over Fianna Fáil move – Eastwood says "the party has spoken"', *Belfast Telegraph*, 11 February 2019.

59 Ó Muilleoir, interviewed by author.

60 Ferguson, A., 'Northern Ireland firms warn of economic, social risks from no-deal Brexit', *Reuters*, 10 March 2019.

61 Manley, interviewed by author.

62 Roberts, interviewed by author.

63 Wilson, personal communication with author.

64 Belfast journalist, interviewed by author, April 2019.

65 Aiken, interviewed by author.

66 Murphy, *Europe and Northern Ireland's Future*, pp. 111–12.

67 Murphy, *Europe and Northern Ireland's Future*, p. 113.

68 Aiken, interviewed by author.

7 From partners to rivals: Anglo-Irish relations after Brexit

1 Quinn, B., 'Sajid Javid criticised for calling Ireland "tail that wags the dog" on Brexit', *Guardian*, 2 June 2019.

Notes

2 Boris Johnson wrote this piece for the *Mail on Sunday* (8 September 2018) attacking Theresa May's Chequers deal and the Irish Backstop dimension of the Withdrawal Agreement specifically. See also O'Rourke, *A Short History of Brexit*, p. 275.

3 Connelly, T., 'Theresa May: how strategic mistakes and the Irish question brought her down', *RTE News*, 25 May 2019.

4 O'Toole, F., 'Britain: The end of a fantasy', *New York Review of Books*, 10 June 2017, www.nybooks.com/daily/2017/06/10/britain-the-end-of-a-fantasy (accessed 8 January 2020).

5 Hanna, interviewed by author.

6 Aiken, interviewed by author.

7 O Beacháin, *From Partition to Brexit*.

8 Hanna, interviewed by author.

9 O Beacháin, *From Partition to Brexit*. See also O'Toole, *Heroic Failure*.

10 Kane, A., 'The past is where we go when we can't agree on the present or future', *Irish News*, 1 December 2017.

11 Makem, T., 'Four green fields', 1967.

12 Makem, 'Four green fields'.

13 See: Aughey, A., *Under Siege: Ulster Unionism and the Anglo-Irish Agreement*, London, Hurst, 1989; Brown, T., *The Whole Protestant Community: The Making of a Historical Myth*, Field Day Pamphlet No. 5, Derry, 1985; Bruce, S., *The Edge of the Union*, Oxford, Oxford University Press, 1994; Akenson, D., *God's People: Covenant and Land in South Africa, Israel and Ulster*, Ithaca, Cornell University Press, 1992.

14 See Cochrane, F., *Unionist Politics and the Politics of Unionism since the Anglo-Irish Agreement*, Cork, Cork University Press, 1997; Millar, D., *Queen's Rebels: Ulster Loyalism in Historical Perspective*, Dublin, Gill & Macmillan, 1978.

15 See Foster, R.F. *Modern Ireland 1600–1972*, London, Penguin, 1989, p. 155.

16 Kinealy, C., *This Great Calamity: The Irish Famine 1845–52*, Dublin, Gill & Macmillan, 2006, p. 297.

17 See Jackson, A., *Home Rule, an Irish History 1800–2000*, Dublin, Phoenix Press, 2003; Stewart, A.T.Q., *The Ulster Crisis, Resistance to Home Rule, 1912–14*, London, Faber and Faber, 1967.

18 Arthur, *Special Relationships*; Aughey, *Under Siege*; Cochrane, *Unionist Politics and the Politics of Unionism*; Kenny, A., *The Road to Hillsborough: The Making of the Anglo-Irish Agreement*, Oxford, Oxford University Press, 1986.

19 Arthur, *Special Relationships*, p. 129.

20 Hayward, K. & Murphy, M., 'The (soft) power of commitment: the EU and conflict resolution in Northern Ireland', *Ethnopolitics*, 11:4 (2012), 439–52.

21 Murphy, *Europe and Northern Ireland's Future*, p. 10.

22 Murphy, *Europe and Northern Ireland's Future*.

23 Murphy, *Europe and Northern Ireland's Future*, p. 11.

24 Thatcher, M., *The Downing Street Years*, London, HarperCollins, 1993.

25 Cochrane, *Northern Ireland: The Reluctant Peace*, p. 129.

26 Cochrane, *Northern Ireland: The Reluctant Peace*, p. 123.

27 Cochrane, *Northern Ireland: The Reluctant Peace*, p. 128.

28 Kentish, B., 'Tories at war over Boris Johnson "suicide vest" jibe at May over her Chequers Brexit plan', *Independent*, 10 September 2018.

29 Powell, J., *Great Hatred, Little Room: Making Peace in Northern Ireland*, London, Vintage, 2009, pp. 28–9.

30 Important to point out for the record – Ireland won the game by 43 points to 13.

31 RTE News, 'State visit an extraordinary moment – McAleese', 16 May 2011.

32 Connelly, 'Theresa May: how strategic mistakes and the Irish question brought her down'.

33 BBC News, 'Brexit: Leo Varadkar warns of Brexit deal "miscalculation"', 11 June 2019.

34 BBC News, 'NI live – EU referendum results and reaction', 24 June 2016.

35 Murphy, *Europe and Northern Ireland's Future*, p. 113.

36 Boffey, D., 'Irish PM warns UK could crash out of EU without Brexit deal if no progress soon', *Guardian*, 17 May 2018.

37 Stone, J., 'Brexit: no deal in Brussels after DUP torpedoes Theresa May and Jean-Claude Juncker's Northern Ireland agreement', *Independent*, 4 December 2017.

38 Stewart, H., Sabbagh, D. & Walker, P., 'Gavin Williamson: "I was tried by kangaroo court – then sacked"', *Guardian*, 1 May 2019.

39 Grant, J., 'Patel accused of "famine threats" as she says risk of food shortages could be used against Republic', *Belfast Telegraph*, 8 December 2018.

40 Grant, 'Patel accused of "famine threats"'.

41 Kentish, B., 'Britain should highlight risk of economic damage in Ireland to get better Brexit deal, suggests Priti Patel', *Independent*, 7 December 2018.

42 Lehane, M., 'Ambassador accuses UK magazine of publishing anti-Irish articles', *RTE News*, 12 April 2019.

Epilogue: Brexit – do or die?

1 Elgot, J., 'Boris Johnson's victory speech: what he said and what he meant', *Guardian*, 23 July 2019.

2 Johnson, B., 'Boris Johnson's first speech as prime minister: 24 July 2019', *Gov.UK*, 24 July 2019.

3 *Guardian*, 'No-deal Brexit would be a "failure of statecraft", says Boris Johnson', *Guardian*, 9 September 2019.

Notes

4   Proctor, K., & Walker, P., 'Boris Johnson: I'd rather be dead in ditch than agree Brexit extension', *Guardian*, 5 September 2019.

5   Sparrow, A., 'Chaotic scenes in the Commons as parliament is suspended – as it happened', *Guardian*, 10 September 2019.

6   Bowcott, O., Quinn, B. & Carrell, S., 'Johnson's suspension of parliament unlawful, supreme court rules', *Guardian*, 24 September 2019.

7   Staunton, D. & Leahy, P., 'Brexit: Varadkar sees "pathway to an agreement in coming weeks"', *Irish Times*, 10 October 2019.

8   Quinn, A., 'Watch Boris Johnson tell the DUP in 2018 he would never put border in the Irish Sea – today he put a border in the Irish Sea', *Belfast News Letter*, 17 October 2019.

9   Moore, C., 'De Gaulle knew it: Britain does not belong in the EU', *Spectator*, 30 April 2016.

Select bibliography

Akenson, D., *God's People: Covenant and Land in South Africa, Israel and Ulster*, Ithaca, Cornell University Press, 1992.

Allen, K., Treanor, J. & Goodley, S., 'Pound slumps to 31 year low following Brexit vote', *Guardian*, 24 June 2016, www.theguardian.com/business/2016/jun/23/british-pound-given-boost-by-projected-remain-win-in-eu-referendum (accessed 8 January 2020).

Allen, N., Consterdine, E., Cochrane, F., Salter, J-P. & Garcia, M., 'Britain's Brexit plan revealed: experts react', *The Conversation*, 12 July 2018, https://theconversation.com/britains-brexit-plan-revealed-experts-react-99862 (accessed 8 January 2020).

Archer, B., 'Leo Varadkar: UK has got it wrong in Emma DeSouza citizenship case', *Irish News*, 15 May 2019, www.irishnews.com/paywall/tsb/irishnews/irishnews/irishnews//news/northernirelandnews/2019/05/15/news/leo-varadkar-uk-has-got-it-wrong-on-emma-desouza-1620007/content.html (accessed 8 January 2020).

Arthur, P., *Government and Politics of Northern Ireland* (2nd ed.), London, Longman, 1984.

Arthur, P., *Special Relationships: Britain, Ireland and the Northern Ireland Problem*, Belfast, Blackstaff Press, 2000.

Arthur, P., 'The British–Irish relationship: confusion, complexity and (ultimately) consensus', in O'Dochartaigh, N., Hayward, K. & Meehan, E. (eds), *Dynamics of Political Change in Ireland Making and Breaking a Divided Island*, London, Routledge, 2017.

Associated Press, 'Northern Ireland multi party peace talks update', AP Archive, *YouTube*, 21 July 2015, www.bing.com/videos/search?q=If+Tony+BLair+wants+peace+he%27d+better+get+over+here+Alderdice&view=detail&mid=A62A0917B4A3E07C34DEA62A0917B4A3E07C34DE&FORM=VIRE (accessed 8 January 2020).

Asthana, A., Mason, R. & Elgot, J., 'Andrea Leadsom pulls out of Conservative leadership race', *Guardian*, 11 July 2016, www.theguardian.com/politics/2016/

jul/11/conservative-leadership-andrea-leadsom-pulls-out-of-race (accessed 8 January 2020).

Asthana, A., Mason, R. & Elgot, J., 'Theresa May calls for UK General Election on 8 June', *Guardian*, 18 April 2017, www.theguardian.com/politics/2017/apr/18/theresa-may-uk-general-election-8-june (accessed 8 January 2020).

Asthana, A. & Mason, R., 'General Election: May falters during challenge over record on public services', *Guardian*, 2 June 2017, www.theguardian.com/politics/2017/jun/02/general-election-may-falters-during-challenge-over-record-on-public-services (accessed 8 January 2020).

Aughey, A., *Under Siege: Ulster Unionism and the Anglo-Irish Agreement*, London, Hurst, 1989.

Bardon, S., 'Sinn Féin to campaign against Brexit in EU referendum', *Irish Times*, 24 December 2015, www.irishtimes.com/news/politics/sinn-féin-to-campaign-against-brexit-in-eu-referendum-1.2476720 (accessed 8 January 2020).

BBC News, 'Northern Ireland: garden centre Unionism', 17 October 2003, http://news.bbc.co.uk/1/hi/programmes/politics_show/3190894.stm (accessed 8 January 2020).

BBC News, 'Brexit "would create serious difficulties for Northern Ireland"', 25 January 2016, www.bbc.co.uk/news/uk-northern-ireland-35395135 (accessed 8 January 2020).

BBC News, 'Major and Blair say an EU exit could split the UK', 9 June 2016, www.bbc.co.uk/news/uk-politics-eu-referendum-36486016 (accessed 8 January 2020).

BBC News, 'EU referendum: DUP takes out four-page "Vote Leave EU" ad in British Metro free newspaper', 21 June 2016, www.bbc.co.uk/news/uk-northern-ireland-politics-36587807 (accessed 8 January 2020).

BBC News, 'Brexit: David Cameron to quit after UK votes to leave the EU', 24 June 2016, www.bbc.co.uk/news/uk-politics-36615028 (accessed 8 January 2020).

BBC News, 'NI live – EU referendum results and reaction', 24 June 2016, www.bbc.co.uk/news/live/uk-northern-ireland-36500476 (accessed 8 January 2020).

BBC News, 'EU referendum: Scotland backs Remain as UK votes Leave', 24 June 2016, www.bbc.co.uk/news/uk-scotland-scotland-politics-36599102 (accessed 8 January 2020).

BBC News, 'EU referendum: Arlene Foster says Brexit vote offers "opportunities"', 27 June 2016, www.bbc.co.uk/news/uk-northern-ireland-36635182 (accessed 8 January 2020).

BBC News, 'Brexit: hard border for island of Ireland says Sinn Féin', 17 January 2017, www.bbc.co.uk/news/uk-northern-ireland-38650350 (accessed 8 January 2020).

Select bibliography

BBC News, 'Stick border where sun doesn't shine – Martina Anderson', 14 March 2017, www.bbc.co.uk/news/video_and_audio/headlines/39269305/stick-border-where-sun-doesn-t-shine-says-martina-anderson (accessed 8 January 2020).

BBC News, 'BBC One UK General Election 2017 leaders' debate: the battle for No. 10', *YouTube*, 31 May 2017, www.youtube.com/watch?v=xmopAnM_exA (last accessed 27 January 2020).

BBC News, 'DUP–Tory deal secures extra spending in Northern Ireland', 26 June 2017, www.bbc.co.uk/news/uk-northern-ireland-40402352 (accessed 8 January 2020).

BBC News, 'Tory/DUP deal an outrageous straight bung, Carwyn Jones says', 26 June 2017, www.bbc.co.uk/news/uk-wales-politics-40406396 (accessed 8 January 2020).

BBC News, 'In full: Theresa May's Conservative conference speech 2017', 4 October 2017, www.bbc.co.uk/news/av/uk-politics-41503214/in-full-theresa-may-s-conservative-conference-speech-2017 (accessed 8 January 2020).

BBC News, 'Brexiteers branded "reckless" over NI peace process', 20 February 2018, www.bbc.co.uk/news/uk-northern-ireland-43126409 (accessed 8 January 2020).

BBC News, 'Boris Johnson likens Irish border challenge to congestion charge', 27 February 2018, www.bbc.co.uk/news/uk-politics-43210156 (accessed 8 January 2020).

BBC News, 'Brexit: Leo Varadkar warns of Brexit deal "miscalculation"', 11 June 2019, www.bbc.co.uk/news/world-europe-48602072 (accessed 8 January 2020).

Belfast Telegraph, 'Thatcher misgivings over Anglo-Irish Agreement revealed', *Belfast Telegraph*, 30 December 2015, www.belfasttelegraph.co.uk/news/republic-of-ireland/thatcher-misgivings-over-angloirish-agreement-revealed-34323146.html (accessed 8 January 2020).

Belfast Telegraph, 'DUP confirms it will campaign for Brexit in Leave/Remain referendum', *Belfast Telegraph*, 20 February 2016, www.belfasttelegraph.co.uk/news/northern-ireland/dup-confirms-it-will-campaign-for-brexit-in-leaveremain-referendum-34470806.html (accessed 8 January 2020).

Belfast Telegraph, 'Ulster Unionist Party supports staying in EU', *Belfast Telegraph*, 5 March 2016, www.belfasttelegraph.co.uk/news/northern-ireland/ulster-unionist-party-supports-staying-in-eu-34514128.html (accessed 8 January 2020).

Belfast Telegraph, 'Sinn Féin "campaigning vigorously" for Remain vote in referendum', *Belfast Telegraph*, 3 June 2016, www.belfasttelegraph.co.uk/news/republic-of-ireland/sinn-fein-campaigning-vigorously-for-remain-vote-in-referendum-34770636.html (accessed 8 January 2020).

Bellamy, A., *Responsibility to Protect: The Global Effort to End Mass Atrocities*, Cambridge Polity, 2009.

Berdal, M., 'Beyond greed and grievance – and not too soon …', *Review of International Studies*, 31 (2005), 687–98.

Blair, T., '1998 speech on foreign affairs', *UKPOL*, 15 December 1998, www.ukpol.co.uk/tony-blair-1998-speech-on-foreign-affairs (accessed 8 January 2020).

Boffey, D., 'Is it West Ham? Or is it Villa? Cameron mocked on Twitter as he forgets which team he backs', *Guardian*, 25 April 2015, www.theguardian.com/politics/2015/apr/25/david-cameron-mocked-for-aston-villa-gaffe (accessed 8 January 2020).

Boffey, D., 'Irish PM warns UK could crash out of EU without Brexit deal if no progress soon', *Guardian*, 17 May 2018, www.theguardian.com/politics/2018/may/17/leo-varadkar-theresa-may-sofia-brexit-deal (accessed 8 January 2020).

Bowcott, O., Quinn, B. & Carrell, S., 'Johnson's suspension of parliament unlawful, supreme court rules', *Guardian*, 24 September 2019, www.theguardian.com/law/2019/sep/24/boris-johnsons-suspension-of-parliament-unlawful-supreme-court-rules-prorogue (accessed 8 January 2020).

Braniff, M. & Whiting, S., 'Deep impact: the fiction of a smooth Brexit for Northern Ireland', *Juncture*, 23:4 (2017), 249–53.

Britain Stronger in Europe, '6 reasons you need to vote Remain on June 23rd', *YouTube*, 3 June 2016, www.strongerin.co.uk/#1KyquBoBoxf9B8Fy.97 (accessed 8 January 2020).

Britain Stronger in Europe, 'Get the Facts', www.strongerin.co.uk/get_the_facts#fEPIjQZqjJIwptf4.97 (accessed 8 January 2020).

Brown, T., *The Whole Protestant Community: The Making of a Historical Myth*, Field Day Pamphlet No. 5, Derry, 1985.

Bruce, S., *The Edge of the Union*, Oxford, Oxford University Press, 1994.

Carmichael, P. & Knox, C., 'Devolution, governance and the peace process', *Terrorism and Political Violence*, 16:3 (2004), 593–621.

Castle, S., 'With Good Friday Agreement under threat, voters urged to "stand up"', *New York Times*, 9 April 2018, www.nytimes.com/2018/04/09/world/europe/peace-in-ireland-blair.html (accessed 8 January 2020).

Cochrane, F., *Unionist Politics and the Politics of Unionism since the Anglo-Irish Agreement*, Cork, Cork University Press, 1997.

Cochrane, F., *Ending Wars*, Cambridge, Polity, 2008.

Cochrane, F., *Northern Ireland: The Reluctant Peace*, New Haven, Yale University Press, 2013.

Cochrane, F., 'Chilcot Report: Tony Blair's sad and shameful political epitaph', *The Conversation*, 6 July 2016, https://theconversation.com/chilcot-report-tony-blairs-sad-and-shameful-political-epitaph-62135 (accessed 8 January 2020).

Cochrane, F., 'Most Brexit voters feel a hard border in Northern Ireland would be worth it to leave the customs union – we shouldn't be surprised',

Independent, 24 June 2018, www.independent.co.uk/voices/brexit-voters-hard-border-northern-ireland-customs-union-leave-eu-a8414196.html (accessed 8 January 2020).

Cochrane, F., Loizides, N. & Bodson, T., *Mediating Powersharing: Devolution and Consociationalism in Deeply Divided Societies*, Abingdon, Routledge, 2018.

Collier, P. & Hoeffler, A., 'Greed and grievance in civil war', *World Bank Policy Research Working Paper*, Washington, 2002.

Connelly, T., *Brexit and Ireland: The Dangers, the Opportunities, and the Inside Story of the Irish Response*, Dublin, Penguin Ireland, 2018.

Connelly, T., 'Theresa May: how strategic mistakes and the Irish question brought her down', *RTE News*, 25 May 2019, www.rte.ie/news/analysis-and-comment/2019/0525/1051593-theresa-may-brexit/ (accessed 8 January 2020).

Connelly, T., 'EU report highlights Brexit effect on north–south cooperation', *RTE News*, 20 June 2019, www.rte.ie/news/ireland/2019/0619/1056392-eu-commission-paper-on-north-south-cooperation (accessed 8 January 2020).

Conservative Party, *Forward, Together: Our Plan for a Stronger Britain and a Prosperous Future. The Conservative and Unionist Party Manifesto 2017*, London, 2017, available at https://blogs.spectator.co.uk/2017/05/2017-conservative-manifesto-in-full/ (accessed 8 January 2020).

Cooper, C., 'Michael Gove to stand in Tory leadership contest and says "Boris is not a leader"', *Independent*, 30 June 2016, www.independent.co.uk/news/uk/politics/michael-gove-to-stand-as-tory-leader-a7110591.html (accessed 8 January 2020).

Coulter, C. & Nagle, A. (eds), *Ireland under Austerity: Neoliberal Crisis, Neoliberal Solutions*, Manchester, Manchester University Press, 2015.

Cowburn, A., 'Theresa May says "Brexit means Brexit" and there will be no attempt to remain inside EU', *Independent*, 11 July 2016, www.independent.co.uk/news/uk/politics/theresa-may-brexit-means-brexit-conservative-leadership-no-attempt-remain-inside-eu-leave-europe-a7130596.html (accessed 8 January 2020).

Cowley, P. & Kavanaugh, D., *The British General Election of 2017*, London, Palgrave, 2018.

Cunningham, C., 'Northern Ireland and the "War on Terror": political perceptions', *Irish Political Studies*, 24:3 (2009), 285–302.

Dáil Éireann Debates, 'EU–UK relations: statements' 21 April 2016, www.oireachtas.ie/en/debates/debate/dail/2016-04-21/2/ (accessed 8 January 2020).

Dallison, P. & Khetani-Shah, S., 'Brexit quotes of 2017', *Politico*, 12 December 2017, www.politico.eu/article/brexit-quotes-of-the-year-2017/ (accessed 8 January 2020).

Davidson, L., Curry, R. & Dean, S., 'Business world reacts to Brexit vote as Britain's EU Commissioner Lord Hill announces resignation', *Telegraph*, 25

Select bibliography

June 2016, www.telegraph.co.uk/business/2016/06/23/markets-live-will-sterling-surge-or-slump-as-the-eu-referendum-c/ (accessed 8 January 2020).

De Mars, S., Murray, C., O'Donoghue, A. & Warwick, B., *Bordering Two Unions: Northern Ireland and Brexit*, Bristol, Policy Press, 2018.

DeSouza, E., 'It is not up to the UK government to decide whether I'm Irish or not', *Guardian*, 6 May 2019, www.theguardian.com/commentisfree/2019/may/06/home-office-british-citizenship-northern-ireland–good-friday-agreement (accessed 8 January 2020).

DUP, *DUP European Election Manifesto 2019*, Belfast, May 2019, www.mydup.com/images/uploads/publications/European_manifesto_-_Final.pdf (accessed 8 January 2020).

Eastwood, C., 'Eastwood calls for strong IN campaign', SDLP press release, 20 February 2016, www.sdlp.ie/news/2016/eastwood-calls-for-strong-in-campaign/ (accessed 8 January 2020).

Eastwood, C., 'Northern Ireland Affairs Committee: devolution and democracy in Northern Ireland, witness evidence', 21 February 2018, www.parliamentlive.tv/Event/Index/bd83d93a-5a17-4d08-832a-9498cffi7232 (accessed 8 January 2020).

Edwards, M., 'Claire Hanna resigns SDLP whip over Fianna Fáil move – Eastwood says "the party has spoken"', *Belfast Telegraph*, 11 February 2019, www.belfasttelegraph.co.uk/news/northern-ireland/claire-hanna-resigns-sdlp-whip-over-fianna-fil-move-eastwood-says-the-party-has-spoken-37804167.html (accessed 8 January 2020).

Elgot, J., 'Theresa May calls for "red white and blue Brexit"', *Guardian*, 6 December 2016, www.theguardian.com/politics/2016/dec/06/theresa-may-calls-for-red-white-and-blue-brexit (accessed 8 January 2020).

Elgot, J., 'Boris Johnson's victory speech: what he said and what he meant', *Guardian*, 23 July 2019, www.theguardian.com/politics/ng-interactive/2019/jul/23/boris-johnsons-victory-speech-what-he-said-and-what-he-meant (accessed 8 January 2020).

Elgot, J. & Walker, P., 'Theresa May tells MPs: no Brexit deal comes without a backstop', *Guardian*, 26 November 2018, www.theguardian.com/politics/2018/nov/26/theresa-may-tells-mps-no-brexit-deal-comes-without-a-backstop (accessed 8 January 2020).

Embassy of Ireland, Great Britain, 'Remarks by Ambassador Mulhall, House of Commons, 10 February 2016', www.dfa.ie/irish-embassy/great-britain/news-and-events/2016/ambassador-mulhall-niac-ni-and-eu-referendum/ (accessed 8 January 2020).

European Commission, TF50 (2017) 19 – Commission to EU 27, 8 December 2017, https://ec.europa.eu/commission/sites/beta-political/files/joint_report.pdf (accessed 8 January 2020).

European Commission, 'Speech by Michel Barnier at the All-Island Civic Dialogue', European Commission press release, speech delivered at Dundalk, 30

April 2018, http://europa.eu/rapid/press-release_SPEECH-18-3624_en.htm (accessed 8 January 2020).

European Research Group, *A Better Deal and a Better Future*, 19 January 2019, pp. 4–5. http://2mbg6fgb1kl380gtk22pbxgw-wpengine.netdna-ssl.com/wp-content/uploads/2019/01/A-Better-Deal-and-a-Better-Future.pdf (accessed 8 January 2020).

Ferguson, A., 'Northern Ireland firms warn of economic, social risks from no-deal Brexit', *Reuters*, 10 March 2019, https://uk.reuters.com/article/uk-britain-eu-nireland/northern-ireland-firms-warn-of-economic-social-risks-from-no-deal-brexit-idUKKBN1QR003 (accessed 8 January 2020).

Fine Gael, *Fine Gael General Election Manifesto 2016 – Let's Keep the Recovery Going*, Dublin, 2016, www.ifa.ie/wp-content/uploads/2016/02/manifesto.pdf (accessed 8 January 2020).

Foster, A., 'It is right to vote to leave the EU and to take back control of our future', DUP press release, 17 June 2016, www.mydup.com/news/article/it-is-right-to-vote-to-leave-the-eu-and-to-take-back-control-of-our-future (accessed 8 January 2020).

Foster, A., & McGuinness, M., 'Open letter from Arlene Foster and Martin McGuinness', Northern Ireland Executive Office, 10 August 2016, www.executiveoffice-ni.gov.uk/sites/default/files/publications/execoffice/Letter%20to%20PM%20from%20FM%20%26%20dFM.pdf (accessed 8 January 2020).

Foster, P., '"Ready as soon as UK is": how Europe's leaders reacted to Theresa May's Brexit speech', *Telegraph*, 17 January 2017, www.telegraph.co.uk/news/2017/01/17/ready-soon-uk-europes-leaders-reacted-theresa-mays-brexit-speech/ (accessed 8 January 2020).

Foster, R.F., *Modern Ireland 1600–1972*, London, Penguin, 1989.

Garry, J., 'House of Lord's European Union Select Committee, witness evidence', 16 January 2018, www.parliamentlive.tv/Event/Index/cf14934 6-742d-4afb-904f-f49c5d372e92 (accessed 8 January 2020).

Garry, J., McNicholl, K., O'Leary, B. & Pow, J., *Northern Ireland and the UK's Exit from the EU: What Do People Think? Evidence from Two Investigations: A Survey and a Deliberative Forum, UK in a Changing Europe*, ESRC report, May 2018, https://ukandeu.ac.uk/wp-content/uploads/2018/05/Northern-Ireland-and-the-UK's-Exit-from-the-EU.pdf (accessed 8 January 2020).

Geoghegan, P. & Ramsey, A., 'The dark money that paid for Brexit', *Open Democracy UK*, 15 February 2017, www.opendemocracy.net/uk/peter-geoghegan-adam-ramsay/you-aren-t-allowed-to-know-who-paid-for-key-leave-campaign-adverts (accessed 8 January 2020).

Gilligan, C., 'Northern Ireland ten years after the Agreement', *Ethnopolitics*, 7:1 (2008), 1–19.

Select bibliography

Government of Ireland, 'Brexit: Ireland's priorities', Dublin (undated), https://dbei.gov.ie/en/What-We-Do/EU-Internal-Market/Brexit/Government-Brexit-Priorities/Brexit-Irelands-Priorities.pdf (Last accessed 27 January 2020).

Grant, J., 'Patel accused of "famine threats" as she says risk of food shortages could be used against Republic', *Belfast Telegraph*, 8 December 2018, www.belfasttelegraph.co.uk/news/brexit/patel-accused-of-famine-threats-as-she-says-risk-of-food-shortages-could-be-used-against-republic-37605632.html (accessed 8 January 2020).

Guardian, 'IRA arms decommissioned', *Guardian*, 26 September 2005, www.theguardian.com/uk/2005/sep/26/northernireland.northernireland1 (accessed 8 January 2020).

Guardian, 'No-deal Brexit would be a "failure of statecraft", says Boris Johnson', *Guardian*, 9 September 2019, www.theguardian.com/politics/video/2019/sep/09/no-deal-brexit-would-be-a-failure-of-statecraft-says-boris-johnson-video (accessed 8 January 2020).

Gurr, T.R., *People versus States: Minorities at Risk in the New Century*, Washington, United States Institute of Peace, 2000.

Hanna, C., 'Picking up the pieces – restoring relationships after Brexit', Jean Monnet Lecture Series, University College Cork, 27 March 2019, www.ucc.ie/en/government-and-politics/news/ucc-jean-monnet-lecture-series-march-2019-claire-hanna-mla-south-belfast-picking-up-the-pieces-restoring-relationships-after-brexit-.html (accessed 8 January 2020).

Hayward, K., *Irish Nationalism and European Integration: The Official Redefinition of the Island of Ireland*, Manchester, Manchester University Press, 2009.

Hayward, K., *Brexit at the Border: Voices of Local Communities in the Central Border Region of Ireland/ Northern Ireland*, Belfast, Irish Central Border Network and Queen's University Belfast, 2018.

Hayward, K., 'Can technology and "max fac" solve the Irish border question? Expert explains', *The Conversation*, 23 May 2018, https://theconversation.com/can-technology-and-max-fac-solve-the-irish-border-question-expert-explains-96735 (accessed 8 January 2020).

Hayward, K. & Murphy, M., 'The (soft) power of commitment: the EU and conflict resolution in Northern Ireland', *Ethnopolitics*, 11:4 (2012), 439–52.

HM Government, *Why the Government Believes that Voting to Remain in the European Union is the Best Decision for the UK*, EU referendum leaflet, April 2016, https://assets.publishing.service.gov.uk/government/uploads/system/uploads/attachment_data/file/517014/EU_referendum_leaflet_large_print.pdf (accessed 8 January 2020).

Hogan, P., 'Now is the time to cut our ties with Brexiting Britain', *Irish Times*, 9 January 2017, www.irishtimes.com/opinion/phil-hogan-now-is-the-time-to-cut-our-ties-with-brexiting-britain-1.2928074 (accessed 8 January 2020).

Holzgrefe, J. & Keohane, R. (eds), *Humanitarian Intervention: Ethical, Legal and Political Dilemmas*, Cambridge, Cambridge University Press, 2003.

Hume, J., 'John Hume Nobel Lecture', Oslo, 10 December 1998, www.nobelprize.org/prizes/peace/1998/hume/lecture/ (accessed 8 January 2020).

Humphreys, R., *Beyond the Border: The Good Friday Agreement and Irish unity after Brexit*, Newbridge, Merrion Press, 2018.

Hunt, A., 'Theresa May and the DUP deal: what you need to know,' BBC News, 26 June 2017, www.bbc.co.uk/news/election-2017-40245514 (accessed 8 January 2020).

Independent, 'Theresa May's Tory leadership launch statement: full text', *Independent*, 30 June 2016, www.independent.co.uk/news/uk/politics/theresa-mays-tory-leadership-launch-statement-full-text-a7111026.html (accessed 8 January 2020).

Institute of International and European Affairs, 'Brexit, the Good Friday Agreement and the European Convention on Human Rights', 9 January 2017, www.iiea.com/brexit/brexit-the-good-friday-agreement-and-the-european-convention-on-human-rights/ (accessed 8 January 2020).

Irish Times, 'Full text of Martin McGuinness's resignation letter', *Irish Times*, 9 January 2017, www.irishtimes.com/news/politics/full-text-of-martin-mcguinness-s-resignation-letter-1.2930429 (accessed 8 January 2020).

Irish Times, 'Chilling DUP deal raises prospect of change to UK abortion law', *Irish Times*, 10 June 2017, www.irishtimes.com/news/world/uk/chilling-dup-deal-raises-prospect-of-change-to-uk-abortion-law-1.3115505 (accessed 8 January 2020).

ITV News, 'EU referendum debate', 9 June 2016, part 1: www.bing.com/videos/search?q=ITV+EU+referendum+debate%e2%80%99%2c+9+June+2016++youtube&&view=detail&mid=55C9634E090FCD5C91AE55C9634E090FCD5C91AE&&FORM=VRDGAR&ru=%2Fvideos%2Fsearch%3Fq%3DITV%2BEU%2Breferendum%2Bdebate%25e2%2580%2599%252c%2B9%2BJune%2B2016%2B%2Byoutube%26qpvt%3DITV%2BEU%2Breferendum%2Bdebate%25e2%2580%2599%252c%2B9%2BJune%2B2016%2B%2Byoutube%26FORM%3DDVDRE; part 2: www.bing.com/videos/search?q=ITV+EU+referendum+debate%e2%80%99%2c+9+June+2016++youtube&qpvt=ITV+EU+referendum+debate%e2%80%99%2c+9+June+2016++youtube&view=detail&mid=0CAEB35753CFD4449F8C0CAEB35753CFD4449F8C&&FORM=VRDGAR&ru=%2Fvideos%2Fsearch%3Fq%3DITV%2BEU%2Breferendum%2Bdebate%25e2%2580%2599%252c%2B9%2BJune%2B2016%2B%2Byoutube%26qpvt%3DITV%2BEU%2Breferendum%2Bdebate%25e2%2580%2599%252c%2B9%2BJune%2B2016%2B%2Byoutube%26FORM%3DDVDRE (accessed 27 January 2020).

ITV News, 'Sinn Féin calls for referendum on United Ireland', 24 June 2016, www.itv.com/news/story/2016-06-24/sinn-fein-calls-for-referendum-on-united-ireland/ (accessed 8 January 2020).

Select bibliography

ITV News, 'Ulster Unionists call for Executive's plan following EU vote', 24 June 2016, www.itv.com/news/utv/update/2016-06-24/ulster-unionists-call-for-executives-plan-following-eu-vote/ (accessed 8 January 2020).

Jackson, A., *Home Rule, an Irish History 1800–2000*, Dublin, Phoenix Press, 2003.

Johnson, B., 'Boris Johnson's first speech as prime minister: 24 July 2019', *Gov. UK*, 24 July 2019, www.gov.uk/government/speeches/boris-johnsons-first-speech-as-prime-minister-24-july-2019 (accessed 8 January 2020).

Kane, A., 'The past is where we go when we can't agree on the present or future', *Irish News*, 1 December 2017, www.irishnews.com/opinion/columnists/2017/12/01/news/alex-kane-the-past-is-where-we-go (accessed 8 January 2020).

Karlsson, L., *Smart Borders 2.0: Avoiding a Hard Border on the Island of Ireland for Customs Control and the Free Movement of Persons*, AFCO Committee European Parliament, PE 596828-November 2017, www.europarl.europa.eu/RegData/etudes/STUD/2017/596828/IPOL_STU(2017)596828_EN.pdf (accessed 8 January 2020).

Keen, D., 'Incentives and disincentives for violence', in Berdal, M. & Malone, D. (eds), *Greed and Grievance: Economic Agendas in Civil Wars*, Boulder, Lynne Rienner, 2000.

Kenny, A., *The Road to Hillsborough: The Making of the Anglo-Irish Agreement*, Oxford, Oxford University Press, 1986.

Kenny, E., 'Why Ireland is so fearful of our closest neighbour leaving the EU', *Guardian*, 20 June 2016, www.theguardian.com/commentisfree/2016/jun/20/ireland-fearful-neighbour-leaving-eu-northern-ireland (accessed 8 January 2020).

Kentish, B., 'Tories at war over Boris Johnson "suicide vest" jibe at May over her Chequers Brexit plan', *Independent*, 10 September 2018, www.independent.co.uk/news/boris-johnson-disgusting-criticism-theresa-may-conservative-row-chequers-plan-suicide-vest-a8529621.html (accessed 8 January 2020).

Kentish, B., 'Britain should highlight risk of economic damage in Ireland to get better Brexit deal, suggests Priti Patel', *Independent*, 7 December 2018, www.independent.co.uk/news/uk/politics/brexit-ireland-food-shortages-threat-risk-priti-patel-negotiate-better-deal-a8672326.html (accessed 8 January 2020).

Kentish, B., 'EU Council president savages Brexit campaigners who failed to plan for departure: "Special place in hell"', *Independent*, 6 February 2019, www.independent.co.uk/news/uk/politics/brexit-donald-tusk-press-conference-leo-varadkar-ireland-border-backstop-theresa-may-a8765606.html (accessed 8 January 2020).

Kinealy, C., *This Great Calamity: The Irish Famine 1845–52*, Dublin, Gill & Macmillan, 2006.

Kipling, R., 'Ulster', *Morning Post*, 9 April 1912, www.youtube.com/watch?v=esggToJF2fo (accessed 8 January 2020).

Know, K.B., 'Compromise is not a dirty word – Bill Clinton delivers keynote speech to mark 20th anniversary of Good Friday Agreement', *Independent.ie*, 9 April 2018, www.independent.ie/irish-news/news/compromise-is-not-a-dirty-word-bill-clinton-delivers-keynote-speech-to-mark-20th-anniversary-of-good-friday-agreement-36791338.html (accessed 8 January 2020).

Kriesberg, L., *Constructive Conflicts: From Escalation to Resolution* (3rd ed.), Lanham, Rowman and Littlefield, 2007.

Labour In for Britain, YouTube video, 30 November 2015, www.bing.com/videos/search?q=Labour+in+for+Britain+&view=detail&mid=EA925DEB84034E02AFCFEA925DEB84034E02AFCF&FORM=VIRE (accessed 8 January 2020).

Labour Party, *For the Many Not the Few: The Labour Party Manifesto 2017*, London, Labour, 2017, https://labour.org.uk/wp-content/uploads/2017/10/labour-manifesto-2017.pdf (accessed 8 January 2020).

Laffan, B. & O'Mahony, J., *Ireland and the European Union*, Houndmills, Palgrave Macmillan, 2008.

Lederach, J.P., *Preparing for Peace*, New York, Syracuse University Press, 1995.

Lederach, J.P., *Building Peace: Sustainable Reconciliation in Divided Societies*, Washington, United States Institute of Peace, 1997.

Lehane, M., 'Ambassador accuses UK magazine of publishing anti-Irish magazines', *RTE News*, 12 April 2019, www.rte.ie/news/2019/0412/1042276-ambassador-britain-spectator/ (accessed 8 January 2020).

Lund, M., *Preventing Violent Conflicts*, Washington, United States Institute of Peace, 1996.

McBride, S., 'UUP grandees urge party's supporters to quit "out of control" EU', *Belfast News Letter*, 17 June 2016, www.newsletter.co.uk/news/uup-grandees-urge-party-s-supporters-to-quit-out-of-control-eu-1-7437838 (accessed 8 January 2020).

McBride, S., 'EU referendum: more UUP councillors backing Brexit', *Belfast News Letter*, 21 June 2016, www.newsletter.co.uk/news/eu-referendum-more-uup-councillors-backing-brexit-1-7440607 (accessed 8 January 2020).

McBride, S., 'RHI inquiry: Arlene Foster admits she didn't even read her own "cash for ash" legislation', *inews.co.uk*, 13 April 2018, https://inews.co.uk/news/northern-ireland/rhi-inquiry-arlene-foster-admits-she-didnt-even-read-her-own-cash-for-ash-legislation/ (accessed 8 January 2020).

McClements, F., 'Mark Durkan: "I regret that only Derry voice in Commons is Gregory Campbell"', *Irish Times*, 13 June 2017, www.irishtimes.com/news/ireland/irish-news/mark-durkan-i-regret-that-only-derry-voice-in-commons-is-gregory-campbell-1.3118577 (accessed 8 January 2020).

McCrudden, C., *The Good Friday Agreement, Brexit, and Rights*, Dublin and London, Royal Irish Academy/British Academy, 2017.

McCrudden, C., McGarry, J., O'Leary, B. & Schwartz, A., 'Why Northern Ireland institutions need stability', *Government and Opposition*, 51:1 (2016), 30–58.

McDonald, H., 'Sinn Féin calls for vote on Irish reunification if UK backs Brexit', *Guardian*, 11 March 2016, www.theguardian.com/politics/2016/mar/11/sinn-fein-irish-reunification-vote-brexit-eu-referendum (accessed 8 January 2020).

McEvoy, J., *The Politics of Northern Ireland*, Edinburgh, Edinburgh University Press, 2008.

McGarry, J. & O'Leary, B., 'Consociational theory, Northern Ireland's conflict, and its Agreement. Part 1: What consociationalists can learn from Northern Ireland', *Government and Opposition*, 41:1 (2006), 43–63.

McGarry, J. & O'Leary, B., 'Consociational theory, Northern Ireland's conflict, and its Agreement. Part 2: What critics of consociation can learn from Northern Ireland', *Government and Opposition*, 41:2 (2006), 249–77.

McGowen, M., 'Remembering John Hume's key role in NI's Good Friday Agreement', *Metro Eireann*, 15 April 2018, www.metroeireann.com/news/1203/remembering-john-humes-key-role-in-nis-good-friday-agreement.html (accessed 8 January 2020).

McGuinness, M., 'Foreword', in Sinn Féin, *Better with Sinn Féin Níos fearr le Sinn Féin, Sinn Féin Manifesto, Assembly Election 2016*, Belfast, Sinn Féin, 2016, www.sinnfein.ie/files/2017/2016_Assembly_Manifesto.pdf (accessed 8 January 2020).

McHugh, M., 'Sinn Féin calls for Ireland reunification poll if UK votes to leave EU – Do you agree?', *Belfast Telegraph*, 12 March 2016, www.belfasttelegraph.co.uk/news/northern-ireland/sinn-fein-calls-for-ireland-reunification-poll-if-uk-votes-to-leave-eu-do-you-agree-34532443.html (accessed 8 January 2020).

McKeown, L.A., 'Tony Blair and John Major warn a Brexit could threaten peace process during visit to Derry', *Irish News*, 9 June 2016, www.irishnews.com/news/brexit/2016/06/10/news/tony-blair-and-john-major-warn-a-brexit-could-threaten-peace-process-during-visit-to-derry-555717/ (accessed 8 January 2020).

Makem, T., 'Four green fields', 1967, www.makem.com/lyrics/lyricpage/fourgreenfields.php (accessed 8 January 2020).

Malnick, E., 'DUP to support minority government after "confidence and supply" deal reached', *Telegraph*, 10 June 2017, www.telegraph.co.uk/news/2017/06/10/dup-support-minority-government-confidence-supply-deal-reached/ (accessed 27 January 2020).

May, J., 'Read in full: Theresa May's Conservative Conference speech on Brexit', *PoliticsHome*, 2 October 2016, www.politicshome.com/news/uk/political-parties/conservative-party/news/79517/read-full-theresa-mays-conservative (accessed 8 January 2020).

May, J., 'In full: Arlene Foster statement on DUP-Conservative confidence and supply deal', *PoliticsHome*, 26 June 2017, www.politicshome.com/news/uk/uk-regions/northern-ireland/news/86999/full-arlene-foster-statement-dup-conservative (accessed 8 January 2020).

May, T., 'The government's negotiating objectives for exiting the EU: PM speech', *Gov.UK*, 17 January 2017, www.gov.uk/government/speeches/the-governments-negotiating-objectives-for-exiting-the-eu-pm-speech (accessed 8 January 2020).

Miall, H., 'Conflict transformation: a multi-dimensional task', in *Berghof Handbook*, Berlin, Berghof Research Centre for Constructive Conflict Management, 2004.

Millar, D., *Queen's Rebels: Ulster Loyalism in Historical Perspective*, Dublin, Gill & Macmillan, 1978.

Minihan, M., 'John Hume's single-transferable speech', *Irish Times*, 30 December 2015, www.irishtimes.com/news/politics/john-hume-s-single-transferable-speech-1.2479853 (accessed 8 January 2020).

Moore, C., 'De Gaulle knew it: Britain does not belong in the EU', *Spectator*, 30 April 2016, www.spectator.co.uk/2016/04/de-gaulle-knew-it-britain-does-not-belong-in-the-eu/ (accessed 8 January 2020).

Morgan, A. & Purdie, B., *Ireland: Divided Nation, Divided Class*, London, Ink Links, 1980.

Moriarty, G., 'Northern Ireland on election footing as Martin McGuinness resigns as deputy First Minister', *Irish Times*, 9 January 2017, www.irishtimes.com/news/politics/northern-ireland-on-election-footing-as-martin-mcguinness-resigns-as-deputy-first-minister-1.2930300 (accessed 8 January 2020).

Morris, N., 'Tory–DUP "confidence and supply" deal facing legal challenge', *inews.co.uk*, 9 July 2017, https://inews.co.uk/news/politics/tory-dup-confidence-supply-deal-facing-legal-challenge/ (accessed 8 January 2020).

Murphy, J. & Cecil, N., 'Donald Tusk slams Brexit saying there's a "special place in hell" for people who promoted Leave without a plan', *Evening Standard*, 6 February 2019, www.standard.co.uk/news/world/european-council-president-donald-tusk-says-theres-a-special-place-in-hell-for-people-who-promoted-a4059126.html (accessed 8 January 2020).

Murphy, M., *Northern Ireland and the European Union: The Dynamics of a Changing Relationship*, Manchester, Manchester University Press, 2014.

Murphy, M., *Europe and Northern Ireland's Future: Negotiating Brexit's Unique Case*, Newcastle, Agenda Publishing, 2018.

Northern Ireland Affairs Committee, *The Land Border between Northern Ireland and Ireland: 2nd Report of Session 2017–19*, House of Commons, HC329, 16 March 2018, https://publications.parliament.uk/pa/cm201719/cmselect/cmniaf/329/329.pdf (accessed 27 January 2020).

O'Beacháin, D., *From Partition to Brexit: The Irish Government and Northern Ireland*, Manchester, Manchester University Press, 2018.

O'Carroll, L., 'Kate Hoey accused of putting Brexit before peace', *Guardian*, 21 February 2018, www.theguardian.com/uk-news/2018/feb/21/mps-accuse-kate-hoey-of-putting-brexit-before-northern-ireland-peace (accessed 8 January 2020).

O'Dochartaigh, N., Hayward, K. & Meehan, E. (eds), *Dynamics of Political Change in Ireland: Making and Breaking a Divided Island*, Abingdon, Routledge, 2017.

O'Kane, E., 'To cajole or compel? The use of incentives and penalties in Northern Ireland's peace process', *Dynamics of Asymmetric Conflict*, 4:3 (2011), 272–84.

Ó Riain, S., *The Rise and Fall of Ireland's Celtic Tiger: Liberalism, Boom and Bust*, Cambridge, Cambridge University Press, 2014.

O'Rourke, K., *A Short History of Brexit: From Brentry to Backstop*, London, Penguin, 2018.

O'Toole, F., *Heroic Failure: Brexit and the Politics of Pain*, London, Head of Zeus, 2018.

Payton, M., 'Ian Paisley Jr urges Northern Irish citizens to apply for Republic of Ireland passports', *Independent*, 25 June 2016, www.independent.co.uk/news/uk/politics/unionist-ian-paisley-jr-mp-constituents-apply-republic-of-ireland-eire-passports-a7102761.html (accessed 8 January 2020).

Phinnemore, D., 'Northern Ireland and Brexit: limits and opportunities for a new relationship with the EU', *Northern Ireland Assembly Knowledge Exchange Series 2016–2017*, 12 October 2016, http://qub.ac.uk/home/EUReferendum/Brexitfilestore/Filetoupload,728117,en.pdf (accessed 8 January 2020).

Phinnemore D. & McGowan, L., 'After the EU referendum: establishing the best outcome for Northern Ireland', briefing paper, Centre for Democracy and Peace Building, Belfast, August 2016.

Political Studies Association, '20 years of the Good Friday Agreement', 10 April 2018, www.psa.ac.uk/psa/news/20-years-good-friday-agreement (accessed 8 January 2020).

Powell, J., *Great Hatred, Little Room: Making Peace in Northern Ireland*, London, Vintage, 2009.

Proctor, K., & Walker, P., 'Boris Johnson: I'd rather be dead in ditch than agree Brexit extension', *Guardian*, 5 September 2019, www.theguardian.com/politics/2019/sep/05/boris-johnson-rather-be-dead-in-ditch-than-agree-brexit-extension (accessed 8 January 2020).

Quinn, A., 'Watch Boris Johnson tell the DUP in 2018 he would never put border in the Irish Sea – today he put a border in the Irish Sea', *Belfast News Letter*, 17 October 2019, www.newsletter.co.uk/news/politics/watch-boris-johnson-tell-the-dup-in-2018-he-would-never-put-border-in-the-irish-sea-today-he-put-a-border-in-the-irish-sea-1-9110754 (accessed 8 January 2020).

Quinn, B., 'Irish prime minister says border controls could return if Britain exits EU', *Guardian*, 29 May 2016, www.theguardian.com/uk-news/2016/

may/29/irish-leader-says-border-controls-may-return-if-brexit-vote-prevails (accessed 8 January 2020).

Quinn, B., 'Sajid Javid criticised for calling Ireland "tail that wags the dog" on Brexit', *Guardian*, 2 June 2019, www.theguardian.com/politics/2019/jun/02/sajid-javid-criticised-for-calling-ireland-tail-that-wags-the-dog-on-brexit (accessed 8 January 2020).

Ramsbotham, O., Woodhouse, T. & Miall, H., *Contemporary Conflict Resolution* (3rd ed.), Cambridge, Polity, 2011.

Ramsbotham, O., Woodhouse, T. & Miall, H., *Contemporary Conflict Resolution* (4th ed.), Cambridge, Polity, 2015.

Rankin, J. & Boffey, D., 'Risk of no-deal Brexit "very high", says key EU negotiator', *Guardian*, 28 January 2019, www.theguardian.com/politics/2019/jan/28/risk-of-no-deal-brexit-very-high-says-key-eu-negotiator-sabine-weyand (accessed 8 January 2020).

Reimann, C., 'Assessing the state of the art in conflict transformation', in *Berghof Handbook*, Berlin, Berghof Research Centre for Constructive Conflict Management, 2003.

Roberts, R., 'Sinn Féin accuses the DUP of "betraying Northern Ireland" by entering into deal to prop up Conservative government', *Independent*, 11 June 2017, www.independent.co.uk/news/uk/politics/sinn-fein-michelle-oneil-accuses-dup-betraying-northern-ireland-confidence-and-supply-deal-theresa-a7784051.html (accessed 8 January 2020).

Routledge, P. & Hoggart, S., 'Major hits out at cabinet', *Guardian*, 25 July 1993, www.theguardian.com/politics/1993/jul/25/politicalnews.uk (accessed 8 January 2020).

Rupesinghe, K., *Conflict Transformation*, New York, St Martin's Press, 1995.

Schiek, D., 'What does the 23 June mean for Northern Ireland specifically? Legal perspectives no 2: peace', Queen's Policy Engagement, 17 June 2016, http://qpol.qub.ac.uk/23-june-ni-peace-process/ (accessed 8 January 2020).

Schofield, K., 'Kate Hoey condemned by her own Labour branch for attacking the Good Friday Agreement', *PoliticsHome*, 23 February 2018, www.politicshome.com/news/uk/constitution/northern-ireland-assembly/news/93079/kate-hoey-condemned-her-own-labour-branch (accessed 8 January 2020).

Scottish Government, *Scotland's Place in Government*, Edinburgh, Scottish Government, 2016, https://beta.gov.scot/binaries/content/documents/govscot/publications/publication/2016/12/scotlands-place-europe/documents/00512073-pdf/00512073-pdf/govscot:document/ (accessed 8 January 2020).

SDLP, *Build a Better Future, 2016 Assembly Election Manifesto*, Belfast, SDLP, 2016.

SDLP, 'Durkan warns fissures are being driven into foundations and bedrock of GFA', 8 December 2016, www.sdlp.ie/news/2016/durkan-warns-fissures-are-being-driven-into-foundations-bedrock-of-gfa/ (accessed 8 January 2020).

Shirlow, P. & Coulter, C., 'Northern Ireland: 20 years after the cease-fires', *Studies in Conflict and Terrorism*, 37:9 (2014), 713–19.

Simpson, C., 'Michel Barnier joins Leo Varadkar and Simon Coveney at rugby match', *Irish News*, 11 March 2019, www.irishnews.com/news/politicalnews/2019/03/11/news/michel-barnier-joins-leo-varadkar-and-simon-coveney-at-rugby-match-1569895/ (accessed 8 January 2020).

Simpson, K., 'General Election 2017: what does this mean for Brexit?' *The Conversation*, 9 June 2017, https://theconversation.com/general-election-2017-what-does-this-mean-for-brexit-79185 (accessed 8 January 2020).

Simpson, K., 'The model EU citizen? Explaining Irish attitudes towards the EU', *Political Insight*, 9:1 (2018), 16–19.

Simpson, K. & Loveless, M., 'Another chance? Concerns about inequality, support for the European Union and further European integration', *Journal for European Public Policy*, 24:7 (2017), 1069–89.

Sinn Féin, *Ard Fheis '16*, Dublin, 22–23 April 2016, https://issuu.com/sinnfeinireland/docs/sf_ard_fheis_clar_2016_web (accessed 8 January 2020).

Sinn Féin, *Equality, Respect Integrity: 2017 Assembly Election Manifesto*, Dublin, Sinn Féin, 2017, www.sinnfein.ie/files/2017/MANIFESTO_ENGLISH.pdf (accessed 8 January 2020).

Sinn Féin, 'EU has key role in assisting transition to Irish unity – Anderson', 28 April 2017, www.sinnfein.ie/contents/44389 (accessed 27 January 2020).

Sky News, 'Faisal Islam struggles with Leaver's explanation there is no Brexit plan', 16 January 2017, https://news.sky.com/video/faisal-islam-struggles-with-leavers-explanation-there-is-no-brexit-plan-10325690 (accessed 8 January 2020).

Smith, A., McWilliams, M. & Yarnell, P., 'Does every cloud have a silver lining? Brexit, repeal of the Human Rights Act and the Northern Ireland Bill of Rights', *Fordham International Law Journal*, 40:1 (2016).

Smith, O., 'Brexiteer slams "myth" of Irish border chaos as part of anti-Brexit "blackmail"', *Daily Express*, 26 November 2017, www.express.co.uk/news/uk/884566/Owen-Paterson-Brexit-Irish-border-blackmail-Ireland-EU (accessed 8 January 2020).

Sparrow, A., 'Brexit: government will introduce Article 50 Bill "within days" following Supreme Court ruling as it happened', *Guardian*, 14 February 2018, www.theguardian.com/politics/blog/live/2017/jan/24/supreme-court-article-50-judgement-announces-its-article-50-judgment-politics-live (accessed 8 January 2020).

Sparrow, A., 'Chaotic scenes in the Commons as parliament is suspended – as it happened', *Guardian*, 10 September 2019, www.theguardian.com/politics/

live/2019/sep/09/brexit-latest-news-eu-no-deal-bill-royal-assent-boris-johnson-parliament-politics-live (accessed 8 January 2020).

Staunton, D. & Leahy, P., 'Brexit: Varadkar sees "pathway to an agreement in coming weeks"', *Irish Times*, 10 October 2019, www.irishtimes.com/news/politics/brexit-varadkar-sees-pathway-to-an-agreement-in-coming-weeks-1.4046312 (accessed 8 January 2020).

Staunton, E., *The Nationalists of Northern Ireland 1918–1973*, Dublin, Columba Press, 2001.

Stedman, S.J., 'Spoiler problems in peace processes', *International Security*, 22:2 (1997), 5–53.

Steerpike, 'Sarah Vine reveals the Gove household reaction to Brexit: "you were only supposed to blow the bloody doors off"', *Spectator*, 29 June 2016, https://blogs.spectator.co.uk/2016/06/sarah-vine-lifts-lid-goves-reaction-brexit/ (accessed 8 January 2020).

Stewart, A.T.Q., *The Ulster Crisis, Resistance to Home Rule, 1912–14*, London, Faber and Faber, 1967.

Stewart, H., 'Tony Blair and John Major: Brexit would close the border', *Guardian*, 9 June 2016, www.theguardian.com/politics/2016/jun/09/tony-blair-and-john-major-brexit-would-close-irish-border (accessed 8 January 2020).

Stewart, H., Sabbagh, D. & Walker, P., 'Gavin Williamson: "I was tried by kangaroo court – then sacked"', *Guardian*, 1 May 2019, https://www.theguardian.com/politics/2019/may/01/gavin-williamson-sacked-as-defence-secretary-over-huawei-leak (accessed 20 January 2020).

Stone, J., 'Theresa May officially becomes UK prime minister', *Independent*, 13 July 2016, www.independent.co.uk/news/uk/politics/theresa-may-officially-becomes-uk-prime-minister-a7135126.html (accessed 8 January 2020).

Stone, J., 'Theresa May accuses EU of trying to influence UK election in astonishing attack', *Independent*, 3 May 2017, www.independent.co.uk/news/uk/politics/theresa-may-general-election-brexit-eu-countries-influence-uk-with-leaks-a7715851.html (accessed 8 January 2020).

Stone, J., 'European Commission says it is "too busy" to interfere in UK General Election after Theresa May claim', *Independent*, 4 May 2017, www.independent.co.uk/news/uk/politics/uk-general-election-live-brexit-european-commission-theresa-may-rig-interference-a7717561.html (accessed 8 January 2020).

Stone, J., 'Brexit: no deal in Brussels after DUP torpedoes Theresa May and Jean-Claude Juncker's Northern Ireland agreement', *Independent*, 4 December 2017, www.independent.co.uk/news/uk/politics/ireland-border-deal-uk-latest-updates-brexit-eu-withdrawal-dup-dublin-republic-a8091326.html (accessed 8 January 2020).

Stone, J., 'Brexit: Northern Ireland should keep EU funding to support peace process, European Parliament says', *Independent*, 11 September 2018, www.independent.co.uk/news/uk/politics/brexit-northern-ireland-eu-funding-money-peace-process-a8532496.html (accessed 8 January 2020).

Taylor, R., 'The injustice of a consociational solution to the Northern Ireland problem', in Taylor, R. (ed.), *Consociational Theory: McGarry and O'Leary and the Northern Ireland Conflict*, Abingdon, Routledge, 2009.

Thatcher, M., 'Remarks on becoming prime minister (St Francis's prayer)', 4 May 1979, www.margaretthatcher.org/document/104078 (accessed 8 January 2020).

Thatcher, M., *The Downing Street Years*, London, HarperCollins, 1993.

Telegraph, 'Nigel Farage: "Dawn is breaking over independent UK"', *Telegraph*, 24 June 2016, www.telegraph.co.uk/news/2016/06/24/nigel-farage-dawn-is-breaking-over-independent-uk/ (accessed 8 January 2020).

Telegraph, 'EU papers react with fury the day after Theresa May's Brexit speech', *Telegraph*, 18 January 2017, www.telegraph.co.uk/news/2017/01/17/little-britain-newspapers-europe-mock-uk-theresa-may-pms-brexit/ (accessed 8 January 2020).

Telegraph, '"Little Britain": newspapers in Europe mock UK and Theresa May over PM's Brexit speech', *Telegraph*, 18 January 2017, www.telegraph.co.uk/news/2017/01/17/little-britain-newspapers-europe-mock-uk-theresa-may-pms-brexit/ (accessed 8 January 2020).

TheJournal.ie, 'Brexit has the Irish government worried – Here's why', *TheJournal.ie*, 12 June 2016, www.thejournal.ie/brexit-uk-ireland-2809506-Jun2016/ (accessed 8 January 2020).

TheJournal.ie, 'David Davis: "Irish border can be solved by a whole load of new technology"', *TheJournal.ie*, 25 March 2018, www.thejournal.ie/david-davis-brexit-technology-3923080-Mar2018/ (accessed 8 January 2020).

Todd, J., 'The effectiveness of the agreement: international conditions and contexts', in O'Dochartaigh, N., Meehan, E. & Hayward K. (eds), *Dynamics of Political Change in Ireland: Making and Breaking a Divided Island*, Abingdon, Routledge, 2017.

Tonge, J., *Comparative Peace Processes*, Cambridge, Polity, 2014.

Tonge, J., 'Plus ça change? The 2016 devolved elections in the UK', *Political Insight*, 7 (2016), 12–15.

TUV, *Manifesto 2016: Straight Talking Principled Politics*, Belfast, TUV, May 2016, http://tuv.org.uk/wp-content/uploads/2016/04/TUV-A5-Manifesto-2016-final.pdf (accessed 8 January 2020).

Ury, W., *The Third Side: Why we Fight and How we Can Stop*, Harmondsworth, Penguin, 2000.

UUP, *#MakeitWork 2016 Assembly Election Manifesto*, Belfast, UUP, 2016, https://uup.org/our-vision/policies (accessed 8 January 2020).

Vayrynen, R., 'To settle or to transform? Perspectives on the resolution of national and international conflicts', in Vayrynen, R. (ed.), *New Directions in Conflict Theory: Conflict Resolution and Conflict Transformation*, London, Sage, 1991.

Watts, J., 'Election 2017: "Theresa May to put Brexit at heart of campaign again amid shrinking poll lead"', *Independent*, 31 May 2017, www.independent.co.uk/news/uk/politics/election-2017-brexit-theresa-may-campaign-poll-lead-a7765821.html (accessed 8 January 2020).

Watts, J., 'Theresa May accused of bribing DUP with £1bn deal despite claiming "there is no magic money tree"', *Independent*, 26 June 2017, www.independent.co.uk/news/uk/politics/theresa-may-dup-deal-billion-pound-bribe-magic-money-tree-criticism-latest-a7809416.html (accessed 8 January 2020).

Wearmouth, R., 'Good Friday Agreement "not sustainable" says Brexiteer Kate Hoey', *Huffington Post*, 19 February 2018, www.huffingtonpost.co.uk/entry/hoey-good-friday-agreement_uk_5a8adf6de4b00bc49f46c3ac (accessed 8 January 2020).

Wehr, P., *Conflict Regulation*, Boulder, Westview, 1979.

Williamson, C., 'Brexit: Theresa May responds to letter from Arlene Foster and Martin McGuinness', *Belfast Telegraph*, 18 October 2016, www.belfasttelegraph.co.uk/news/northern-ireland/brexit-theresa-may-responds-to-letter-from-arlene-foster-and-martin-mcguinness-35139845.html (accessed 8 January 2020).

Wilson, R., *Northern Ireland Peace Monitoring Report, Number 4*, Belfast, Community Relations Council, September 2016, www.community-relations.org.uk/sites/crc/files/media-files/NIPMR-Final-2016.pdf (accessed 8 January 2020).

Woodcock, A., 'EU referendum results live: Nigel Farage "concedes defeat" in Brexit vote', *Irish News*, 23 June 2016, www.irishnews.com/news/brexit/2016/06/23/news/eu-referendum-results-live-nigel-farage-concedes-defeat-in-brexit-vote-577784/ (accessed 8 January 2020).

Woodcock, A., 'Theresa May resigns: PM breaks down as she announces departure amid Brexit gridlock and expected European election wipeout', *Independent*, 24 May 2019, www.independent.co.uk/news/uk/politics/theresa-may-resigns-latest-brexit-deal-conservative-leadership-race-european-elections-tory-party-a8928321.html (accessed 8 January 2020).

YouGov, 'YouGov on the day poll: Remain 52%, Leave 48%', 23 June 2016, https://yougov.co.uk/topics/politics/articles-reports/2016/06/23/yougov-day-poll (accessed 8 January 2020).

Young, D., 'Video: Tony Blair's "hand of history upon our shoulder" comment a source of "pride and embarrassment"', *Irish News*, 9 April 2018, www.irishnews.com/news/gfa20/2018/04/09/news/tony-blair-s-hand-of-history-upon-our-shoulder-comment-source-of-pride-and-embarrassment-1299816/ (accessed 8 January 2020).

Select bibliography

Interviews

A number of meetings, briefings and interviews were conducted, some private and unattributed and others on the record. The following is a list of on the record interviews:

Steve Aiken MLA, UUP Brexit spokesperson, interviewed by author, 24 April 2019.

Stephen Farry MLA, Alliance Party Brexit spokesperson, interviewed by author, 26 April 2019.

Claire Hanna MLA, former SDLP Brexit spokesperson, interviewed by author, 23 April 2019.

Alex Kane, journalist and commentator, interviewed by author, 25 April 2019.

Ben Lowry, deputy editor, *Belfast News Letter*, interviewed by author, 23 April 2019.

John Manley, political correspondent, *Irish News*, interviewed by author, 25 April 2019.

Máirtín Ó Muilleoir MLA, Sinn Féin former finance minister in Stormont Executive, interviewed by author, 19 April 2019.

Glyn Roberts, CEO, Retail Northern Ireland, interviewed by author, 22 April 2019.

Peter Sheridan, CEO, Co-Operation Ireland, interviewed by author, 24 April 2019.

Sammy Wilson MP, DUP Brexit spokesperson, personal communication with author, 1 October 2019.

Index

Adams, Gerry 17, 18, 65, 113, 177,
    210, 212
agri-food sector 43–5
Aiken, Steve 1, 21, 23, 27, 30, 55, 57,
    70, 111, 136, 168, 193
Alliance Party 37, 49, 59, 98, 105,
    115, 129
Allister, Jim 25, 26, 37
    see also Traditional Unionist Voice
    (TUV)
Anderson, Martina 98, 153
Anglo-Irish Agreement 132, 142,
    200, 203, 207–9, 213, 231
Anglo-Irish relations 7, 11, 12, 38,
    57, 60, 74, 75, 139, 145, 154,
    170, 172–3, 174, 195–7, 201,
    204–5, 207–9, 210, 212–14,
    222, 224–5
Anglo-Irish Treaty of 1921 141
    see also Baldwin, Stanley;
    Boundary Commission;
    Cosgrave, William; Lloyd
    George, David
Article 50 68–9, 90, 99–101, 104–6,
    101, 125, 145, 150, 219, 233
    full regulatory alignment 149
Aviva Stadium 66, 213

Backstop 13, 73, 133–4, 136, 144,
    152, 157–8, 160–6, 191, 194,
    195, 196, 200, 203, 206,
    208–9, 211, 218, 222, 227–8
alternative arrangements 218
guarantee 134, 141, 222
legally binding/enforceable
    Backstop 157, 158, 162, 166,
    218
Northern Ireland-only Backstop
    132
Baldwin, Stanley 141
Barclay, Stephen 219
Barnier, Michel 66, 104, 165, 177,
    197
    second Programme for Peace and
    Reconciliation in Northern
    Ireland 177
Belfast Agreement see Good Friday
    Agreement (GFA)
Belfast News Letter 19, 30, 107
Belfast Telegraph 40–1
Benn Act 228–9, 232
Bercow, John 69, 229
Blair, Tony 38–9, 41–2, 48–9, 79,
    127, 173, 211–12
border poll 36, 51, 54–6, 67, 73, 85,
    153, 187
Boundary Commission 141
Bradley, Karen 49
breaking peace 4, 12, 13, 196, 201,
    212, 225–6, 233–5

Index

Brexit
  clean 235
  hard 152, 191, 194, 233
  harder 191
  no-deal 13, 70, 104, 163, 178,
     191–2, 194, 205, 220, 224,
     228, 233
  smooth 104
  soft 105, 152
  special status for Northern
     Ireland 6, 85, 87, 101, 113,
     114, 131, 188
  'weaponising' 200
Brexiteers 1, 22, 47, 86, 179, 187,
    215, 218, 221–2, 234
Brexit meteor 2, 4, 8, 46, 50, 52–3,
    56–7, 63, 67–8, 70, 73–5,
    170, 179
Brexit referendum 16–17, 20, 24–6,
    27, 32–4, 43, 47
  campaign 7
    Project Fear 17, 41, 44, 47,
     157
    'taking back control' 16, 25, 40,
     68–9, 144, 159
    Vote Leave 68, 227
  debate 7
Britain Stronger in Europe 31,
    138–9
British Nationality Act 60–1

Cameron, David 16, 18, 27, 29, 32,
    33, 37, 44, 47, 65, 77–80,
    82–4, 90, 92, 94–5, 108, 137,
    198, 213, 216
  Bullingdon Club 92
  legacy 94
Carney, Mark 80, 81
Chequers Deal 65
citizenship *see* British Nationality
    Act; dual citizenship; human
    rights, EU citizens' rights;
    Irish citizenship rights

common rulebook *see* maximum
    facilitation ('max fac')
Common Travel Area (CTA) 5, 10,
    11, 38, 97, 103–4, 141, 146,
    147, 148, 154–6, 162–3, 198,
    215–16
confidence-and-supply 9, 53, 63,
    124–9, 149, 188, 216, 220
conflict resolution 176
conflict transformation 8, 61–2,
    71
  see also peacebuilding
Connelly, Tony 81–2, 146, 198
consent 57, 98, 182
  consent principle 7, 50, 54, 99,
    162, 171–2, 182, 187–8
Conservative Party 21, 22, 28, 48,
    65
consociational democracy 11, 72,
    139, 153
Corbyn, Jeremy 9, 19, 68, 100,
    108–9, 116, 119, 123
  see also Labour Party
Cosgrave, William 141–2
Coveney, Simon 21, 66, 173, 195,
    215, 222
criminal justice system 52, 54, 73,
    185
Croke Park 213
Cummings, Dominic 68, 227
customs union 5, 10, 105, 141, 149,
    157, 159, 162–3, 179–80, 183,
    192

Davis, David 65, 108, 152, 158–9,
    165
De Gaulle, Charles 235
Democratic Unionist Party (DUP)
    1, 5, 9, 19, 20–9, 31, 35, 37,
    39–42, 51, 53–6, 63, 70–1,
    73, 76, 85–6, 88–9, 91–2,
    109–10, 112–15, 120–31,
    133–5, 149–51, 159, 167–9,

172, 187–8, 190–4, 202–3,
206, 216–17, 220, 230–1
DeSouza, Emma 53, 59–61
see also British Nationality Act;
dual citizenship; Irish
citizenship rights
devolved government 9, 122, 185
devolved institutions 1, 4–6, 8,
10–11, 14, 19, 36, 38, 52–4,
57, 67, 71, 121, 127, 128–9,
138, 139, 153, 168, 169,
172–3, 185, 188, 224
restoration of 53
Dodds, Nigel 39, 53, 193
dual citizenship 184

Eastwood, Colum 33, 37, 98, 122–3,
129, 170, 174, 189
endogenous conflicts 57
ethnonationalist 24, 26, 114, 169, 186
conflict 10, 86
dispute 89, 139, 183
divide 22, 91
identity 2, 3
politics 98
EU law 181
legal guarantees 182–3
legal standards 58
see also human rights, EU Charter
of Fundamental Rights;
human rights, EU citizens'
rights; human rights, EU
labour and human rights
legal norms
European Commission 116
European Convention on Human
Rights (ECHR) 181, 184
European Court of Justice 163
European Economic Community
(EEC) 12, 175, 208, 225
European Parliament 160, 178
cross-community initiatives 178

European Research Group (ERG)
22, 160, 172, 231
A Better Deal and a Better Future
160
European Structural Funds 208
Euroscepticism 19, 21, 33, 34, 48,
68, 186
EU Withdrawal Bill *see* Withdrawal
Agreement
existential crisis 122
fear 162
of unionists 132, 133
exogenous shocks 8, 50, 52, 57, 74

Farage, Nigel 76, 82
Farry, Stephen 59, 61, 105
Fianna Fáil 18, 55, 189
Fine Gael 17, 18, 65, 199–200
Foster, Arlene 21, 23, 29, 37, 39, 40,
41, 88, 90, 91, 96–7, 110–13,
115, 128, 134, 193, 217
'blood-red' line 217
see also Renewable Heating
Incentive (RHI)
Fresh Start Agreement 72

Gaelic Athletic Association (GAA)
213
General Election, Westminster 2017
113
see also May, Theresa, 2017
General Election
'God Save the Queen' *see* Aviva
Stadium
Good Friday Agreement (GFA) 1, 3,
4, 7, 11, 12, 14, 11, 18, 19, 22,
29, 33, 34, 36, 38, 42, 48–54,
56–61, 63–4, 67–8, 72, 79,
98–9, 108, 113–14, 121, 127,
129, 132, 133, 134, 137–40,
144, 146–7, 164–7, 168,
169–75, 177, 179–87, 193–6,

203, 205, 207, 209, 212–13, 216, 218, 224, 230
birthright provisions 61
co-guarantors 70, 146, 172, 196, 224
constructive ambiguity 50, 52, 144
cross-border bodies 167
Declaration of Support 182–4
East/West relationships 57
international treaty 57, 168, 181–3
north–south bodies 57, 180
north–south cooperation 146, 149
see also Hoey, Kate
Gove, Michael 78, 83, 99
leadership bid 92–3

Hale, Lady Brenda 229
Hamilton, George 153
Hanna, Claire 16, 19, 55, 58, 70, 76, 98, 123, 186, 189, 199–200
Hardman, Robert 223
Hazzard, Chris 221
Hoey, Kate 172–4
Home Office 53, 59–61
Home Rule 131, 202–3, 205–6, 231
Home Rule Act 132
human rights 52, 58, 181
EU Charter of Fundamental Rights 185
EU citizens' rights 61
EU labour and human rights legal norms 184
see also EU law; European Convention on Human Rights (ECHR); UK domestic law; UK Human Rights Act
Hume, John 122, 175, 186, 189, 193, 210
Hume/Adams talks 210
Irish Peace Initiative 210
Nobel Peace Prize 175

single transferable speech 176
see also Mitchell, George

in/out referendum *see* Brexit referendum
international conflict prevention *see* peacebuilding
IRA *see* Provisional Irish Republican Army (IRA)
Irish border 2, 3, 6, 8, 10, 12, 53, 62, 102, 134–5, 136–8, 139, 140, 142–4, 146, 150–2, 156, 157, 158, 160–3, 168, 170, 216, 217, 222, 224, 234
checks 153, 160–1, 163
frictionless 107–8, 134, 136, 148–9, 154, 156, 157, 161, 163, 179–80, 190, 196
technological solutions 109, 158, 162–3
hard 38, 43, 45, 73, 96, 98, 105, 133, 142, 145, 147–8, 154, 159, 161–2, 165, 167, 168, 179–80, 188, 194–5, 198, 216, 218, 230
infrastructure 145–6, 153, 157
in Irish Sea 132, 230–1
invisible 138, 148
land 63, 142, 91, 146
open 145
policing of 142, 154
smart 157–8, 160
visible 153–4, 156
Irish citizenship rights 60
Irish diaspora 137, 204
Irish Famine 3, 204–5, 221
Irish Farmers' Union (IFU) 44, 45
Irish News 27, 36, 52, 107, 123, 191
Irish passport 61, 86, 183
Irish peace process 3, 12, 14, 138
Irish reunification/unity 36–7, 51, 53–4, 55, 56, 67, 73, 85, 154, 187, 191
Italian Job, The 83

Index

Johnson, Boris 33, 65, 69, 78, 80,
    83, 108, 159–60, 197, 202,
    206, 211–12, 223, 226–33
  Conservative Party leadership
    race 92–3, 227
  extension to Brexit 228
  prorogation of House of
    Commons 69, 229
  see also Benn Act; Supreme Court
Juncker, Jean-Claude 217

Kane, Alex 51, 56, 76, 87, 201
Karlsson, Lars 160
  see also Irish border, smart
Kenny, Enda 17–18, 44–5, 65, 137,
    194, 198–9, 214–15
Kipling, Rudyard 131

Labour in for Britain 139
Labour Party 19, 21, 32, 117
Lansdowne Road *see* Aviva Stadium
Leadsom, Andrea 93–4
Leave campaign *see* Brexit
    referendum, campaign, Vote
    Leave
Lloyd George, David 141, 203
Lowry, Ben 2, 19, 30, 107

MacDonald, Mary Lou 65
MacDonald, Stewart 221
McGuinness, Martin 20, 23, 35, 36,
    64, 85, 88, 90, 91, 96–7,
    101–2, 110–11, 112, 115, 122
Major, John 37, 38, 39, 41–2, 78,
    209–11, 216
Manley, John 27, 36, 52, 107, 123,
    191
maximum facilitation ('max fac')
    157–8, 161–2
  see also Irish border, frictionless
May, Theresa 9, 16, 49, 65, 67–8,
    70, 82, 84, 90, 92, 94–5, 99,
    100, 104, 108–9, 115–20, 125,
    130, 132–3, 146, 147, 149,
    151, 163–4, 166, 171, 190,
    192, 198, 203, 216–19, 222,
    227, 231
  2017 General Election 107,
    115–16, 120–3, 132–5, 150,
    156, 188, 192–3, 216
  aspirational language of 97,
    102–3, 156, 222
  austerity agenda of 95
  Brexit means Brexit 84, 93–4,
    100, 102, 105, 147
  failure 79, 123, 218, 220
  Lancaster House speech 102–5,
    109, 116, 147, 155
  magic money tree 115, 120,
    129–30
  political legacy 94
  red lines 157, 218
  see also Windrush scandal
Miller, Gina 69, 101, 229
Mitchell, George 49, 177
Mulhall, Dan 43, 148

Nesbitt, Mike 41, 42, 87, 88
New Decade New Approach 72
no deal *see* Brexit, no-deal
Northern Ireland Affairs
    Committee 144–6, 170,
    174
Northern Ireland Assembly 1, 73,
    87–8, 111, 184
  election 110, 113–14, 120–1, 128
Northern Ireland Executive 63,
    87–8, 90, 97, 101, 128, 149,
    190

Ó Muilleoir, Máirtín 1, 63, 85, 167,
    187, 191
O'Neill, Adrian 223
O'Neill, Michelle 64–5, 101, 113,
    115, 129
O'Toole, Fintan 198

Index

parity of esteem 58
Patel, Priti 220–2
peacebuilding 8, 71, 177, 208
peace process 4, 7–8, 12, 14–15,
  38–9, 43, 45, 49–50, 54, 67,
  70, 89, 92, 135, 136, 137, 139,
  140, 144, 146, 154, 166, 168,
  170–1, 173, 175–6, 187, 194,
  196, 201, 212, 216, 224–5,
  233
Police Service of Northern Ireland
  153
  see also Royal Ulster Constabulary
  (RUC)
Political Studies Association 170
power-sharing 6, 7, 70, 99, 111, 113,
  151
  institutions 10, 11, 91, 98
Project Fear see Brexit referendum,
  campaign, Project Fear
Provisional Irish Republican Army
  (IRA) 54, 67, 133, 210,
  216

Raab, Dominic 65
Renewable Heating Incentive
  (RHI) 110–12, 115, 120, 128,
  134
Reynolds, Lee 31
Roberts, Glyn 30, 31, 191
Robinson, Peter 23, 112
Royal Ulster Constabulary (RUC)
  142
Rudd, Amber 95, 119, 140

St Andrews Agreement 71
St Francis of Assisi 94
Scottish government 98, 103
Scottish independence 32, 38, 47,
  80
  referendum 17
Scottish National Party (SNP) 79,
  88, 98

self-determination 9, 10, 13, 36, 41,
  70, 80, 85, 88, 98, 105, 141,
  147, 171
Sheridan, Peter 47, 51, 55, 136
single market 5, 105, 141, 157, 160,
  162–3, 180, 183, 192
Sinn Féin 1, 5, 9, 10, 12, 17, 18, 19,
  20, 23, 24, 25, 26, 33, 34, 35,
  36, 37, 52, 54, 63–5, 70–3,
  76, 85, 88, 91–2, 97–8, 98,
  101, 105, 110–15, 120–2, 123,
  127–9, 133, 153–4, 167–9,
  172, 176, 186, 187–8, 190,
  210, 212
Six Nations rugby see Aviva
  Stadium
Social Democratic and Labour
  Party (SDLP) 16, 19, 20, 26,
  33, 34, 37, 55, 58, 98, 121–2,
  127, 129, 170, 174, 186–90,
  193, 199, 210
special status see Brexit, special
  status for Northern
  Ireland
Spectator 223
Stormont House Agreement 72
Sturgeon, Nicola 79–80
Sunningdale Agreement 132
Supreme Court 69, 101, 229

'taking back control' see Brexit
  referendum, campaign,
  'taking back control'
Team GB 132–3
Thatcher, Margaret 78, 94–5, 133,
  142, 200, 203, 207, 209,
  227
Traditional Unionist Voice (TUV)
  25, 26, 29
Trimble, David 42, 54, 175, 193
  Nobel Peace Prize 175
Tusk, Donald 105, 164, 165
Twitter 152

UK domestic law 58, 60
UK Human Rights Act 181
UK Independence Party (UKIP)
    22, 25, 32, 33, 48, 76–7, 82
Ulster Farmers' Union 134, 190–2
Ulster Unionist Party (UUP) 1, 19,
    20–1, 23, 27–8, 30, 37, 41–2,
    54–6, 70, 86–7, 98, 111, 115,
    121–2, 128, 162, 168, 175,
    190, 193–4
united Ireland *see* Irish
    reunification/unity

Varadkar, Leo 60, 65–6, 164, 194–5,
    199–200, 214–15, 217, 222,
    230

Villiers, Theresa 33, 36
Vine, Sarah 83

Wilson, Sammy 1, 89, 109, 132, 159,
    163, 167, 169, 192
Windrush scandal 95
Withdrawal Agreement 65, 70, 73,
    115, 133–4, 160–2, 164–5,
    190–1, 193, 195–6, 200, 203,
    206–8, 211, 214–15, 219, 222,
    228, 231
    Brady Amendment 166
    Withdrawal Agreement Bill 16,
    224, 231–2